INTRODUCTION
TO LAW

SCOTT MYERS

ISBN: 1453693726
ISBN-13: 9781453693728

CONTENTS

TABLE OF CASES

CHAPTER ONE

INTRODUCTION TO THE LAW

The American legal system can be divided into two major component parts, which, in turn, may be subdivided into several areas. The two major divisions of the American legal system are public law and private law.

A. PUBLIC LAW

Public law is that part of the law that covers our rights and obligations as citizens of our nation or state. It deals with those laws that describe how we, as members of society, must act within that society. It must also, therefore, define how the state, on behalf of an orderly and just society, may regulate individuals for the greater good of that society. Public law comprises constitutional law, administrative law, international law, and criminal law.

Constitutional law deals with the interpretations of our Constitution, which, as is true of all constitutions, is the written document agreed upon as the rule and organization of union of the people within a given nation. Our Constitution establishes the form and structure of our government and describes the powers granted to that government by the people. It further delineates the powers of individual citizens within the society and describes the relationship between the government and the individual. As the U.S. Constitution is subject to change and interpretation, our legal system is constantly being called upon to review the meanings of broad constitutional mandates on finite issues.

Administrative law deals with the rules and regulations promulgated by the various and numerous administrative agencies created by the legislature. Such agencies include the Small Business Administration, the Federal Communications Commission, the Environmental Protection Agency, and the ever-popular Internal Revenue Service. Our government has created these agencies to provide for the day-to-day functioning of government. Each of these agencies regulates and monitors governmental authority through the use of its rules and regulations.

International law regulates the conduct of our society as a nation within the broader collection of nations. It establishes the conduct of our nation in relation to the conduct of other nations, and also establishes the conduct of our citizens in relation to the conduct of citizens of other nations. These conducts include international trade, travel between nations, and the conduct of nations at war. Much of international law is a customary law; that is, it is governed by past and existing custom or practice. Our next case deals with this facet of international law. We will see the variations between traditional legal analysis and the respect accorded custom in international law.

Criminal law deals with the punishment of behaviors that are offensive to the public good and safety. It attempts to prohibit those behaviors that are violations of duties owed to the community. The state, through criminal laws or statutes enacted by legislatures, establishes which behaviors are deemed offenses and prohibits them for the public good, so that order and structure may be maintained. These statutes also provide for the punishment of individuals who violate these societal standards or norms. In comparing crimes to torts, which are civil wrongs such as negligence or product liability, crimes are breaches of public right, while torts are breaches of rights each of us owes to other members of society. Crimes are often punishable by prison, while civil wrongs usually require the payment of money by one person to another.

The importance and applicability of criminal law can be seen in our first case opinion. Case opinions are the judicial decisions which resolve disputes between the adversaries. They include the judge's conclusion as to who wins and who loses, and the rationale behind the decision that the judge has reached. We can learn from these opinions by doing case briefs.

BRIEFING CASES

Before reading our first case, we need to understand the necessity and process of briefing each of our case studies. The law is regularly studied through the use of case excerpts. These excerpts are taken from case opinions and are used to illustrate and expand upon a point of law. Given that, in the law, we are using complex intellectual concepts and applying them to a myriad of real-life disputes, the use of cases for study allows us to accomplish two things. First, it provides knowledge and insight into legal theory. As we are dealing with great ideas that are constantly evolving, to attempt definitions would be a difficult task doomed to failure. We would not want a definition so terse as to be incomplete, nor would we want a definition as large and long as to be practically useless. Indeed, even if we came up with just the right description, it would probably evolve somewhat by the time we could get it to the publisher, rendering it less than we had wanted. Second, the manner and mechanisms in which the courts use these concepts are illustrated through the study of cases. We get to see what the processes are for utilizing our legal theories. For these reasons, the law is typically taught, in part, through the use of case studies.

Our case excerpts are pieces of judicial opinions rendered by judges as decisions that resolve disputes between participants in a lawsuit. This creates some difficulties that need to be addressed, no matter how good a technique the case study method is. Our first consideration is that these opinions are not primarily intended as teaching tools; rather, they are written to resolve disputes. Second, the participants know the facts of the case; after all, it's their problem. The court might choose, therefore, not to reiterate all of the facts in the decision, leaving us to occasionally struggle with somewhat incomplete facts. Third, the judges who write these opinions use varying styles and write with varying skill. Fourth, the language used might be difficult in older cases, as English, like the law, evolves and changes. Lastly, we, as beginning students, have little knowledge of the concepts being used. These difficulties make the practice of case briefing, at least initially, a difficult task. But the difficulties, I assure you, are overcome with just a little practice, leaving us with useful case briefs that illuminate and explain a particular concept for us.

In legal practice, case briefs are done after reading an entire opinion. This provides the practitioner with a standardized summary of the case opinion so that he or she will not need to reread the case in the future when drafting a memorandum of law or other piece of legal work. Thus, one has a usable summary.

A case brief, which is really just a standardized synthesis of the case excerpt, should only be done after the case has been read and reviewed.

At the top of the case brief, the name of the case and the citation should appear. Cases in our system are named for the participants. The citation, or cite, for the case is the reference to the location of the case opinion in a case reporter. Case reporters are the sets of volumes in which decisions of a particular court or court system are compiled. These case reporters are arranged in chronological order; the citation allows us to access the entire opinion, if we are working from an excerpt, or to locate an entire opinion we have used for our brief. Citations are typically a number, followed by an abbreviation, followed by another number. The abbreviation is for the particular case reporter or set of volumes in which the case would be found. The first number is the volume number within the set, and the second number is the page within the particular volume. For example, the case titled <u>International Shoe Company v. Washington</u>, 326 U.S. 310, could be found in the case reporter United States Reports, volume 326, page 310.

Next in our brief, we will draft a summary of the relevant facts of the case. For our purposes, a one- or two-sentence summary should provide enough detail to be useful. As is true with all the pieces of the brief that we will be writing, the facts should be in our own words. It is important not to copy extensively from the case excerpt. If we do, we just end up with an excerpt of an excerpt, and have not done the necessary analysis that writing it on your own requires.

Next, we need to summarize the issue or issues presented by the case. These are the questions the court is required to answer in its resolving of the dispute. For our briefs, we present these issues in the form of a question or questions.

Next, we need to summarize the holding of the case. The holding really is a discussion of how the court answers the questions asked of it, along with an analysis of how it arrived at those answers. It is the holding that provides us with the opportunity to understand the rationale for the court's decision. It is the synthesis of the rationale that, for us as students, gives the educational purpose for the case excerpt. That is, why is this case in the book? What am I supposed to gather from the case? The holding may use the relevant facts, summarized before, and see what law the court applied to these facts, to answer the question or questions before the court. This paragraph is the meat and potatoes of the case brief.

Lastly, in our form of case brief, we need to include a short summary of the dissenting opinions, if any occur. Dissenting opinions are written by appellate judges who disagree with the majority of judges within the court. In the

Supreme Court of the United States, for instance, a winning litigant needs to persuade five of the nine judges that he is correct. That leaves, potentially, four of the nine judges who disagree with the majority's opinion. They, either individually or collectively, may write a dissenting opinion or opinions explaining why they feel the Court's majority opinion is flawed.

Our first case concerns the authority of courts over individual citizens. Here, in U.S. v. Nixon, the ability of the courts to resolve disputes that involve any citizen, including the president of the United States, is brought into question by the executive branch of government.

✻ ✻ ✻

CASE #1-1

U.S. v. Nixon
418 U.S. 683, 94 Sect. 3090, 41 L.Ed.2d 1039 (1974)

BURGER, C.J. We turn to the claim that the subpoena should be quashed because it demands "confidential Conversations between a President and his close advisors that would be inconsistent with the public interest to produce." The first contention is a broad claim that the separation of powers doctrine precludes judicial review of the President's claim of privilege. The second contention is that if he does not prevail on the claim of absolute privilege, the court should hold, as a matter of Constitutional Law that the privilege prevails over the subpoena duces tecum.

In the performance of assigned Constitutional duties, each branch of the government must initially interpret the Constitution, and the interpretation of its powers by any branch is due great respect from the others. The President's counsel...reads the Constitution as providing an absolute privilege of confidentiality for all Presidential communications. Many decisions of this court, however, have unequivocally reaffirmed the holding of <u>Marbury v. Madison</u> (1803) that "it is emphatically the province and duty of the judicial department to say what the law is."

Since we conclude that the legitimate needs of the judicial process may outweigh presidential privilege, it is necessary to resolve those competing interests in a manner that preserves the essential functions of each branch. The right and indeed the duty to resolve that question does not free the judiciary from according high respect to the representations made on behalf of the President. <u>U.S. v. Burr</u> (1807)

The expectation of a President to the confidentiality of his conversations and correspondence, like the claim of confidentiality of judicial deliberations, has all the values to which we accord deference...

But this presumptive privilege must be considered in light of our historic commitment to the rule of law. This is nowhere more profoundly manifest than in our view that "the two-fold aim (of Criminal Law) is that guilt shall not escape nor innocence suffer." <u>Berger v. U.S.</u> (1935)

We conclude that when the ground for asserting privilege as to subpoenaed material sought for use in a criminal trial is based only on the generalized interest of confidentiality, it cannot prevail over the fundamental demands of due process of law in the fair administration of criminal justice. The generalized assertion of privilege must yield to the demonstrated specific need for evidence in a criminal trial.

☆ ☆ ☆

B. PRIVATE LAW

<u>Private law</u> covers the regulations and rules that are concerned with the behavior of one private citizen towards

another private citizen. It incorporates those standards of behavior that are needed to allow for a degree of order in our daily lives with one another. Private law includes the law of contracts, property law, torts, wills and estates, family law, and all other areas in which the law forms some order in our formal relations with each other.

The law of contracts deals with those promises we make each other that are binding by the law. Not all promises are legally binding but, of course, all contracts are some form of judicially enforceable promise. When we buy a car, for example, we enter into and sign a contract for the vehicle that outlines our promises in purchasing the car and that outlines the manufacturer's promises in selling it.

Property law defines the rights and duties of ownership of that which belongs to an individual. Property law can be further divided into real property law, which governs the ownership of land, and personal property law, which governs the ownership of all other types of property. In Blackstone's *Commentaries*, a famous description of English law published in 1765, the right of property is described as "that sole and despotic dominion which one man claims and exercises over the external things of the world, in total exclusion of the right of any other individual in the universe." Describing whether or not an individual even has such a right, to own and possess exclusively, was a defining challenge in the twentieth century as the struggle to preeminence between capitalistic cultures and communistic cultures provided a dominant international theme.

Torts are those civil wrongs, excluding those within a contractual situation, done by one party to another in violation of a duty of care owed. Damages for injuries may arise from personal injury or property injury, but must arise from a breach of a duty of care. Torts result from behavior that may be characterized as either careless or intentionally harmful, and provide for compensation for these injuries that so arise. Examples of torts include medical malpractice, auto accidents, slip-and-fall cases, and assaults.

Wills and estates deals with the ability to pass property that one owns along to one's heirs or beneficiaries. A will is a legal statement of how one's own properties are to be disposed of after one's death. The general area of wills and estates also defines what happens to a person's property if he should die without a will.

Family law governs the legal responsibilities of members of the basic social unit, the family. In the twenty-first century, the American description of family has broadened to include a variety of social arrangements, although the baseline definition remains father, mother, and children. Necessarily, family law deals extensively with families in trouble; divorce, separation, child or spousal abuse, and a variety of other difficulties are important facets of family law. Other issues, not necessarily crisis related, that occur in this field include marriage and adoption.

C. COURT SYSTEMS

Within the United States, there are at least fifty-two separate court systems, one for each of the fifty states, one for the District of Columbia, and one federal court system. There is a great deal of independence in the management and power of each of these court systems. The basic structure of each of the systems, however, is similar. Each has a hierarchical structure, with trial courts at the lowest level, and one or two levels of appeals courts above the trial court. Although the names of each level vary from system to system, the basic structure of each system is similar. Cases begin at the lowest level and work upwards through the system, if necessary. Each level contains a decreasing number of courts, with the highest level of appeals containing only one court in each system.

In addition to the levels of trial and appellate courts, most state court systems contain a number of courts often referred to as courts of limited jurisdiction. These courts, such as small claims court, traffic court, and town court, are available to parties that are involved in disputes that have only a small dollar amount in dispute, or who have violated a town or local ordinance. Proceedings in these courts may be less formal than in trial courts of general jurisdiction, and parties may present their own cases without an attorney.

✯ ✯ ✯

LEGAL LIGHT

The Supreme Court of the United States has seen a dramatic increase in its caseload in recent years. In the 2009-2010 term, there were some ten thousand cases on the docket. In 1960, only 2,313 cases were on the docket, and in 1945, only 1,460. Plenary review, with full oral presentations, is granted in about one hundred cases per term. The publication of the Term's written opinions approaches five thousand printed pages.

✯ ✯ ✯

Our next case combines a view of the structure of courts that goes beyond our initial discussion, along with a view of the power of a court that may relate to that structure. Structure and power can be interrelated and symbiotic.

✯ ✯ ✯

CASE #1-2

Ex Parte Milligan
71 U.S. (4 Wall.) 2, 18L.Ed. 28 (1866)

DAVIS, J. The importance of the main question presented by this record cannot be overstated, for it involves the very framework of the government and the fundamental principles of American liberty.

During the late wicked rebellion (the Civil War) the temper of the times did not allow that calmness in deliberation and discussion so necessary to a correct conclusion of a purely judicial question. Then, considerations of safety were mingled with the exercise of power, and feelings and interests prevailed which are happily terminated. Now that the public safety is assured, this question, as well as all others, can be discussed and decided without passion....

The controlling question in this case is this: Upon the facts stated in Milligan's petition, and the exhibits filed, had the Military Commission mentioned in it the jurisdiction, legally, to try and then sentence him? Milligan, not a resident of one of the rebellious states, or a prisoner of war, but a citizen of Indiana for twenty years past, and never in the military or naval service, is, while at his home, arrested by the military power of the United States, imprisoned, and, on certain criminal charges preferred against him, tried, convicted, and sentenced to be hanged by a military commission, organized under the direction of the military commander of the military district of Indiana. Had this tribunal the legal power and authority to try and punish this man?...

Every trial involves the exercise of judicial power; and from what source did the Military Commission that tried him derive their authority? Certainly, no part of the judicial power of the country was conferred upon them; because the Constitution expressly vests it "in one Supreme Court and such inferior courts as the Congress may from time to time ordain and establish," and it is not pretended that the commission was a court ordained and established by Congress. They cannot justify the mandate of the President; because he is controlled by law, he has an appropriate sphere of duty, which is to execute, not to make the laws; and there is no "unwritten criminal code to which resort can be had as a source of jurisdiction."

But it is said that the jurisdiction is complete under the "laws and usages of war." It can serve no useful purpose to inquire what those laws and usages are, whence they originated, where found, and on whom they operate; they never can never be applied to citizens in states which have upheld the authority of the government, and where the courts are open and their process unobstructed. This court has judicial knowledge that in Indiana the Federal authority was always unopposed, and its courts always open to hear criminal accusations and redress grievances; and no usage of war could sanction a military trial there for any offense whatever of a citizen in civil life, in no way connected with the military service. Congress could grant no such power; and to the honor of our national legislature be it said, it has never been provoked by the state of the country to even attempt its exercise. One of the plainest constitutional provisions was, therefore, infringed when Milligan was tried by a court not ordained and established by Congress, and not composed of judges appointed during good behavior....

It is claimed that martial law covers with its broad mantle the proceedings of this Military Commission. The proposition is this: That in a time of war the commander of an armed force...has the power, within the lines of his military district, to suspend all civil rights and their remedies, and subject citizens as well as soldiers to the rule of his will....

The statement of this proposition shows its importance; for, if true, republican government is a failure, and there is an end to liberty regulated by law...Civil liberty and this kind of martial law cannot endure together; the antagonism is irreconcilable and, in the conflict, one or the other must perish....

This nation, as experience has proved, cannot always stay at peace, and has no right to expect that it will always have wise and humane rulers, sincerely attached to the principles of the Constitution....If our fathers had failed to provide for such a contingency, they would have been false to the trust reposed in them....

* * *

LEGAL LIGHT

Some may say we have too many lawyers. However, just in the area of personal injury for auto accidents, the growth of disputes has exploded. In 2003, there were some 7,000,000 auto accidents in the United States, resulting in almost 3,500,000 injuries. The first recorded auto accident, by the way, occurred in 1896, when a collision occurred in Saint Louis between two of the four automobiles registered in the United States.

* * *

D. SOURCES OF LAW

The sources of the law, or where the law may be found, can be viewed in two ways. The first is where courts or judges find the law, and the second is where a given society finds the values and standards that are reflected and formalized into the legal system.

Where the courts find the law may be divided into two categories, primary sources of law and secondary sources of law. Primary sources of law are those five basic cornerstones of our legal system that are definitive sources for determining what the law is in a certain type of dispute or problem. They are the authoritative statements of that which constitutes the law. These five primary sources of law are the U.S. Constitution, cases, statutes, treaties, and administrative law.

The first primary source of law in our system is the U.S. Constitution, which serves as the basic contract of governance for the American people. It establishes both a framework of government and a philosophy of governance that have served us well for over two hundred years. Written in 1789, it is the world's oldest constitution. It forms a government of limited, enumerated powers; the structure established for this government consists of three co-equal branches, the legislative branch, the executive branch, and the judicial branch. There are checks and balances built into the authorities of each of the three branches to ensure a distribution of power. The philosophy of governmental theory that is expressed in the Constitution provides that all the powers not directly granted to one of these three branches shall be granted to the people. Great care is given in the Constitution to form a government that maintains power in the hands of citizens rather than in the hands of government.

The second primary source of law is cases, or previous decisions of judges, which form the backbone of our legal system. The dependence on precedence, or previous cases, allows a great deal of continuity and consistency in our courts and is a necessary element in the credibility of our law. Citizens essentially have faith in the legal system because the application of law to our disputes is fairly constant. Keep in mind, however, that the law applies intellectual concepts to an enormous variety of disputes with an infinite number of variations; some variations of solutions are inevitable. It is to the great credit of our legal system that these variations are as infrequent as they are. These judicial decisions still allow for change within the legal system, but this change is, as an inevitable consequence, evolutionary rather than revolutionary. We derive our reliance on previously decided cases from the English Common Law. Oran's *Dictionary of the Law* defines the Common Law as "the legal system that originated in England and is composed of case law and statutes that grow and change, influenced by ever-changing custom and tradition."

The third primary source of law is statutes or laws enacted by elected representatives in legislatures. Both state legislatures and Congress enact statues, which are compiled for us in sets of volumes called codes. Local legislative bodies enact laws as well; these are often called ordinances. The sum of the statutes that are passed by legislative bodies is enormous, and covers a great variety of topics.

The fourth primary source of law is treaties. Treaties are agreements between nations. Our Constitution provides that the executive branch of government drafts treaties and the legislative branch ratifies them. These treaties, once ratified, are the formal understandings between countries; they may cover such topics as trade, mutual defense, or monetary policy, and are the supreme law of the land.

Our third case in this chapter addresses the judicial interpretation of a treaty. The court uses an extradition treaty between the United States and Mexico as a primary source of law.

☆ ☆ ☆

CASE # 1-3

U.S. v. Alvarez-Machain
504 U.S. 655, 112 S.Ct. 2188 (1992)

REHNQUIST, C.J. The issue in this case is whether a criminal defendant, abducted to the United States from a nation with which it has an extradition treaty, thereby acquires a defense to the jurisdiction of this country's courts....

Respondent, Humberto Alvarez-Machain is a citizen and resident of Mexico. He was indicted for participating in the kidnap and murder of United States Drug Enforcement Administration (DEA) special agent Enrique Camarene-Salazar and a Mexican pilot working with Camarena, Alfredo Zavala-Avelar. The DEA believes that respondent, a medical doctor, participated in the murder by prolonging Agent Camarena's life so that others could torture and interrogate him. On April 2, 1990, respondent was forcibly kidnapped from his medical office in Guadalajara, Mexico, to be flown by private plane to El Paso, Texas, where he was arrested by DEA officials. The District court concluded that DEA agents were responsible for respondent's abduction, although they were not personally involved in it.

Respondent moved to dismiss the indictment, claiming that his abduction constituted outrageous governmental conduct, and that the District court lacked jurisdiction to try him because he was abducted in violation of the extradition treaty between the United States and Mexico....

More critical to respondent's argument is Article 9 of the Treaty, which provides:

"1. Neither Contracting Party shall be bound to deliver up its own nationals, but the executive authority of the requested Party shall, if not prevented by the laws of that Party, have the power to deliver them up if, in its discretion, it be deemed proper to do so.

"2. If extradition is not granted pursuant to paragraph 1 of this Article, the requested Party shall submit the case to its competent authorities for the purpose of prosecution, provided that Party has Jurisdiction over the offense."

According to respondent, Article 9 embodies the terms of the bargain which the United States struck: If the United States wishes to prosecute a Mexican national, it may request that individual's extradition. Upon a request from the United States, Mexico may either extradite that individual or submit the case to the proper authorities for prosecution in Mexico. In this way, respondent reasons, each nation preserved its right to chose whether its nationals would be tried in its own courts or by the courts of the other nation. This preservation of rights would be frustrated if either nation were free to abduct nationals of the other nation for the purpose of prosecution. More broadly, respondent reasons, as did the Court of Appeals, that all the processes and restrictions on the obligation to extradite established by the Treaty would make no sense if either nation were free to resort forcible kidnapping to gain the presence of an individual for prosecution in a manner not contemplated by the Treaty.

We do not read the Treaty in such a fashion. Article 9 does not purport to specify the only way in which one country may gain custody of a national of the other country for the purposes of prosecution. In the absence of an extradition treaty, nations are under no obligation to surrender those in their country to foreign authorities for prosecution. Extradition treaties exist so as to impose mutual obligations to surrender individuals in certain defined sets of circumstances, following established procedures. The Treaty thus provides a mechanism which would not otherwise exist, requiring, under certain circumstances, the United States and Mexico to extradite individuals to the other country, and establishing the procedures to be followed when the Treaty is invoked.

The history of negotiation and practice under the Treaty also fails to show that abductions outside of the Treaty constitute a violation of the Treaty....

Thus, the language of the Treaty, in the context of its history, does not support the proposition that the Treaty prohibits abductions outside of its own terms....

The judgment of the Court of Appeals is therefore reversed, and the case is remanded for further proceedings consistent with this opinion.

STEVENS, J. dissenting.

The court correctly observes that this case raises a question of first impression. The case is unique for several reasons. It does not involve an ordinary abduction by a private kidnapper or bounty hunter....Rather, it involves this country's abduction of another country's citizen; it also involves a violation of the territorial integrity of that other country, with which this country has signed an extradition treaty....

It is true, as the court notes, that there is no express promise by either party to refrain from forcible abductions in the territory of the other nation. Relying on that omission, the Court, in effect, concludes that the Treaty merely creates an optional method of obtaining jurisdiction over alleged offenders, and that the parties silently reserved the right to resort to self-help whenever they deem force more expeditious than legal processes....

I respectfully dissent.

The fifth primary source of law is administrative law. Administrative law, as we have seen before, encompasses the rules and regulations of administrative agencies. These agencies are sub-branches of the government that are set up to carry out the law. In this case, the court is asked to resolve a dispute involving how an agency carrying out a regulatory policy.

Case #1-4

New York v. F.E.R.C.
535 U.S. 1, 122S.Ct. 1012, 152 L.Ed.2d. 47 (2002)

STEVENS, J. These cases raise two important questions concerning the jurisdiction of the Federal Energy Regulatory Commission (FERC or Commission) over the transmission of electricity. First, if a public utility "unbundles"—i.e., separates—the cost of transmission from the cost of electrical energy when billing its retail customers, may FERC require the utility to transmit competitors' electricity over its lines on the same terms that the utility applies to its own energy transmissions? Second, must FERC impose that requirement on utilities that continue to offer only "unbundled" retail sales?

...FERC answered yes to the first question and no to the second....

In the face of this clear statutory language, New York advances three arguments in support of its submission that the statute draws a bright jurisdictional line between wholesale transactions and retail transactions. First, New York contends that the Court of Appeals applied an erroneous standard of review because it ignored the presumption against Federal pre-emption of state law; ... These arguments are unpersuasive.

...This is the sort of case we confront here—defining the scope of federal power. Such a case does not involve a "presumption against pre-emption," as New York argues, but rather requires us to be certain that Congress has conferred authority on the agency. As we have explained, the best way to answer such a question—i.e., whether federal power may be exercised in an area of preexisting state regulation—"is to examine the nature and scope of the authority granted by Congress to the agency." Louisiana Pub. Serv. Comm. v. FCC, 476 U.S. 355, 106 S.Ct. 1890, 90 L.Ed.2d. 369 (1986). In other words, we must interpret the statute to determine whether Congress has given FERC the power to act as it has, and we do so without any presumption one way or the other.

...[W]e nevertheless conclude that the agency had the discretion to decline to assert such jurisdiction in this proceeding in part because of the complicated nature of the jurisdictional issues. Like the Court of Appeals, we are satisfied that FERC's choice not to assert jurisdiction over bundled retail transmissions in a rulemaking proceeding focusing on the wholesale market "represents a statutorily permissible policy choice." 225 F.3d., at 694-695.

Accordingly, the judgment of the Court of Appeals is affirmed.

✯ ✯ ✯

In addition to these primary sources of law, judges may turn to other places for help and guidance in determining what the law applies in a particular dispute. These other places are known as secondary sources of law and may include law review articles, legal treatises, dictionaries, encyclopedias, or any other possible source available. These secondary sources are inferior to primary sources, but may be used as supplements to the primary sources.

Within any society, the laws must reflect the standards of that particular society; if they do not reflect these widespread standards, the laws and the legal system will fail. Prohibition, no matter how well intended and moral, simply did not reflect the prevailing societal sentiment. These societal values are passed from one segment of society to another and from one generation to another through a variety of mechanisms. These methods for continuity in societal values include parents, peers, teachers, religious leaders, and the media.

Here is an example of the way courts use primary sources of law.

✵ ✵ ✵

CASE #1-5

In re ORSO
283 F.3d 686 (2002)

WIENER and DENNIS, Circuit Judges:

In this appeal we decide whether, under the laws of Louisiana that establish exemptions from seizure, the proceeds of annuity contracts purchased by obligors to fulfill a personal injury settlement structured to comply with 26 U.S.C. §§ 104(a)(2) and 130 [FN 1] are exempt from claims of creditors of the payee who is a debtor in bankruptcy. A divided panel of this court [FN2] concluded that our opinion in Young v. Adler [FN3] required it to hold the instant annuity payments are not exempt under the Louisiana exemption statute as it existed when bankruptcy proceedings were commenced, and that a post-petition, expressly-interpretive amendment of that statute could not be considered when ascertaining its meaning as of the date of filing for bankruptcy protection. A majority of the judges in active service voted to rehear the case en banc. [FN4] Disagreeing with the panel majority, we affirm the bankruptcy and district courts' conclusion that the annuity payments in question are exempt from seizure, and thus exempt from claims asserted by Creditor-Appellant Valerie Canfield in Debtor-Appellee Paul William Orso's bankruptcy proceedings.

✵ ✵ ✵

I. FACTS AND PROCEEDINGS

Orso suffered serious injuries in an automobile accident in November 1986, a few months after he and Canfield were wed. The closed-head injuries Orso sustained in the accident left him permanently and severely brain damaged, rendering him mildly mentally retarded, with an I.Q. of less than 70. In November 1987, Canfield and Orso sued for damages resulting from his injuries.

In September 1989, Orso and Canfield entered into a consent judgment with the defendants in the tort litigation. On the same day, the parties executed a settlement agreement, the pertinent provision of which specified that Orso would receive two payments each month for the longer of * thirty years or his lifetime, one such payment for $1,180 and another for $850.

To ensure Orso's full and timely receipt of these periodic payments, annuity contracts ("the Annuities") were purchased. Orso is the named payee or annuitant in both contracts, but is not the owner of either; the defendant tortfeasors' insurers obtained the policies and retained ownership. The annuity contract that pays $1,180 per month was issued by Liberty Life Assurance Company of Boston in connection with Orso's settlement with one of the tortfeasors, Cook Construction Co., Inc., and its insurer, Liberty Mutual Insurance Co. The annuity contract that pays Orso $850 per month was issued by Western National Life Insurance Company in connection with his settlement with the State of Louisiana, having been purchased by the Conseco Annuity Guarantee Company, the company to which the State had assigned the obligation to make the periodic payments. The tortfeasors and their respective insurers were released from further tort liability but remained obligated for the periodic payments to Orso, who presumably could thereafter look to his original judgment debtors and their insurers in the unlikely event that the issuers of the Annuities should be unable or unwilling to continue making the specified monthly payments.

✼ ✼ ✼

2. Interpretation of Applicable State Law

For Orso to prevail, he must demonstrate that the payments produced by the particular annuities purchased by or on behalf of his tort debtors in the structured settlement of their consent judgment are covered by § 22:647. In determining whether the proceeds and avails of the structured settlement annuities fall within the Louisiana exemption, we resort to the acts of the state legislature and to the pronouncements of the state's courts as well.

Having established the applicable framework for resolution of the question whether Orso's proceeds from the Annuities are exempt, we now examine the Louisiana annuity exemption statute, § 22:647.

C. Construction of the Louisiana Statute

[8] As noted, Orso contends that his property right in the stream of annuity payments from his structured settlement comes within the purview of the version of § 22:647, specifically subsection (B) that existed on the day his bankruptcy petition was filed. For the following reasons, we agree.

When, in 1948, the Louisiana Legislature enacted that state's Insurance Code, it specified that the proceeds and avails of annuity contracts are exempt from all debt liability. The language of that enactment is largely retained in the current version of the statute. [FN20] The term "annuity contract" was not modified; neither was it limited to particular types, classes, or categories of annuity. That being the case, the term's grasp is co-extensive with its reach.

✼ ✼ ✼

[11][12][13][14][15] Because Louisiana stands alone among the 50 states as a hybrid Civil Law/common law jurisdiction, its situation is unique: The State's constitution, its codes and its statutes, are the **primary sources** of law; court decisions are treated as secondary sources of law, without *stare decisis* precedential effect. [FN29] When interpreting the law of Louisiana, as we do today, we are bound to honor, among other things, Louisiana's distinction between substantive and interpretive laws, recognizing that:

✻ ✻ ✻

The character of interpretive legislation is evident in a civil law system such as Louisiana. "Judicial opinions, although invaluable interpretations of the law are merely that; interpretations of the legislative will. The supreme expression of legislative will in Louisiana is of course the codes and statutes." Interpretive laws provide the Legislature with the opportunity to pronounce the "correct" interpretation to be given to existing laws. [FN30]

✻ ✻ ✻

*696 [16][17] The Louisiana Legislature expressly characterized the 1999 Amendment as *interpretive*, meaning that it is not new law and not a retroactive change, but is the correct construction of existing law. In Louisiana, "interpretative legislation does not create new rules, but merely establishes the meaning that the interpreted statute had from the time of its enactment. It is the original statute, not the interpretive one, that establishes the rights and duties." [FN31] Although other states allot similar interpretive roles to the judiciary alone, the Louisiana approach is within the broad latitudes states enjoy in choosing which roles are performed by which state institutions. [FN32] When, as here, federal courts must interpret a state statute that is functioning under a congressional delegation of exclusive authority to declare the law, we properly include in our consideration and treat as instructive, legislative enactments and judicial decisions of the State that postdate filing of the bankruptcy petition yet properly bear on our construction of the statute in question to conform with the way the State interprets it. This is especially true of unmistakably interpretive declarations of the Louisiana Legislature. [FN33]

II. CONCLUSION

We hold that the periodic payments to Orso under his structured settlement, flowing as they do from annuity contracts, are exempt from his bankruptcy creditors under Louisiana law, a conclusion bolstered by (but not wholly reliant on) the 1999 Amendment to § 22:647. Because they are proceeds of annuity contracts, the payments to Orso are exempt from his bankruptcy estate under clearly established Louisiana law extant on the day that his petition in bankruptcy was filed. And, as today we are rehearing this case en banc, we expressly overrule Young and McGovern, as well as anything in Guidry that conflicts with the foregoing. The judgment of the bankruptcy court, as affirmed by the district court, recognizing the exemption of the monthly annuity payments to Orso, is
AFFIRMED.

✿ ✿ ✿

E. SCHOOLS OF LEGAL THOUGHT AND THEORY

A variety of basic schools of legal theory have evolved over the centuries. These philosophies of legal thought have an impact on both the type of legal system we have and on the goals of that legal system.

Natural law is a school of legal thought that believes that there is a higher law than man-made law which applies to all men and is unchangeable. It puts forth the idea that people have certain absolute rights as a matter of nature, and that these rights cannot be impaired by the state. The Declaration of Independence, which includes reference to certain unalienable rights endowed upon us by our Creator, reflects the essence of this philosophy of law. The document goes on to describe these rights as life, liberty, and the pursuit of happiness, and to explain that these natural rights cannot be infringed upon by governments. Natural law presumes the basic goodness of man, and relies upon man's intellect to discover appropriate laws and behaviors.

A second school of legal theory is the historical school of law. This philosophy emphasizes the continuity in the law and believes that current laws should be constructed on that which has been done in the past. One can see the influence of this school of law in our system's reliance on case law and precedence. Also, some judges rely on the original intent of our Constitution's authors when attempting to interpret the Constitution.

A third school of legal thought is the analytical school. This group relies on logical examination to reach inevitable conclusions about legal principles. The correctness of a particular law would depend on whether or not it agrees with broad legal principles gleaned from the review of the law.

The fourth school is referred to as the legal realism school of law. This group bases its study of the law on the view that social forces and desired societal results should shape the law. It is highly pragmatic in its philosophy of law; it assesses the success of a law on how efficiently it serves social needs.

✳ ✳ ✳

CHAPTER ONE
KEY TERMS

Administrative Law
Appellate Courts
Constitutional Law
Criminal Law
Estates
Extradition
Family Law
International Law
Jurisdiction
Primary Sources of Law
Private Law
Property
Public Law
Secondary Sources of Law
Subpoena
Subpoena Duces Tecum
Torts
Trial Courts
Wills

☆ ☆ ☆

CHAPTER SUMMARY

The vast field of the law can be divided into two major components, private law and public law. Private law covers how individuals deal with each other. Public law deals with how society, either in the form of the government or as a nongovernmental entity, deals with individual members of the society.

The law is usually studied both in a traditional pedagogical structure and also through the use of case studies. The case studies serve as examples and illustrations of the application of abstract legal concepts to concrete, real problems. This case study method of learning is greatly enhanced by the use of case briefs, devices to synthesize and standardize the highly complex and diverse case opinions that are used in the case study method. These case briefs are also used in the practice of law as a building block in legal research.

The American legal system has a variety of legal entities, both on a state and on a federal level. While these entities are diverse, the basic structure of the various court systems is the same within each state system and within the federal court system. The basic common structure is pyramidal in form, with the trial courts as the base and the two appellate levels higher up.

When we attempt to glean from whence the law has come, we divide the various sources of law into two parts. Primary sources, which are the Constitution, treaties, cases, statutes, and administrative law, are definitive and controlling. Secondary sources, which are any other sources of law, are suggestive and subsidiary to primary sources.

THINK AND WRITE

1. What are three specific standards or behavior that we Americans impose on our society in each of the areas of public law?
2. What are three specific standards of behavior that we Americans impose on our society in each of the areas of private law?
3. Why are there fewer appellate courts than trial courts in each court system?
4. What are the advantages and disadvantages of each state and the federal government having separate court systems?

5. How can the various schools of legal thought work in harmony or in disharmony?
6. Name four administrative agencies within the federal government. What does each do?

✲ ✲ ✲

PROJECTS

1. Look up and review a schematic diagram of the federal court system.
2. Look up and review a schematic of your state's court system.
3. Review the legal system of a Muslim country. How does it differ from ours?
4. Review the legal system of a Common Law country. How does it differ from ours?
5. Review the legal system of an ancient civilization. How does it differ from ours?

✲ ✲ ✲

ETHICAL QUESTIONS

1. In most states, the average amount of judgments varies from county to county. Should an attorney encourage his client to move to a county where the judgment for matters like his plaintiff-client's are larger?
2. I am an attorney whose practice is in a New York town that borders New Jersey. In New York, divorces based on a separation cause of action require a written agreement be in place before the separation period begins tolling; in New Jersey, the time begins to toll when one party moves out. Should I suggest to my client that she move

out to a New Jersey, rather than a New York address, knowing the time period and the costs would be less?

☆ ☆ ☆

RELATED WEBSITES

1. Current legal cases with commentary: http://www.cnn.com/LAW/
2. "Everyday law for everyday people": http://www.nolo.com/
3. General legal information: http://wwwlawguru.com/
4. Directory of law schools: http://www.usnews.com/usnews/edu/grad/directory/dir-law/dirlawindex_brief.php

CHAPTER TWO

JUDICIAL POWER

Courts have a variety of powers to hear cases that are brought before them. Equally as important, the courts have a variety of powers not to hear a case brought before them. We need to understand the rules that govern the powers of courts to hear disputes in order to understand the types of problems that are appropriate for resolution in our court system. It is important to understand that not all problems belong in courts; some problems are not appropriate for judicial resolution. Further, even if a case is appropriate for our courts, some rules of order are necessary to determine where in our large court structures a particular case belongs. The rules for whether or not a case will be heard and for where a case will be heard fall within the study of the powers of courts.

I. TYPES OF JURISDICTION

A. STATE JURISDICTION

Jurisdiction is defined as the power of a tribunal to hear and decide a case. At least one of the jurisdictions that we are going to discuss must be identified as being present as part of a given dispute, or a court would not have the power to hear the case. That is, if a court cannot identify a specific jurisdiction that it has over a particular case, the court would be powerless to hear the dispute. Courts exercise a variety of jurisdictions, including *in personam* jurisdiction, *in rem* jurisdiction, and *quasi in rem* jurisdiction.

More than one of these bases of jurisdiction may be present in a given dispute, and some of these powers may overlap one another in a particular problem. In personam jurisdiction, in rem jurisdiction, and quasi in rem jurisdiction are primarily applicable to state level courts; federal courts have a different set of powers, as we will see later. Original jurisdiction, appellate jurisdiction, and subject matter jurisdiction are all applicable to both state level and federal courts.

1. In Personam Jurisdiction

In personam jurisdiction means the power over the person or persons involved in a dispute or lawsuit. Courts have authority over the people who live in, or who have some significant contact with, the state in question. If, for example, the two parties in a civil law suit are both residents of New York, then New York courts would have in personam jurisdiction to hear the dispute involving these two parties. But, what if the two parties are from different states? Suppose one of the parties is from New York but the other party is from Connecticut. Then New York would still have in personam jurisdiction over the lawsuit, as New York would still have power over its residents, Connecticut, though, would also have in personam jurisdiction over the dispute, as it would have power over its residents. Notice, only one of the participants need be from a state for that state's courts to have the power to hear the case. This gives rise to two questions. First, can more than one state have the power to hear a lawsuit? As we've seen here, more than one state can have the ability to hear a case. As each state's courts should have the ability to hear the cases involving its citizens, in some disputes more than one court may have the authority to hear the suit. The second question that arises is, can the case be heard in more than one state? The answer is no, but in which state it will be heard depends on the area of law called conflict of laws. Conflict of laws exists when the laws of more than one state or country may apply to a case and a judge must choose among them.

The rules concerned with the determination of the state or country in which the case will be heard is called conflict of laws.

In personam jurisdiction may be satisfied in several ways. First, as we have seen, citizens of the state are subject to the in personam jurisdiction of that state's courts. Further, if a business is regularly transacting business in a given state, then it is subject to the state courts' in personam jurisdiction. Third, if a party to a dispute has an agent or official representative within the state, then the party is subject to in personam jurisdiction in that state and the agent will receive all the documents associated with the suit. Fourth, if a party is served with the summons and complaint while it is in the state, whether it is a resident or not, then it would be subject to the power of that state's court. These four facets of in personam jurisdiction comprise the vast majority of state rules covering in personam jurisdiction.

Our next case involves a dispute as to whether a state court has in personam jurisdiction over parties in a dispute. In the Internet age, technology can raise issues where none existed before.

✲ ✲ ✲

CASE #2- 1

Young v. New Haven Advocate
315 F.3d 256 (2002)

MICHAEL, J. The question in this case is whether two Connecticut newspapers and certain of their staff... subjected themselves to personal jurisdiction in Virginia by posting on the Internet news articles that, in the context of discussing the State of Connecticut's policy of housing its prisoners in Virginia institutions, allegedly defamed the warden of a Virginia prison....

Sometime in the late 1990's the State of Connecticut was faced with substantial overcrowding in its maximum security prisons. To alleviate the problem, Connecticut contracted with the Commonwealth of Virginia to house Connecticut prisoners in Virginia's correctional facilities. Beginning in late 1999, Connecticut transferred about 500 prisoners, mostly African-American and Hispanic, to the Wallens Ridge State Prison, a "supermax" facility in Big Stone Gap, Virginia....

...On March 30, 2000, the Advocate published a news article, written by one of its reporters, defendant Camille Jackson, about the transfer of Connecticut inmates to Wallens Ridge. The article discussed the allegedly harsh conditions at the Virginia prison and pointed out that the long trip to southwestern Virginia made visits by prisoners' families difficult or impossible....Finally, a paragraph at the end of the article reported that a Connecticut state senator had expressed concern about the presence of Confederate War memorabilia in Warden Young's office...

The newspaper defendants filed motions to dismiss the complaint under Federal Rule of Civil Procedure 12(b)(2) on the ground that the...court lacked personal jurisdiction over them....

They (defendants) do not live in Virginia, solicit any business there, or have any assets or business relationships there. The newspapers do not have any offices or employees in Virginia and they do not regularly solicit or do business in Virginia. Finally, the newspapers do not derive any substantial revenue from goods used or services rendered in Virginia....

Warden Young argues that the district court has specific personal jurisdiction over the newspaper defendants... because of the following contacts between them and Virginia: (1) the newspapers, knowing that Young was a Virginia resident, intentionally discussed and defamed him in their articles, (2) the newspapers posted the articles on their websites, which were accessible in Virginia and (3) the primary effects of the defamatory statements on Young's reputation were felt in Virginia. Young emphasizes that he is not arguing jurisdiction is proper in any location where defamatory Internet content can be accessed, which would be anywhere in the world. Rather, Young argues personal jurisdiction is proper in Virginia because the newspapers understood that their defamatory articles, which were available to Virginia residents on the Internet, would expose Young to public hatred, contempt, and ridicule in Virginia, where he lived and worked...

...In ALS Scan we went on to adapt the traditional standard...for establishing...jurisdiction so that it makes sense in the Internet context. We "conclude(d) that a State may, consistent with due process, exercise judicial power over a person outside the State when that person (1) directs electronic activity into that State, (2) with the manifest intent of engaging in business or other interactions within the State, and (3) that activity creates, in a person within the State, a potential cause of action cognizable in the State's courts."...

...The overall content of both websites is decidedly local, and neither newspaper's websites contains advertisements aimed at a Virginia audience...

The facts in this case establish that the newspapers' websites, as well as the articles in question, were aimed at a Connecticut audience. The newspapers did not post materials on the Internet with the manifest intent of targeting Virginia readers....In sum, the newspapers do not have sufficient Internet contacts with Virginia to permit the district court to exercise...jurisdiction over them.

✲ ✲ ✲

2. In Rem Jurisdiction

In rem jurisdiction means having power over the thing involved in the lawsuit. The courts have the power to hear disputes involving things that are within the state's borders. A typical example of in rem jurisdiction involves a dispute over the ownership of a piece of real property. Suppose two people both claim that they are the rightful owner of a piece of real estate. One of the parties is a resident of Kansas, one of the parties is a resident of Wyoming, and the land is located in Colorado. The courts in the state of Colorado would have the authority to hear the dispute, as they have in rem jurisdiction over the thing involved in the dispute, here the land located in Colorado. Notice also that the courts in Kansas and Wyoming would still have in personam jurisdiction over the dispute as well.

Our next two cases are interesting variations on in rem jurisdiction.

✫ ✫ ✫

Case #2-2 In Rem Jurisdiction

In re FRENCH
303 B.R. 774 (2003)

JAMES F. SCHNEIDER, Chief Judge.

This matter is before the Court upon the defendants' motion to dismiss the trustee's complaint to recover fraudulently transferred estate property. For the reasons set forth, the motion will be denied.

FINDINGS OF FACT

On October 20, 2000, the Peninsula Bank filed the instant involuntary Chapter 7 bankruptcy petition in this Court against the debtor, Betty Irene French. On January 29, 2001, an order for relief was entered.

On August 22, 2002, George W. Liebmann, the Chapter 7 trustee, filed the instant complaint to avoid and recover an alleged fraudulent transfer made by the debtor to her son, Randy French, and her daughter, Donna Shaka, of certain real property located in Nassau in the Bahama Islands for no consideration within 12 months of the filing of the petition. The verified complaint alleged that the debtor did not list the property in her schedules or disclose its existence in her Statement of Affairs which she filed in her bankruptcy case. It further alleged that the property was purchased by the debtor and titled in her name by deed dated November 11, 1976, and recorded in the Bahamas; that she deeded the property to the defendants by deed dated December 1981 but not recorded in the Bahamian land records until June 21, 2000.

The trustee also filed a motion [P. 2] for temporary restraining order ("TRO"), which this Court granted by order [P. 3] entered August 26, 2002. The TRO prohibited the defendants from Transferring or encumbering the Bahamian property for a period of ten days. On September 4, 2002, Judge E. Stephen Derby granted the plaintiff's request for a preliminary injunction [P. 7].

On October 10, 2002, the defendants filed the instant motion to dismiss [P. 9]. The motion was premised upon two legal arguments. First, that the transfer in question occurred upon the date the unrecorded deed was executed, namely, December 1981, well outside the one-year period authorized for the recovery of fraudulent conveyances. Second, that Sections 548 and 550 of the Bankruptcy Code [FN1] providing for the recovery of fraudulent transfers, do not apply to property located outside the borders of the United States, citing <u>Maxwell Communication Corp. v. Barclays Bank (In re Maxwell Communication Corp.)</u>, 170 B.R. 800 (Bankr.S.D.N.Y.1994), aff'd, 186 B.R. 807 (S.D.N.Y.1995), aff'd, 93 F.3d 1036 (2d Cir.1996), and principles of International comity.

✵ ✵ ✵

They also cited the case of <u>Kojima v. Grandote Intern., LLC (In re Grandote Country Club Co., Ltd.)</u>, 252 F.3d 1146 (10th Cir.2001), for the proposition that foreign law can never apply to property located in another country.

The defendants claim that there are no cases standing for the proposition that Sections 547 and 548 may be applied outside the United States to permit a trustee to recover property.

CONCLUSIONS OF LAW

[1] To the extent that the motion to dismiss contests the date of the transfer, it must fail. "When ruling upon a motion to dismiss a complaint for failure to state a claim for which relief can be granted pursuant to Federal Rule 12(b)(6), the Court must accept as true all well-pleaded allegations in the complaint, including all reasonable inferences that may be drawn from them, in the light most favorable to the plaintiff." <u>Hemelt v. Pontier (In re Pontier)</u>, 165 B.R. 797, 798 (Bankr.D.Md.1994). As stated in the complaint, the transfer in this case occurred on June 21, 2000, when the deed to the property was recorded among the Bahamian land records by the defendants. This comports with Section 548(d)(1) of the Bankruptcy Code, which provides that a transfer occurs "when such transfer is so perfected that a bona fide purchaser from the debtor against whom applicable law permits such transfer to be perfected cannot acquire an interest in the property transferred that is superior to the interest in such property of the transferee, but if such transfer is not so perfected before the commencement of the case, such transfer is made immediately before the date of the filing of the petition."

[2] The motion to dismiss could be denied without even addressing the extraterritoriality of the Bankruptcy Code,

because the complaint does not allege that the transfer occurred outside this country, which the motion to dismiss assumes. Nevertheless, to the extent that the avoidance of the transfer at issue requires a discussion of extraterritoriality, it is noted that the extraterritorial application of the Bankruptcy Code has been upheld in the context of the discharge injunction of Section 524, the worldwide effect of the automatic stay of Section 362, and the prohibition against litigation against a reorganized debtor after confirmation of a plan, pursuant to Sections 524 and 1141, considerations that have some application to the present controversy.

✲ ✲ ✲

The district court properly concluded that as to actions against the bankruptcy estate, Congress clearly intended extraterritorial application of the Bankruptcy Code. The filing of a bankruptcy petition under 11 U.S.C. §§ 301, 302 or 303 creates a bankruptcy estate. 11 U.S.C. § 541(a). With certain exceptions, the estate is comprised of the debtor's legal or equitable interests in property *"wherever located and by whomever held" Id.* (emphasis supplied). The district court in which the bankruptcy case is commenced obtains exclusive ***in* rem jurisdiction** over all of the property in the estate. 28 U.S.C. § 1334(e); Commodity Futures Trading Comm'n v. Co Petro Marketing Group, Inc., 700 F.2d 1279, 1282 (9th Cir.1983) (interpreting 28 U.S.C. § 1471, the statutory precursor to 28 U.S.C. § 1334(e)). The court's exercise of "custody" over the debtor's property, via its exercise of *in rem* jurisdiction, essentially creates a fiction that the property—regardless of actual location—is legally located within the jurisdictional boundaries of the district in which the court sits. *See* Katchen v. Landy, 382 U.S. 323, 327, 86 S.Ct. 467, IS L.Ed.2d 391 (1966) (noting that bankruptcy courts have "constructive possession" over estate property) (internal quotation marks and citations omitted); Commodity Futures, 700 F.2d at 1282 (noting that under the bankruptcy code, "all property of the debtor, wherever located, is in *custodia legis* of the bankruptcy court."). This includes property outside the territorial jurisdiction of the United States. *See* Stegeman, 425 F.2d at 986 (construing extraterritorial jurisdictional reach of prior Bankruptcy Act); *see also* Underwood v. Hilliard (In re Rimsat, Ltd.), 98 F.3d 956, 961 (7th Cir.1996).

Given this clear expression of intent by Congress in the express language of the Bankruptcy Code, we conclude that Congress intended extraterritorial application of the Bankruptcy Code as it applies to property of the estate. Although Hong Kong-Shanghai concedes this point, it questions whether such an extraterritorial application may operate to enjoin a foreign proceeding. As a matter of general principle, protection of **in rem** or **quasi in rem jurisdiction** is a sufficient basis for a court to restrain another court's proceedings. Donovan v. City of Dallas, 377 U.S. 408, 412, 84 S.Ct. 1579, 12 L.Ed2d 409 (1964). In such cases "the state or federal court having custody of such property has exclusive jurisdiction to proceed." *Id.* This rationale extends to foreign proceedings. *See* Seattle Totems Hockey Club v. National Hockey League, 652 F.2d 852, 855 (9th Cir.1981); *see also* Gau Shan Co. v. Bankers Trust Co., 956 F.2d 1349, 1356 (6th Cir.1992); China Trade & Develop. Corp., v. MY. Choong Yong, 837 F.2d 33, 36 (2d Cir.1987).

In the bankruptcy context, the Seventh Circuit has expressly held that protection of the bankruptcy court's **in rem jurisdiction** over estate property allows an international proceeding to be enjoined pursuant to the automatic stay in 11 U.S.C. § 362.

Underwood, 98 F.3d at 961. As Chief Judge Posner explained: "The efficacy of the bankruptcy proceeding depends on the court's ability to control and marshal the assets of the debtor wherever located...." *Id.*

As applied to the concept of **in rem** bankruptcy **jurisdiction**, there is no functional difference between the automatic stay imposed by 11 U.S.C. § 362 upon the commencement of a bankruptcy and the injunction prohibiting collection actions against the bankruptcy estate provided in 11 U.S.C. § 524(a)(3). Each stay operates to protect the estate and the **in rem jurisdiction** of the bankruptcy court. Accordingly, we join the Seventh Circuit's logic and hold that a bankruptcy court may validly exercise its **in rem jurisdiction** to protect estate property wherever the property is located in issuing a discharge injunction under 11 U.S.C. § 524. Thus, the district court correctly held in this case that the 11 U.S.C. § 524 discharge enjoined Hong Kong-Shanghai from commencing collection against any bankruptcy estate properly regardless of its geographic location.

Simon, 153 F.3d at 995-96.

According to Section 541(a) of the Bankruptcy Code [FN2] property of the bankruptcy estate includes every interest of a debtor in property "wherever located and by whomever held." In <u>Nakash v. Zur (In re Nakash)</u>, 190 B.R. 763 (Bankr.S.D.N.Y.1996), this provision was held to indicate congressional intent that the automatic stay provisions of Section 362 of the Code be given extraterritorial application to protect a debtor from the filing of an insolvency proceeding against it in Israel.

☆ ☆ ☆

[3][4] Regardless of the fact that the land in question is located in the Bahamas, it is property of the estate within the subject matter jurisdiction of this Court pursuant to Section 541(a). This Court enjoys primary jurisdiction over the subject property because there is no competing insolvency proceeding involving the debtor now pending in the Bahama Islands. *Cf.* <u>Stonington Partners, Inc. v. Lernout & Hauspie Speech Products, NV.</u>, 310 F.3d 118 (3d Cir.2002) (U.S. Bankruptcy Court erroneously entered "anti-suit"

injunction against pending Belgian insolvency proceeding according to the <u>Maxwell</u> analysis); and <u>Official Committee of Unsecured Creditors v. Transpacific Corp. Ltd. (In re Commodore Intern., Ltd.)</u>, 242 B.R. 243 (Bankr.S.D.N.Y.1999) (Bahamian insolvency proceedings were given deference under the principle of comity, where a competing insolvency proceeding was pending in the Bahamas).

This Court has personal jurisdiction as well over the parties, including the defendants, both of whom are domiciliaries of the United States who were properly served. As the debtor's children, the defendant-transferees are insiders of the debtor. This matter is a core proceeding over which this Court is exercising **in rem jurisdiction**. 28 U.S.C. § 157(b)(2)(F) and (H).

For all these reasons, the defendants' motion to dismiss will be DENIED.

☆ ☆ ☆

CASE #2-3 IN REM II

POLKOWSKI v. POLKOWSKI
854 So.2d 286 (2003)

☆ ☆ ☆

[1] The effect of state boundaries on a court's jurisdiction over property to be distributed in a dissolution proceeding frames the issue in this appeal. The husband challenges the final judgment dissolving his marriage and distributing the marital property. He raises two issues on appeal. First, the husband argues that the trial court lacked the authority to order the partition of the marital residence located in Plantation, Florida. Second, he

argues that the trial court lacked jurisdiction to order the sale of real property located in North Carolina. We reverse that portion of the final judgment ordering the sale of the North Carolina property and affirm in all other respects.

[2] The final judgment provides, "The real property located in Murphy, North Carolina shall be sold and the net proceeds of the sale shall be equally divided by the parties." Like lines in the sand, state boundaries determine a court's jurisdiction over real property. In this case, the trial court lacked **in rem jurisdiction** over the North Carolina property. It erred in that portion of the final judgment ordering the partition and sale of the North Carolina property. *See* <u>Pawlik v. Pawlik</u>, 545 So.2d 506, 507 (Fla. 2d DCA 1989); *see also* <u>Sammons v. Sammons</u>, 479 So.2d 223, 225 (Fla. 3d DCA 1985); <u>Farley v. Farley</u>, 790 So.2d 574 (Fla. 4th DCA 2001).

We therefore reverse the judgment in part and remand the case to the trial court. Upon remand, the court may reconsider the distribution of all marital assets in light of this opinion. *See* <u>Pawlik</u>, 545 So.2d at 507.

Affirmed in part, reversed in part, and remanded. STEVENSON, MAY, JJ., and CHAVIES, MICHAEL B., Associate Judge, concur.

☆ ☆ ☆

3. Quasi In Rem Jurisdiction
Quasi in rem jurisdiction means the power over the thing involved that the plaintiff wants to get out of the lawsuit. Unlike in rem jurisdiction, which is authority over the actual thing involved in the dispute, quasi in rem jurisdiction is an authority over the thing that the plaintiff wants to get from the court as an end product. Generally, quasi in rem jurisdiction is used when the plaintiff can't find in personam or in rem jurisdiction, but can identify assets of the defendant that will be a necessary part of the judgment that he hopes to win.

Suppose a dispute develops between two Missouri residents over an accident that occurred in Missouri. The payment of the judgment, however, depends upon a liability insurance policy that was issued in, and is payable by, an Arkansas insurance company. The Arkansas company is not a party to the dispute, the accident occurred in Missouri, and the parties are residents of Missouri, but the plaintiff can only collect the money in Arkansas. Arkansas courts would have quasi in rem jurisdiction over the dispute, as that which can be recovered in the suit is in Arkansas, even though that which can be recovered is not directly involved in the suit.

☆ ☆ ☆

B. STATE AND/OR FEDERAL JURISDICTION

4. Original Jurisdiction

The first three types of jurisdiction we examined all help to determine in which state or states a case might be heard. Once a case is in a particular state, or in the federal courts, methods are needed for determining which court within the system will have the authority to hear the case. The first of these internal jurisdictions is <u>original jurisdiction</u>. Courts within the trial court level of a given system are said to have original jurisdiction over a dispute, since it is at this court level that cases originate or begin. As our state courts have a hierarchical structure, it is at the base layer in which cases are begun.

5. Appellate Jurisdiction

Courts within the appeals levels of a system are said to have <u>appellate jurisdiction,</u> which is the power to hear appeals. The appeals courts cannot hear cases' original presentations, nor, then, do they make original decisions, as they do not have original jurisdiction over disputes. These appeals courts must hear appeals from original decisions;

hence, they are said to have appellate jurisdiction over cases. Both the concepts of original jurisdiction and appellate jurisdiction apply to federal courts as well.

6. Subject Matter Jurisdiction

Some courts have the authority to hear only particular types of disputes. These courts have subject matter jurisdiction over particular issues. That is, they are empowered to hear only certain categories of cases. Usually, these types of courts are established to resolve case that are frequently occurring and have special problems or rules associated with them. As an example, Chuck, who is a resident of New Jersey, has a dispute with the New Jersey Department of Taxation. The department feels that Chuck has underpaid his taxes, and Chuck disagrees and refuses to pay the amount demanded of him. As both Chuck and the department are domiciled in New Jersey, New Jersey courts would have in personam jurisdiction over both parties, satisfying the initial need to identify the New Jersey court system's authority over the dispute. Next, as this case is just being started in the system, it would begin in the trial court level of the New Jersey system, as this level has original jurisdiction over disputes. Finally, within the trial court level in the New Jersey court system, there are special tax courts established to hear only tax disputes, so this dispute could only be heard in those subject matter jurisdiction courts in New Jersey, not in just any trial court in the system. Additionally, if Chuck wants to appeal the trial court decision, then he would have to go to the tax appeals court in New Jersey, as this state has a subject matter jurisdiction court in the first appeals level for tax disputes, as well as the trial court level tax court subject matter jurisdiction court.

C. FEDERAL JURISDICTION

The federal courts have different powers to hear cases than the three state court jurisdictions that we have seen. The two types of jurisdictions that are exclusive to the federal courts are <u>federal question jurisdiction</u> and <u>diversity jurisdiction</u>. These two powers comprise the bulk of the authority the federal courts have to hear disputes. Remember, original jurisdiction, appellate jurisdiction, and subject matter jurisdiction also apply to federal courts.

1. Federal Question Jurisdiction

The power of the federal courts to hear cases that involve federal questions comes directly from the U.S. Constitution. Article III, Section 2 of the Constitution gives the federal courts the jurisdiction over cases arising from federal law, from treaties, or from the Constitution itself. The cases arising under federal question jurisdiction need only be involved in part with a federal question. If a plaintiff has other causes of action above and beyond the federal question, then the federal court will hear those as well, as long as the requirement of federal question jurisdiction has been met. If Harry Smith, for instance, feels that he has been denied a promotion due to his race, then this violates federal antidiscrimination laws, as well as the Constitution. This would satisfy the federal question standard, such that the federal courts would have the power to hear this suit brought by Mr. Smith against his employer. Furthermore, if Mr. Smith also has a dispute concerning being shortchanged in his paycheck, the federal court would hear this as well.

2. Diversity of Citizenship Jurisdiction

Diversity of citizenship jurisdiction in federal courts arises when the parties to a lawsuit are citizens of different states, or are citizens of a state and a foreign country. Diversity jurisdiction for federal courts is also enumerated in Article III, Section 2 of the Constitution and was written into the document by the framers, who felt that a state court would be biased in favor of its own citizens if a suit also involved citizens of other states. Suppose Bill, a citizen of Nevada, wished to commence a lawsuit for $150,000 against a corporation that is incorporated in the state of Delaware.

As corporations are considered citizens of the state in which they are incorporated, this suit could be instituted in federal court, as it would have diversity of citizenship jurisdiction.

One additional feature or requirement of diversity jurisdiction has been added by federal legislation. Each lawsuit which is begun in federal court and which relies on diversity jurisdiction must have, at a minimum, $75,000 as the amount in controversy. The plaintiff must have the reasonable expectation that the lawsuit is worth at least the required amount in order to be heard in federal court. This dollar threshold has been placed on federal diversity jurisdiction to attempt to make the federal system more cost efficient. Given the large expense of trials in federal court, the amount in controversy must be of a significant financial value.

✻ ✻ ✻

LEGAL LIGHT

There are two special trial courts that have nationwide jurisdiction over certain types of cases. The Court of International Trade addresses cases involving international trade and customs issues. The United States Court of Federal Claims has jurisdiction over claims for money damages against the United States, disputes over federal contracts, and unlawful "takings" of private property by the federal government.

✻ ✻ ✻

II. JUDICIAL SELF-RESTRAINT

The concept of judicial self-restraint flows from the court's own interpretation of our system as an adversarial system of law. Simply by starting with this description of the legal system as an adversarial one, the courts have developed a variety of self-imposed limits or parameters on the types of problems and disputes that may be heard by the judicial system. These concepts of judicial self-restraint act as the parameters of the cases that may be heard. The specific limits that are parts of judicial self-restraint are <u>feigned controversies</u>, <u>moot controversies</u>, <u>unripe controversies</u>, <u>standing to sue</u>, <u>advisory opinions</u>, <u>political questions</u>, and <u>justiciability of the controversy</u>.

A. Feigned Controversy

At the core of our adversarial system of law is the requirement that the dispute brought to court not be a <u>feigned controversy</u> or faked dispute. The dispute must be a real disagreement between the parties to the suit. It must not be a device to get the court to hear a particular issue, but must present a real conflict for resolution. As an example, the courts will not hear cases between individuals who construct what looks to be a case or controversy, but is not. If two members of a special-interest group decided that the court should be forced to take a position on their issue, and they constructed a dispute between themselves, this would be a feigned controversy and the courts would not resolve the dispute.

B. Moot Controversy

A <u>moot controversy</u> is a dispute whose time for decision has passed. The courts feel that in an adversarial system such as ours, in which disputes are to be won or lost, cases should only be decided by the courts when the decision still matters to the participants. Let us suppose Bill Jones and Sharon White are the plaintiff and defendant in a lawsuit to determine the ownership of a particular painting done by a friend of the two parties to the suit. The painting itself has virtually no economic value but is of great sentimental value to Ms. White and Mr. Jones. Unfortunately, after the commencement of the lawsuit, the painting is destroyed by fire. The question of ownership is rendered moot by its destruction. The courts will not spend time on a lawsuit when the decision in that suit no longer has any practical impact on the participants.

C. Unripe Controversy

An unripe controversy is a dispute in which the time has not yet come to make a decision. In a way, it is the opposite limit to a moot controversy, as both relate to the appropriate timing of court decisions in a dispute. Courts will only decide cases in which the core problem has already occurred. That is, the basis for a lawsuit cannot be something which you think will happen, or might happen, or even that you are quite sure will happen. The basis for a lawsuit must be a completed activity. If, for instance, in our last example, Ms. Jones threatened to take the painting that she felt she owned away from Mr. White's apartment, the civil issue of recovering the painting would, as yet, be unripe for the court's review.

In Cole, the court addresses both the questions of the mootness and unripeness of the issue presented to it for resolution.

✲ ✲ ✲

Case#2-4

Cole v. Chief of Police of Fall River
312 Mass. 523, 45 N.E. 2d 400 (1942)

RONAN, J. The plaintiff, a candidate for the office of representative in Congress from the Fourteenth Congressional District of Massachusetts, equipped an automobile and trailer, both registered in his name, with signs directing attention to the record of his opponent and informing the public that he was a candidate for the office. The trailer carried a large board, approximately fifteen feet long and seven feet wide, on each of the two faces of which was a sign attacking the public record of his opponent. The automobile bore a sign approximately four feet long and three feet high which announced the candidacy of the plaintiff and referred to his opponent as an ex-congressman. On the morning of May 30, 1942, while the automobile and trailer were being operated along a public street in Fall River by an agent of the plaintiff, the said agent was informed by the defendant Verville, a captain of the Police Department of Fall River, that he was violating the law and, subsequently, the defendant Violette, chief of police, informed the defendant that he intended to enforce against him an ordinance which provided that "No person shall operate or park on any street or highway for the primary purpose of displaying advertising signs." The plaintiff then (commenced an action) against the chief of police, a police captain, the police board of the city of Fall River, and the mayor...The plaintiff has appealed from a final decree dismissing the bill.

When this case was reached for argument in this court on November 10, 1942, it was properly represented by an affidavit filed by the defendants stating that the plaintiff had been defeated in the primary election of his party held on September 15, 1942, and that the successful candidate at this primary of the political party of which the plaintiff was a member was defeated at the election held on November 3, 1942, by the candidate of the opposing party. The plaintiff, on the other hand, has filed an affidavit stating that he intends to use upon the streets of Fall River in another political campaign this equipment with different messages upon it.

(The purpose of this action) is a permanent injunction, restraining the defendants from interfering with the operation of the plaintiff's automobile and trailer bearing the signs described in the bill upon the streets of Fall River. The occasion for the use of such signs has passed and there is now no actual controversy based upon any factual foundation existing between the parties. While there still may be a difference of opinion as to the validity of the ordinance in question, there is no longer any present clash of contending rights. Parties are not entitled to decisions upon abstract propositions of law unrelated to some live controversy...The possibility that the same issue might arise in the future and that it might be advantageous for the parties to have their rights determined in advance is not enough to call for the rendition of a judgment, which the future might show was of little practical value and merely settled a matter that had become no more than a theoretical dispute...

☆ ☆ ☆

D. STANDING TO SUE

The injury in a lawsuit must be a direct, measurable injury to the party who is participating in the suit. An individual has <u>standing to sue</u> if the injury is directly to him and is a measurable and quantifiable injury. The parameter of standing to sue precludes lawsuits by individuals who might be taking the place of another party who is really the party that has been injured. Similarly, the direct injury must be sufficiently large to be quantifiable by the court. If, for example, Sarah Lewis punches Harriet Sims in the jaw, Ms. Sims would have both a broken jaw and standing to sue. The injury would be direct to Ms. Sims and would be of sufficient magnitude to be measured; that is, the damages to Ms. Sims would include such measurable items as medical bills, loss of wages, and the pain and suffering caused to her by Ms. Lewis's battery. If, on the other hand, Ms. Lewis simply touched Ms. Sims on the jaw, although the basic action would be the same, there would be no direct and measurable damage for the court to assess and award, so, in this instance, Ms. Sims would lack the standing to sue, no matter how she disliked being touched. Also, if Bertram

Lee wanted to sue Ms. Lewis on Ms. Sims's behalf because he was so enraged by the dirty deed, he could not, as the injury was not directly to him.

E. ADVISORY OPINIONS

In an adversarial system of law, there need to be two parties or participants to a dispute in order for the court to issue an opinion that settles a dispute. The courts will not offer advisory opinions that do nothing more than give advice as to how they would or would not resolve a dispute when and if it comes before the court in a proper fashion. Let us suppose that our state legislature has just passed a law that requires the Department of Motor Vehicles in our state to issue special license plates to people who have been convicted of drunk driving. The plates would have a large skull and crossbones in their centers, with the express purpose of the legislature being to safeguard and warn other drivers of the potential for dangerous behavior from the convicted drivers. We work for the state Department of Motor Vehicles, and we know that the labeled drivers will sue to protect their privacy; in fact, several of the potential plate holders have told us that they would sue. As we are not quite sure of the constitutionality of the plates, and before we spend a great number of tax dollars in making the plates, we turn to the court to seek advice as to the constitutionality of such a statute. The courts would decline to offer an opinion, as no advisory opinions will issue from a court whose business is settling disputes, not giving advice.

F. POLITICAL QUESTIONS

The concept of political questions arises from the core constitutional concept that our government is one of co-equal, separate branches, with each branch having limited, enumerated powers. Political questions are issues that courts will refuse to address, because to do so would clearly encroach on an enumerated power of a separate, co-equal branch of the government. If the court could evaluate each and every act of another governmental branch when that branch is acting within its constitutional authority, then the court would be superior to, not equal to, that branch. This also allows the court to avoid questions that might be better solved within the political process.

G. JUSTICIABILITY

Justiciability, or a justiciable controversy, is a dispute in which there are inappropriate parties or disputes in question. As the actual appropriateness of parties and disputes is inherently a judgment of the court, it is difficult to describe with great precision those controversies that are inappropriate and, therefore, nonjusticiable, but the courts feel that some problems and disputes, while seeming to satisfy all the requirements that we have discussed so far, are too personal or intimate for judicial review. In some ways, listening to the courts discuss justiciability conjures up an unsophisticated description of art that we have all heard; that is, "although I can't describe it, I know it when I see it." The courts have not made great strides in improving their description of justiciability beyond this rudimentary level, but we can generalize that the types of cases that the courts feel lack justiciability do have a sense of inappropriateness about them. These cases may deal with privacy or intimate personal interactions that may meet all the requirements of a controversy that would be heard by the courts, but which are still inappropriate for judicial consideration. As an example, early attempts to have cases brought to the Supreme Court which dealt with laws that outlawed the sale of birth control devices were not heard by the court, because, on one occasion, the court stated that the relationships between doctor and patient and between husband and wife were so personal that they lacked justiciability. While certainly not always the case, the perceived nonjusticiability of the issues within the case may allow the court to not settle an issue that it feels is inappropriate in its timing. In <u>Poe</u>, we see the court's reliance on the nonjusticiability of the issue, the same issue as to the constitutionality of the laws dealing with the illegality of providing birth control devices that it heard a year later.

✿ ✿ ✿

Case#2-5

<u>Poe v. Ullman</u>
367 U.S. 497, 81 S.Ct. 1752 (1961)

FRANKFURTER, J. These appeals challenge the constitutionality, under the Fourteenth Amendment, of Connecticut statutes which, as authoritatively construed by the Connecticut Supreme Court of Errors, prohibit the use of contraceptive devices and the giving of medical advice in the use of such devices. In proceedings seeking declarations of law, not on review of convictions for violations of the statutes that the court has ruled that these statutes would be applicable in the case of married couples and even under claim that contraception would constitute a serious threat to the health or life of the female spouse.

...The complaint in the first alleges that the plaintiffs, Paul and Pauline Poe (...fictitious names), are a husband and wife, thirty and thirty-six years old respectively, who live together and have no children. Mrs. Poe has had three consecutive pregnancies terminating in infants with multiple congenital abnormalities from which each died shortly after birth. Plaintiffs have consulted Dr. Buxton, an obstetrician and gynecologist of eminence and it is Dr. Buxton's opinion that the cause of the infants' abnormalities is genetic, although the underlying mechanism is unclear....Plaintiffs know that the best and safest medical treatment which could be prescribed for their situation is advice in methods of preventing contraception....Plaintiffs, however, have been unable to obtain this information for the sole reason that its delivery and use may or will be claimed by the defendant State's Attorney (Ullman) to constitute offenses against Connecticut law....

The restrictions of our jurisdiction to cases and controversies within the meaning of Article III of the Constitution...is not the sole limitation on the exercise of our appellate powers, especially in cases raising constitutional questions. The policy reflected in numerous cases and over a long period was thus summarized in the oft quoted statement of Mr. Justice Brandeis: "The Court (has) developed, for its own governance in the case confessedly within its jurisdiction, a series of rules under which it has avoided passing upon a large part of all the constitutional questions pressed upon it for decision."...

Justiciability is of course not a legal concept with a fixed content or susceptible of scientific verification. Its utilization is the result of many subtle pressures, including the appropriateness of the issues for decision by this Court and the actual hardship to the litigants of denying them the relief sought. Both these factors justify withholding adjudication of the constitutional issue raised under the circumstances and in the manner in which they are know before the Court.

Dismissed.

DOUGLAS, J., Dissenting. These cases are dismissed because a majority of the members of this Court conclude, for varying reasons, that this controversy does not present a justiciable question. That conclusion is too transparent to require an extended reply....

If there is a case where the need for this remedy in the shadow of a criminal prosecution is shown, it is this one, as Mr. Justice Harlan demonstrates. Plaintiffs...are two sets of husband and wife. One wife is pathetically ill, having delivered a stillborn fetus....

What are these people—doctor and patients—to do? Flout the law and go to prison? Violate the law surreptitiously and hope they will not get caught? By today's decision we leave them no other alternatives....We should not turn them away and make them flout the law and get arrested.... They are entitled to an answer to their predicament here and now....

☆ ☆ ☆

LEGAL LIGHT

Three territories of the United States, the Virgin Islands, Guam, and the Northern Mariana Islands have federal district courts that hear all federal cases, including bankruptcy cases.

☆ ☆ ☆

III. VENUE

Venue is the place or county within a system in which a particular case is to be heard. The question of venue does not arise until the question of jurisdiction is well settled. Once the proper system for the case is determined, then the issue of where specifically within that court system the case should be heard arises. The venue of a case is determined by ascertaining the most appropriate and convenient location for the action. If venue is successfully challenged as improper by one of the parties, then the remedy is to change the location of the case, not to dismiss the action from the court, as would happen if jurisdiction were to be successfully challenged. Venue may be predetermined by the choice of defendant. For example, if the plaintiff is suing a corporation, then the proper venue for the case would be the county of residence as stated in the corporation's certificate of incorporation. If the defendant is a municipality, then the suit must be in the county in which the municipality exists. Primarily, the venue for a lawsuit is the county of residence of the plaintiff, or the county in which the basis for in rem jurisdiction exists.

In <u>Union Carbide</u>, we see an analysis of place for a dispute.

✲ ✲ ✲

Case#2-6

In re Union Carbide Corporation Disaster
809 F. 2d 1987 (1987)

MANSFIELD, J. This appeal raises the question of whether thousands of claims by citizens of India and the Government of India arising out of the most devastating industrial disaster in history should be tried in the United States or in India.

The accident occurred on the night of December 2-3, 1984, when winds blew a deadly gas from the plant operated by Union Carbide India, Limited, into densely occupied parts of the city of Bhopal. UCIL is incorporated under the laws of India. Fifty and nine-tenths of its stock is owned by the Union Carbide Corporation, 22% is owned or controlled by the Government of India, and the balance is held by approximately 23,500 Indian citizens.

Four days after the Bhopal accident, on December 7, 1984, the first of some purported class actions in federal district courts in the United States was commenced on behalf of the victims of the disaster...On July, 31, 1985, Union Carbide Corporation moved to dismiss the complaints on the grounds of forum non conveniens...

The many witnesses and sources of proof are almost entirely located in India, where the accident occurred, and could not be compelled to appear for trial in the United States. The Bhopal plant at the time of the accident was operated by 193 Indian nationals, including the managers of seven operating units employed by the Agricultural Products Division of Union Carbide India, Limited, who reported to Indian Works Managers in India. The great majority of documents bearing on the design, safety, start-up, and operation of the plant, as well as the safety training of the plant's employees, are located in India.

The plaintiffs seek to prove that the accident was caused by negligence on the part of Union Carbide Corporation (an American corporation) in originally contributing to the design of the plant and its provision for storage of excessive amounts of gas at the plant...

In short, the plant has been constructed and managed by Indians in India. No Americans were employed at the plant at the time of the accident. In the five years from 1980 to 1984, although more than 1,000 Indians were employed at the plant, only one American was employed there and left in 1982. No Americans visited the plant for more than one year prior to the accident, and during the five year period before the accident, the communications between the plant and the United States were almost non-existent.

The vast majority of material witnesses and documentary proof bearing on causation of and liability for the accident is located in India, not the United States, and would be more accessible to an Indian court than to a United States court. The records are almost all in Hindu or other Indian language, understandable to an Indian court without translation. The witnesses, for the most part, do not speak English but Indian languages understood by an Indian court but not by an American court....

...Indeed, a long trial of the 145 cases here would unduly burden an already overburdened court, involving both jury hardship and heavy expenses. It would face the court with numerous practical difficulties, including an almost impossible task of attempting to understand extensive relevant Indian regulations published in a foreign language and the slow process of receiving testimony of scores of witnesses through interpreters.

Having made the foregoing conclusions, Judge Keenan (at the trial court) dismissed the actions against Union Carbide Corporation on the grounds of forum non conveniens...

...[T]he district court's order is affirmed.

☆ ☆ ☆

CHAPTER TWO
KEY TERMS

Advisory Opinions
Appellate Jurisdiction
Diversity of Citizenship Jurisdiction
Federal Question Jurisdiction
Feigned Controversy
In Personam Jurisdiction
In Rem Jurisdiction
Justiciability
Moot Controversy
Original Jurisdiction
Political Question
Quasi In Rem Jurisdiction
Standing
Unripe Controversy

☆ ☆ ☆

CHAPTER SUMMARY

Jurisdiction is the power that different courts have over people and disputes. On the state level, these powers are in personam jurisdiction, in rem jurisdiction, and quasi in rem jurisdiction. On the federal level, federal question jurisdiction and diversity jurisdiction are the methods of control and access to the courts. Common to both federal and state courts are original jurisdiction, appellate jurisdiction, and subject matter jurisdiction.

Courts also have the power to control access through the self-imposed concepts of judicial self-restraint. These limitations include mootness, unripeness, political questions, standing, justiciability, feigned controversies, and advisory opinions. These limitations flow from the courts views of our system as an adversarial system of law devoted to the resolution of disputes.

THINK AND WRITE

1. Discuss the types of connections that might allow a court to have jurisdiction over an Internet company.
2. How can courts place the limits on judicial self-restraint?
3. Please concoct a story for each element of judicial self-restraint that uses the element.
4. Why, in <u>Union Carbide</u>, do the Indian plaintiffs want to be in the United States, and why does the American defendant want to be in India?
5. What things would make a court change the venue of a case?

PROJECTS

1. Long-arm statutes are state laws that allow state courts to exercise in personam jurisdiction over out-of-state residents, provided that the non-residents have "minimum contacts" within the state. What does your state's long-arm statute provide as acceptable service on out-of-state defendants?
2. Contact the American Arbitration Association and ascertain the type of disputes that they accept. Review the pluses and minuses of having a dispute resolved in this fashion, rather than in court.
3. Review the index of your state's court rules. What topics are covered, and how do they relate to judicial power?
4. Research how a corporation can be a resident of more than one state.
5. When the court of more than one state has jurisdiction over a dispute, what are some of the ways that the courts determine in which state the case will be heard?

☆ ☆ ☆

ETHICAL QUESTIONS

1. Harry works for an attorney who has a court appearance in a civil matter and in a deposition scheduled for the same time. The attorney asks Harry, a paralegal, to appear at the deposition and fill in for him. What should Harry do?
2. Jack is an attorney who is working on a lawsuit filed in federal district court whose jurisdiction is based on diversity of citizenship. Jack discovers that his client's Florida home is a winter address and that his client files his tax returns based on New York residence, which is the same residence as his client's opponent. What should Jack do?

✵ ✵ ✵

RELATED WEBSITES

1. Books and articles on judicial power: http://www.questia. com/popularSearches/judicial_power.jsp
2. Definition of judicial power with link to a lengthy piece on the rule of law: http://encyclopedia.thefreedictionary. com/judicial%20power
3. Article on judicial power: http://www.ielrc.org/content/ n0202.htm
4. Article on standing and the impact on cases: http:// www.luten.com/standing.htm

CHAPTER THREE

LITIGATION

The civil trial process is a cornerstone of our legal system. It affords all citizens the right to access a legal forum for their disputes. The formal process begins with the filing of a complaint.

A. THE COMPLAINT

The <u>complaint</u> does precisely what its name states; it complains that the plaintiff has been injured. The complaint is a formal document, filed with the appropriate court, which serves to notify the court and the defendant of a pending lawsuit. The complaint must contain a variety of items in order to be valid. First, the name of the plaintiff and the name of the defendant must appear. The complaint then often states the jurisdiction, or power, of the court to which it is sent over the matter contained in the suit. The complaint then states a factual summary of the facts as viewed by the plaintiff. This factual presentation needs to have within it the cause of action, or legal basis, of the lawsuit. The cause of action is essential to demonstrate that the type of problem stated in the facts of the complaint is a type of problem that the law recognizes and for which the law may supply a remedy. Lastly, the complaint must state what the plaintiff wants to get as a remedy for the lawsuit.

The complaint is first filed with the court, where it is assigned a docket or index number that serves as a clerical link for all of the paperwork in the suit. The complaint is then served, or delivered, on the defendant, putting the defendant on notice that he is being sued, in what court the suit is taking place, a summary of the plaintiff's facts, and a demand for damages. This element of notification and openness is an important feature of our legal system. Other systems may allow lawsuits to occur in secret, without notification to the other party or without access to the facts or demands, clearly an unacceptable premise for our legal system. Complaints need to be filed within a certain time period from the occurrence of the act that allegedly injured the plaintiff. These prescribed time frames are outlined in a state's <u>statute of limitations</u>. This law sets out the time limits for starting a lawsuit in different areas of the law. Each state has its own set of limits, and, within a given state, different types of limits are set for different types of lawsuits.

* SAMPLE COMPLAINT

✿ ✿ ✿

UNITED STATES DISTRICR COURT
FOR THE DISTRICT OF OHIO

JOHN H. SMITH and)
FRED JONES,) No. 444444
Plaintiffs)
) COMPLAINT FOR TORT
vs.)
)
HARVEY MUDD and)
LUCY MUDD) JURY TRIAL DEMANDED
)
)

_____

1. Plaintiffs are and were at all the times herein mentioned, residents and citizens of the state of Ohio. Defendants, Harvey Mudd and Lucy Mudd, are and were at all times mentioned herein residents and citizens of the state of Nebraska. This is a civil action involving, exclusive of interests and costs, a sum in excess of $75,000.
2. On or about June 6, 2003, plaintiff John H. Smith was driving northbound on Route 9 in the city of Cleveland, Ohio at or about 9:00 A.M. Plaintiff Fred Jones was a passenger in the automobile being driven by John H. Smith.
3. A truck being driven by defendant Harvey Mudd struck plaintiff's auto from the rear after plaintiff's auto had stopped for a red light at the intersection of Route 9 and Route 100.
4. The truck being driven by defendant Harvey Mudd is believed to be owned jointly by defendants Harvey Mudd and Lucy Mudd.
5. As a result of defendant's negligence, plaintiffs received injuries and sustained losses of $200,000.

WHEREFORE, plaintiffs pray for judgment against the defendants as follows:

1. For judgment in the sum of $200,000.
2. For costs of the suit.
3. For such other relief as the court deems just.

Dated: September 25, 2003   By: _____
Harold Johnson
Attorney at Law
555 Main Street
Smithtown, Ohio

☆ ☆ ☆

LEGAL LIGHT

In the state of California alone, there were some 195,000 attorneys as of 2004. About 20,000 legal assistants work in California.

✫ ✫ ✫

B. THE ANSWER

The answer acts as a response to the complaint that has been delivered to the defendant. In it, the defendant answers the allegations of the plaintiff. In the answer, the defendant has an opportunity to deny any and all allegations made in the complaint. The answer is also filed with the court and then delivered to the plaintiff. At this point, the plaintiff, the defendant, and the court are all on notice as to the outlines of the suit, and the positions of the parties with the suit.

In addition, some affirmative defenses can or must be raised in the answer. Affirmative defenses are those defenses which assume the facts in the complaint are true, but, nonetheless, offer protection from the lawsuit. For example, the previously mentioned statute of limitations may offer an affirmative defense to the suit. That is, even if the complaint is all true, if the plaintiff failed to file the complaint with the proper time frame, the defendant has a successful defense to the suit.

Also, in the answer, the defendant may raise counterclaims, or countersuits, against the plaintiff. Depending on the state, these counterclaims may be either in the answer itself, or in a separate countercomplaint attached to the answer. These countersuits claim that the plaintiff was really the individual at fault in the matter involved in the lawsuit, and it is, therefore, the defendant who is entitled to compensation for injuries and damages. A counterclaim really acts as a complaint on behalf of the defendant against the plaintiff. It is more efficient, however, than requiring the defendant to file a separate complaint in those instances where the two parties disagree as to who is at fault in a given set of circumstances. The original plaintiff must then file an answer to the counterclaim, just as the original defendant had to file an answer to the complaint. Notice that these documents allow both parties to complain that they are the injured party, and allow both parties to respond to the others allegations. This evenhanded treatment of the parties demonstrates the lack of importance placed upon being labeled "plaintiff" or "defendant" in those suits where there is a counterclaim. Unlike in the criminal law, there are no clearly defined benefits or handicaps placed on plaintiffs or defendants in the civil law; a party's only obligation here is to demonstrate one's case.

Simon v. Jackson gives us an opportunity to view an example of a countersuit.

☆ ☆ ☆

CASE #3-1 COUNTERSUITS

SIMON v. JACKSON
855 So.2d 1026 (2003)

JOHNSTONE, Justice.

Thomas Simon appeals from a default judgment entered against him in favor of Anthony Jackson and Carol Jackson on their claim for money damages. We affirm.

*1028 Simon originally sued the Jacksons to evict them from certain premises they were occupying. The Jacksons countersued Simon for money damages on two theories. One was that he fraudulently misrepresented his title to the same property in negotiating a contract with the Jacksons for their purchase of the property. The other theory was that Simon negligently or wantonly failed to obtain good title to convey to the Jacksons.

After the Jacksons vacated the property, Simon's eviction claim was dismissed as moot. Simon has not appealed that dismissal.

After the dismissal of Simon's eviction claim, only the claims in the Jacksons' **countersuit** remained pending. In the context of the countersuit, Simon was, of course, the defendant, and the Jacksons were the plaintiffs. This obvious alignment is noteworthy simply to correlate the parties in this case with the parties in cases this opinion will cite as authority. Simon appeals only the judgment entered against him as counterclaim defendant.

On appeal, Simon argues that the default judgment against him should be reversed on two grounds: first, that the trial court erred in denying Simon's motion to dismiss the Jacksons' counterclaim, and, second, that the trial court erred in denying Simon's motion to set aside the default judgment. Because procedural considerations require that the judgment of the trial court be affirmed, the operative facts are purely procedural.

Simon's first response to the Jacksons' counterclaim was a motion to dismiss grounded on the failure of the counterclaim "to state a claim upon which relief can be granted," Rule 12(b)(6), an interlocutory order the trial court denied this motion to dismiss.

Simon then filed his answer to the Jacksons' counterclaim. The answer merely joined issue on the merits of the Jacksons' two counterclaim theories by denying the allegations and demanding strict proof of each. Simon's answer did not include as a defense the failure of the Jacksons' counterclaim to state a claim on which relief could be granted.

Simon then failed to appear at the trial. After moving for entry of a default judgment against Simon, the Jacksons, by oral testimony, proved their damages. The Jacksons also introduced some evidence on some of the other elements of their theories. Thereupon, on October 18, 2001, the trial court entered judgment for $107,600 in compensatory damages against Simon and in favor of the Jacksons on their counterclaim. While the case action summary and the separate judgment document, see Rule 58(a)(2), Ala. R. Civ. P., do not characterize the judgment as a default judgment, the parties and the trial judge have invariably treated it as a default judgment.

On November 19, 2001, a Monday, Simon filed a post judgment motion for judgment as a matter of law or, alternatively, to alter, to amend, or to vacate the judgment. The motion was not denominated as a motion to set aside a default judgment. Simon's original post judgment motion contained two grounds:

"That on information and belief, Counter-Defendant asserts that the evidence presented at trial is insufficient to support the judgment and Counter-Defendant is entitled to a judgment as a matter of law.
"Alternatively, Counter-Defendant asserts that the judgment is due to be vacated because he did not receive notice of the setting of the counterclaim for trial."

The post judgment motion did not assert that the counterclaim failed to state a claim upon which relief could be granted. Nor did the post judgment motion originally assert in any way or words that Simon had a meritorious defense.

We need not decide whether Simon's January 31, 2002 affidavit meets the Kirtland, *1031 605-06, substantive criteria for showing a meritorious defense. The deadline for moving to set aside a default judgment is "thirty (30) days after the entry of the judgment." Rule 55(c), Ala. R. Civ. P. Accord Kirtland, 524 So.2d at 604. While Simon filed his post judgment motion in its original form just before the expiration of the deadline for filing a Rule 55(c) motion to set aside a default judgment, he did not even broach the subject of a meritorious defense until he filed this last affidavit 105 days after entry of the default judgment and 73 days after the deadline. (The deadline was extended two calendar days because the thirtieth calendar day after judgment was a Saturday. Rule 6, Ala. R. Civ. P.) While we question whether a post judgment motion which does not even broach the subject of a meritorious defense before the expiration of the Rule 55(c) deadline can be deemed a timely Rule 55(c) motion at all, the length of Simon's delay and the discretionary prerogative of the trial judge obviate our deciding this precise question.

At some point a party's right to a trial on the merits yields to everybody's right to prompt justice. We cannot hold that the trial judge in this case *abused his discretion* by disregarding a showing of a meritorious defense not filed until 73 days after the Rule 55(c) deadline. Because the defaulting party's showing of a meritorious defense is one of the prerequisites to an order setting aside a default judgment, Kirtland, 524 So.2d at 605-06, we likewise cannot hold that the trial judge abused his discretion by denying Simon's post judgment motion.

AFFIRMED.

☆ ☆ ☆

Both the answer and the counterclaim must be filed with the court and then delivered to the plaintiff. Further, these documents must be filed within a prescribed time period. This time period for an answer begins tolling, or running, when the complaint is served on the defendant or on the defendant's agent. In most states, the answer must be filed within twenty or thirty days. Failure to answer within the proper time may result in penalties being imposed by the court upon the defendant, up to and including being unable to actually answer the complaint.

C. MOTIONS

Motions are court filings that, typically, precede a trial and are formal requests by one party for a court order. These requests for an order may involve any issues that may arise at trial, such as for the exclusion of evidence, for the request of additional documents or other evidence, or for a summary judgment, among many other items.

The request for a motion will be filed with the court, and then served on the other party to the suit. Court rules prescribe the amount of notice required for motions, and describe the additional documentation that is required for a particular motion. The court may request oral arguments, oral testimony, affidavits, or any combination thereof prior to issuing or declining to issue an order.

D. DISCOVERY

Discovery is the period in which the parties have the opportunity to gather information that is available through the other participant in the suit. Our system of law, being based on openness, provides each party to a suit access to the pool of information of the other party. This access, however, is not automatic; one must enquire and search for the documents and testimony of the other side. The law provides for a number of methodologies to access this information during the discovery period.

The first of these methods for discovering information held by the other party is called a deposition. A deposition is the questioning of one of the parties to the suit, or of one of their witnesses, by the opposing attorney. Depositions take place prior to the trial proper, are done under oath, and are transcribed by a court reporter. Depositions most commonly occur at the office of one of the attorneys involved in the suit. The individual being deposed, or questioned, typically has his or her attorney present. Depositions are effective methods for acquiring information, as they are spontaneous, detailed, and done under oath. They do, however, present some difficulties. First, the logistics of the deposition may be difficult. Each party and the respective attorneys must meet at the prescribed location, which may be a difficult task to orchestrate. More significantly, depositions are expensive. The participants must pay their attorneys for the time spent at the deposition, as well as for preparation time and follow-up time, at the agreed-upon hourly rate. Additionally, the court reporter is a professional whose time is costly. Further, the copies made from lengthy depositions can be costly as well.

For those interested in a career in litigation, let the following case involving depositions serve as an insight.

☆ ☆ ☆

CASE #3-2 DEPOSITIONS

TERRELL v. ALLRED
2004 WL 293342 (Cal.App. 1 Dist.)

HAERLE, J.

I. INTRODUCTION

*1 This is an appeal from an order and judgment of the Alameda County Superior Court dismissing appellant's wrongful eviction lawsuit for her failure to properly and adequately respond to discovery. We affirm.

II. FACTUAL AND PROCEDURAL BACKGROUND

On July 31, 2000, appellant, acting *in pro per* as she has throughout, filed this action asking for damages for an "Illegal Lockout, General Negligence, Willful Negligence," etc., against respondent Allred, a business firm named as "Marian Associates," three Oakland police officers, the Alameda County Sheriffs Department and one of its employees, and an Oakland attorney named Donald Kirby. Without going into unnecessary detail, suffice it to say that the lawsuit concerned an allegedly unlawful eviction of appellant by her landlady (respondent), an eviction which was allegedly aided or facilitated in some way by the actions of the other named defendants.

☆ ☆ ☆

Meanwhile, on October 31, 2002, respondent filed a motion to either dismiss the complaint as to her or for sanctions for appellant's failure to provide discovery. Via that motion and its supporting papers, respondent related the extensive efforts made by her and the other defendants to attempt to secure discovery from appellant in both this case and a companion case filed in the same court (No. 824425-5). The court was provided with deposition transcripts and other record citations indicating that appellant, who had first resisted any deposition because of alleged medical problems, had thereafter been totally uncooperative at her first deposition session, was sanctioned by the court for that conduct, but continued to resist discovery at a reconvened session of her deposition. As a result, the court ordered the companion case dismissed and denied appellant's efforts to reinstate it.

Appellant was also resistant to discovery in this case. More specifically, she had to be deposed in three separate sessions in January, March and June 2002. After the first of these sessions, on January 4, 2002, some of the other defendants moved for either monetary or terminating sanctions based on appellant's behavior at that session of her deposition, including her refusal to answer questions.

On March 11, 2002, the court denied those defendants' motion for terminating sanctions but granted their motion for monetary sanctions. The court stated in its order: "1) As a preliminary matter, the Court finds that Defendants' request for sanctions is well-taken. Having reviewed the transcript of Plaintiffs deposition, the Court finds that Plaintiff is not acting in good faith, and that Plaintiffs conduct appears designed to prevent Defendants from taking Plaintiffs deposition, as set forth below. [¶] 2) At deposition, Plaintiff contended under oath that she cannot take her medication and then drive herself home from a deposition. Plaintiff further contended that not taking her medication would endanger her health. [¶] 3) At deposition, Defendants offered to try to accommodate Plaintiffs travel needs; Defendants also proposed that Plaintiffs deposition be taken at a location to which Plaintiff would not need to drive (e.g., Plaintiffs home). Plaintiff refused Defendants' offers. [¶] 4) Further, Plaintiff contended under oath that, even if travel to and from the deposition was not an issue, Plaintiff would not be able both to take her medication and be deposed in light of the fact that her medication would cause her to fall asleep. [¶] ... [¶] ...Defendants' request for terminating sanctions is DENIED. Based on Plaintiffs lack of good faith, Defendants' request for monetary sanctions is GRANTED."

*2 Appellant's deposition continued in March and again in June 2002. On June 12, 2002, counsel for respondent examined appellant for the first time. She continued to be extremely evasive and argumentative with respondent's counsel (as will be detailed more below), eventually declaring: "I will not answer any more questions for you."

Appellant opposed respondent's motion to dismiss or for sanctions, and the matter came on for hearing before the superior court on December 2, 2002. Appellant did not appear. The court ordered appellant's complaint dismissed as to respondent and judgment to that effect was entered on December 16, 2002. Appellant filed a timely notice of appeal on January 31, 2003.

✰ ✰ ✰

A trial court order sanctioning a party for refusal to provide required discovery, including applying terminating sanctions, is reviewed for abuse of discretion. "The power to impose discovery sanctions is a broad discretion subject to reversal only for arbitrary, capricious, or whimsical action. [Citations.] Only two facts are absolutely prerequisite to imposition of the sanction: (1) there must be a failure to comply...and (2) the failure must be willful [citation]." [Citation.] "(<u>Vallbona v. Springer</u> (1996) 43 Cal.App.4th 1525, 1545.) As another of our sister courts has written: "Management of discovery lies within the sound discretion of the trial court. Consequently, appellate review of discovery rulings is governed by the abuse of discretion standard. [Citation.] Where there is a basis for the trial court's ruling and the evidence supports it, a reviewing court will not substitute its opinion for that of the trial court. [Citation.]" (<u>Johnson v. Superior Court</u> (2000) 80 Cal.App.4th 1050, 1061.)

*3 We find no abuse of discretion here. The trial court had before it, as do we, the transcript of that portion of appellant's June 12, 2002, [FN 1] deposition in which respondent's attorney attempted to examine her. That attempt was continually frustrated by appellant's evasions and truculence. Some examples:

FN 1. All further dates noted are in 2002.
"Q [respondent's counsel, William Ginsburg]: Now, did you hear her [respondent] say anything else that night?
"A: I just told you. Don't keep asking me the same thing over and over.

"Q: Did you hear—

"A: I don't remember hearing her saying anything else because I wasn't paying any attention to her.

"Q: Okay, so the only thing you remember her saying that you could repeat here is the two statements I just reminded you of, right?

"A: (No response.)

"Q: Ms. Terrell?

"A: I just answered that question.

"Q: No you haven't answered the question. You need to answer the question. The question is— "A: I just answered the question to you two or three times. I don't want to keep answering the same questions over and over again. You heard me answer the question." (CT 2013-2024)

"…

"Q: Where is that amended court order allowing you to pay $192 in exchange for remaining on the property another month?

"A: I think I have a copy at home, and the other copy may be at an attorney's office.

"Q: What attorney?

"A: That's my private business, what attorney.

"Q: No, it's not.

"A: What do you mean it's not?

"Q: It doesn't matter.

"A: I don't have to tell you whether or not I have an attorney. But if I said it's in an attorney's office, that's where it is.

"Q: But you don't have any privilege to keep you from testifying.

"A: Oh, yes, I do have a privilege. I don't have to tell you whether or not I have an attorney yet. [¶] I said it's in an attorney's office, and I may have an extra copy at home. [¶] Isn't that what I told you, Mr. Hallifax [another defense counsel]?

"Q: What attorney are you talking about?

"A: I don't have to tell you that.

"Q: Do you have an objection to that question?

"A: What do you mean, do I have an objection? I don't have to tell you what attorney I have it in an office.

"Q: What privilege are you relying on?

"A: That it is private. I don't have to tell you that.

"Q: And what law or privilege are you relying on?

"A: Look, I don't want to argue with you about any of that. (CT 2021-2022)

    "...

"Q: Ma'am, you have to answer all the questions.

"A: No, I don't have to answer nothing.

"Q: You have to answer all the questions 1 ask you unless you have some valid objection to the question; so do you have a valid objection to the question about who is the attorney?

"A: That is a valid objection right there. [¶] I don't have to tell you what attorney that 1 have that court order in their possession, okay?

    "...

"Q: And the illegal lockout happened July 3rd, right?

*4 "A: Are you handling it for her? Are you handling it for her? You should know.

"Q: But I ask questions, you answer questions.

"A: What a minute. Wait a minute, Ginsburg. You're not going to keep asking me the same thing over and over again. We can just stop this right here, okay? And then you request your own deposition and go back to court as you have already filed a motion for dismissal. I am not going to sit here and argue.

"Q: I'm trying to get a simple answer to a simple question, but you're not answering it.

"A: Well, I'm not answering it to the way you want it answered, and I can't answer it any better, okay?

"Q: Well, but you can if you try.

"A: No, I'm not going to even try.

"Q: All right.

"A: I already tried to answer it for you.

"Q: All right. So you—

"A: What's pertaining to your Marian Allred? You know what your client did.

"Q: Ma'am, it doesn't matter what I know.

"A: Well, I'm just reminding you, I want to remind you.

"Q: I want your testimony on the record about this litigation.

"A: No. I will not answer any more questions for you."

It is also noteworthy that appellant did not even appear before the superior court to contest respondent's motion for sanctions based on her June 12 performance and behavior.

Finally, it should be remembered that appellant's conduct followed by only a few months the court's March 11 order sanctioning her for her January 4 refusal to be deposed. In that order, the court decided not to grant the-then moving defendants terminating sanctions, although it did grant monetary sanctions and noted that, had those defendants so moved, it would have granted evidentiary sanctions precluding appellant from testifying. After that very significant warning shot across her bow, appellant's behavior at her June 12 deposition was properly sanctioned by the dismissal of her lawsuit pursuant to section 2023, subdivision (b)(4)(C).

IV. DISPOSITION

The judgment is affirmed.

✫ ✫ ✫

A second method for discovery is the <u>interrogatory</u>. Interrogatories are written questions to which the responding person must supply written answers. As these interrogatories are delivered through the mail, arranging to respond to them is easy. Additionally, as no oral testimony is given, no court reporter is required. Interrogatories, as they are logistically easier and require no court reporter, are much less expensive than depositions. Interrogatories, however, do eliminate the spontaneity of the responses that are given. As the person responding also has the opportunity to confer in private before giving answers, the answers tend to be accurate but brief; no extra information is proffered when one uses interrogatories.

A third method used in discovery is a <u>motion to produce</u>. These motions demand the production of witnesses or physical evidence that is relevant to the case. The court order that results from the motion to produce a witness is called a subpoena, said subpoena requiring the person to come and give testimony. The court order that results from a motion to produce documents or other physical evidence is called a subpoena duces tecum and said subpoena duces tecum requires that the evidence be produced.

A fourth method used in discovery is a request for <u>physical or mental examination</u>. Obviously used when physical or emotional damages are claimed, the court may require that a doctor of its own choosing examine the party claiming the injuries, rather than the party's personal physician, who has a professional responsibility to believe that which is claimed by the patient.

Here is a complex example of what may be discovered.

☆ ☆ ☆

Case#3-3

<u>DOI and BIA v. Klamath</u>
532 U.S. 1, 121 S.Ct. 1060 (2001)

SOUTER, J. Document in issue here, passing between Indian Tribes and the Department of the Interior, addressed tribal interests subject to state and federal proceedings to determine water allocations. The question is whether the documents are exempt from the disclosure requirements of the Freedom of Information act, as "intra-agency memorandums or letters" that would normally be privileged in civil discovery....

During roughly the same period, the department's Bureau of Indian Affairs (Bureau) filed claims on behalf of the Klamath Tribe alone in an Oregon state court adjudication intended to allocate water rights. Since the Bureau is responsible for administering land and water rights held in trust for Indian tribes...it consulted with the Klamath Tribe, and the two exchanged written memorandums on the appropriate scope of the claims submitted by the United States for the benefit of the Klamath Tribe. The Bureau does not, however, act as counsel for the Tribe, which has its own lawyers and has independently submitted claims on its own behalf....

Respondent, the Klamath Water Users Protective Association (Association), is a nonprofit association of water users in the Klamath River Basin, most of whom receive water from the Klamath Project, and whose interests are adverse to the tribal interests owing to the scarcity of water. The Association filed a series of requests with the Bureau under the Freedom of Information Act...seeking access to communications between the Bureau and the Basin Tribes during the relevant time period. The Bureau turned over several documents but withheld others as exempt under the attorney work-product and deliberative process privileges....

The District Court granted the Government's motion...It held that each of the documents qualified...and that each was covered by the deliberative process privilege or the attorney work-product privilege, as having played a role in the Bureau's deliberations about the plan....

The Court of Appeals for the Ninth Circuit reversed. 189 F3d. 1034 (1999)....

But again, the dispositive point is that the apparent object of the Tribe's communications is a decision by an agency of the Government to support a claim by the Tribe that is necessarily adverse to the interest of the competitors. Since there is not enough water to satisfy everyone, the Government's position on behalf of the Tribe is potentially adverse to other users, and it might ask for more or less on behalf of the Tribe depending on how it evaluated the tribal claim compared with the claims of its rivals. The ultimately adversarial character of tribal submissions to the Bureau therefore seems the only fair inference, as confirmed by the Department's acknowledgment that its "obligation to represent the Klamath Tribe necessarily coexists with the duty to protect other federal interests, including in particular its interests with respect to the Klamath Project."...The position of the Tribe as beneficiary is thus a far cry from the position of a paid consultant....

The judgment of the Court of Appeals is affirmed.

✻ ✻ ✻

LEGAL LIGHT

Tort reform is currently a popular political topic. Notwithstanding the need to improve the legal system, some statistics undermine the rhetoric. For instance, median payouts for all tort cases decreased 56 percent between 1992 and 2001. According to the U.S. Department of Justice, the median inflation-adjusted payout in all tort cases dropped from $49,700 in 1992 to $28,000 in 2001. In addition, medical malpractice filings per one hundred thousand population decreased 1 percent from 1998 to 2004.

✻ ✻ ✻

E. PRETRIAL CONFERENCES

Pretrial conferences may be requested by either party or by the court. The conference usually occurs after discovery has finished. The conference serves to allow the attorneys and the judge to determine what issues are actually in dispute and to arrange the order of the trial. This also allows the judge to determine the length and schedule for the trial. Pretrial conferences also may be geared towards settlement of the suit prior to trial. These settlement conferences are usually attended by the parties. The judge may advise or encourage the parties to settle the case at hand.

F. SELECTION OF THE JURY

The selection of the jury is the next step in the trial process. Juries are impaneled in civil matters to make determinations of fact after viewing the evidence presented by both sides. Questions of law, that is, which law is to be applied and how it is to be interpreted, are determined by the court.

Potential jurors are randomly selected from compilations of lists; courts use voting lists, homeowners' lists, driver's license lists, food stamp lists, and many other lists to arrive at as complete a representation of residents within the jurisdiction of the court as is possible. In all states, certain groups are exempt from jury duty. These exempt groups are far fewer in number than in the past; these groups include minors, convicted felons, and persons unable to read, write, and understand English. The process by which attorneys query selected individuals for bias prior to their being impaneled on a particular jury is called voir dire. During voir dire, an attorney may exclude, for cause, any prospective juror with a demonstrable bias. Any number of jurors may be excluded by either attorney for cause. Additionally, a limited number of peremptory challenges, or dismissals without a cause or justification, are allotted to each attorney. The number of peremptory challenges varies from state to state, but six is a common number of peremptory challenges. Peremptory challenges cannot be used to discriminate on the basis of race or gender. Historically, juries have been composed of twelve people. Many states, however, have lowered this number to six in civil trials, as it provides a cost savings for the various judicial systems. Indeed, some states have even lowered the number in some criminal matters to six, although the majority of states and the federal criminal courts have maintained the number at twelve.

In <u>Manufacturers</u>, one party's appeal is based upon an alleged flaw in the jury selection process.

☆ ☆ ☆

Case#3-4

<u>Manufacturers Hanover Trust Co. v. Drysdale</u>
801 F.2d 13(1986)

PIERCE, J. The defendant appeals a judgment entered into after a jury returned a verdict against it. The jury awarded the plaintiff $17 million, to which the district judge added interest and costs, in a civil action seeking damages for losses that Manufacturers Hanover Trust Company claimed to have suffered as a result of certain alleged misrepresentations that Arthur Anderson and Co. made on behalf of Anderson's client, Drysdale Securities Corporation.

On appeal, Anderson (and Drysdale) argue...that the empanelment of the jury was fundamentally unfair and flawed....

The parties raise several additional issues which we can dispose of briefly. First, Anderson argues that the empanelment of the jury was fundamentally unfair because the district judge expressly excused venire persons who could not sit for a trial likely to last several weeks.

A jury is fundamentally flawed if it systematically and intentionally discriminates or otherwise deprives a litigant of a chance to have his case heard by a cross-section of the community. In the present case, since there was no per se exclusion of any group, and no systematic and intentional discrimination against any person or persons, the district judge's empanelment procedure was not unconstitutional.

☼ ☼ ☼

Conversely.

☼ ☼ ☼

Case #3-5

Miller-El v. Texas

2003 WL 431659 (U.S.)

KENNEDY, J. In this case, we once again examine when a state prisoner can appeal the denial or dismissal of his petition for writ of habeas corpus. In 1986 two Dallas County assistant district attorneys used peremptory strikes to exclude 10 of the 11 African-Americans eligible to serve on the jury which tried petitioner Thomas Joe Miller-El. During the ensuing seventeen years, petitioner has been unsuccessful in establishing, in either state or federal court, that his conviction and death sentence must be vacated because the jury selection procedures violated the Equal Protection Clause and our holding in Batson v. Kentucky, 476 U.S. 79, 106 S. Ct. 1712, 90 L.Ed.2d 69 (1986)....

Petitioner, his wife Dorothy Miller-El, and one Kenneth Flowers robbed a Holiday Inn in Dallas, Texas. They emptied the cash drawers and ordered two employees, Doug Walker and Donald Hall, to lie on the floor. Walker and Hall were gagged with strips of fabric, and their hands and feet were bound. Petitioner asked Flowers if he was going to kill Walker and Hall. When Flowers hesitated or refused, petitioner shot Walker twice in the back and shot Hall in the side. Walker died from his wounds....

A comparative analysis of venire members demonstrates that African-Americans were excluded from petitioner's jury in a ratio significantly higher than Caucasians were. Of the 108 possible jurors reviewed by the prosecution and defense, 20 were African-American. Nine of them were excused for cause or by agreement of the parties. Of the 11 African-American jurors remaining, all but one was excluded by peremptory strikes exercised by the prosecutors. On this basis, 91% of the eligible black jurors were removed by peremptory strikes. In contrast, the prosecutors used their peremptory strikes against just 13% (4 out of 31) of the eligible non-black prospective jurors qualified to serve on petitioner's jury....

There was an even more pronounced difference, on the apparent basis of race, in the manner the prosecutors questioned members of the venire about their willingness to impose the minimum sentence for murder....

Of more importance, the defense presented evidence that the District Attorney's Office had adopted a formal policy to exclude minorities from jury service. A 1963 circular by the District Attorney's Office instructed its prosecutors to exercise peremptory strikes against minorities: " 'Do not take Jews, Negroes, Dagos, Mexicans or a member of any minority race on a jury, no matter how rich or well educated.' " A manual entitled "Jury selection in a Criminal Case" was distributed to prosecutors. It contained an article authored by a former prosecutor (and later a judge) under the direction of his superiors in the District Attorney's Office, outlining the reasoning for excluding minorities from jury service. Although the manual was written in 1968, it remained in circulation until 1976, if not later, and was available to at least one of the prosecutors in Miller-El's trial.

Some testimony casts doubt on the State's claim that these practices had been discontinued before petitioner's trial....

To secure habeas corpus relief, petitioner must demonstrate that a state court's finding of the absence of purposeful discrimination was incorrect by clear and convincing evidence, 28 U.S.C. s2254(e)(1), and that the corresponding factual determination was "objectively unreasonable" in light of the record before the court. The State represents to us that petitioner will not be able to satisfy his burden. That may or may not be the case. It is not, however, the question before us. The COA (Certificate of Appeal) inquiry asks only if the District Court's decision was debatable. Our threshold examination convinces us that it was.

The judgment of the Fifth Circuit is reversed, and the case is remanded for further proceedings consistent with this opinion.

THOMAS, J., Dissenting ...Because petitioner has not shown, by clear and convincing evidence, that any peremptory strikes were exercised because of race, he does not merit a Certificate of Appeal. I respectfully dissent....

The "historical" evidence is entirely circumstantial, so much so that the majority can only bring itself to say it "casts doubt on the State's claim that (discriminatory) practices had been discontinued before petitioner's trial." And the evidence that the prosecution used jury shuffles no more proves intentional discrimination than it forces petitioner to admit that he sought to eliminate whites from the jury, given that he employed the tactic more than the prosecution did. Ultimately, these two categories of evidence do very little for petitioner, because they do not address the genuineness of prosecutors' proffered race-neutral reasons for making the peremptory strikes of these particular jurors....

Quite simply, petitioner's arguments rest on circumstantial evidence and speculation that does not hold up to a thorough review of the record....Because the petitioner has not demonstrated by clear and convincing evidence that even one of the peremptory strikes at issue was the result of racial discrimination, I would affirm the denial of a COA.

✵ ✵ ✵

And, finally, a third case impacting on our view of the selection of a jury.

✵ ✵ ✵

Case #3-6 JURY SELECTION

J.E.B. v. ALABAMA
511 U.S. 127, 114 S.Ct. 1419 (1994)

Justice BLACKMUN delivered the opinion of the Court.
[1] In Batson v. Kentucky, 476 U.S. 79, 106 S.Ct. 1712, 90 L.Ed.2d 69 (1986), this Court held that the Equal Protection Clause of the Fourteenth Amendment governs the exercise of peremptory challenges by a prosecutor in a criminal trial. The Court explained that although a defendant has "no right to a petit jury composed in whole or in part of persons of his own race," id., at 85, 106 S.Ct., at 1717, quoting Strauder v. West Virginia, 100 U.S. 303, 305, 25 L.Ed. 664 (1880), the "defendant does have the right to be tried by a jury whose members are selected pursuant to nondiscriminatory criteria." 476 U.S., at 85-86, 106 S.Ct., at 1717. Since Batson, we have reaffirmed repeatedly our commitment to **jury selection** procedures that are fair and nondiscriminatory. We have recognized that whether the trial is criminal or civil, potential jurors, as well as litigants, have an equal protection right to **jury selection** procedures that are free from state-sponsored group stereotypes rooted in, and reflective of,

historical prejudice. *See* <u>Powers v. Ohio</u>, 499 U.S. 400, 111 S.Ct. 1364, 113 L.Ed.2d 411 (1991); <u>Edmonson v. Leesville Concrete Co.</u>, 500 U.S. 614, 111 S.Ct. 2077, 114 L.Ed.2d 660 (1991); <u>Georgia v. McCollum</u>, 505 U.S. 42, 112 S.Ct. 2348, 120 L.Ed.2d 33 (1992).

[2] Although premised on equal protection principles that apply equally to gender discrimination, all our recent case defining the scope of <u>Batson</u> involved alleged racial discrimination in the exercise of peremptory challenges. Today we are faced with the question whether the Equal Protection Clause forbids intentional discrimination on the basis of gender, just as it prohibits discrimination on the basis of race. We hold that gender, like race, is an unconstitutional proxy for juror competence and impartiality.

I

On behalf of relator T.B., the mother of a minor child, respondent State of Alabama filed a complaint for paternity and child support against petitioner J.E.B. in the District Court of Jackson County, Alabama. On October 21, 1991, the matter was called for trial and jury selection began. The trial court assembled a panel of 36 potential jurors, 12 males and 24 females. After the court excused three jurors for cause, only 10 of the remaining 33 jurors were male. The State then used 9 of its 10 peremptory strikes to remove male jurors; petitioner used all but one of his strikes to remove female jurors. As a result, all the selected jurors were female.

Before the jury was empanelled, petitioner objected to the State's peremptory challenges on the ground that they were exercised against male jurors solely on the basis of gender, in violation of the Equal Protection Clause of the Fourteenth Amendment. App. 22. Petitioner argued that the logic and reasoning of <u>Batson v. Kentucky</u>, which prohibits peremptory strikes solely on the basis of race, similarly forbids intentional discrimination on the basis of gender. The court rejected petitioner's claim and empanelled the all-female jury. App. 23. The jury found petitioner to be the father of the child, and the court entered an order directing him to pay child support. On post judgment motion, the court reaffirmed its ruling that <u>Batson</u> does not extend to gender-based peremptory challenges. App. 33. The Alabama Court of Civil Appeals affirmed, 606 A.2d 156 (1992), relying on Alabama precedent, see, e.g., <u>Murphy v. State</u>, 596 So.2d 42 (Ala.Crim.App.1991), cert. denied, 506 U.S. 827, 113 S.Ct. 86, 121 L.Ed.2d 49 (1992), and <u>Ex parte Murphy</u>, 596 So.2d 45 (Ala.1992). The Supreme Court of Alabama denied certiorari, No. 1911717 (Oct. 23, 1992).

[3] We granted certiorari, 508 U.S. 905, 113 S.Ct. 2330, 124 L.Ed2d 242 (1993), to resolve a question that has created a conflict of authority—whether the Equal Protection Clause forbids peremptory challenges on the basis of gender as well as on the basis of race. [FN 1] Today we reaffirm what, by now, should be axiomatic: Intentional discrimination on the basis of gender by state actors violates the Equal Protection Clause, particularly where, as here, the discrimination serves to ratify and perpetuate invidious, archaic, and overbroad stereotypes about the relative abilities of men and women.

☆ ☆ ☆

II

Discrimination on the basis of gender in the exercise of peremptory challenges is a relatively recent phenomenon. Gender-based peremptory strikes were hardly practicable during most of our country's existence, since, until the 20th century, women were completely excluded from jury service. [FN2] So well entrenched was this exclusion of women that in 1880 this Court, while finding that the exclusion of African-American men from **juries** violated the Fourteenth Amendment, expressed no doubt that a State "may confine the **selection** [of jurors] to males." <u>Strauder v. West Virginia</u>, 100 U.S., at 310, 25 L.Ed. 664; see also <u>Fay v. New York</u>, 332 U.S. 261, 289-290, 67 S.Ct. 1613, 1628-1629, 91 L.Ed. 2043 (1947).

✯ ✯ ✯

Many States continued to exclude women from jury service well into the present century, despite the fact that women attained suffrage upon ratification of the Nineteenth Amendment in 1920. [FN3] States that did permit women to serve on juries often erected other barriers, such as registration requirements and automatic exemptions, designed to deter women from exercising their right to jury service. See, e.g., Fay v. New York, 332 U.S., at 289, 67 S.Ct., at 1628 ("[I]n 15 of the 28 states which permitted women to serve [on juries in 1942], they might claim exemption because of their sex"); Hoyt v. Florida, 368 U.S. 57, 82 S.Ct. 159, 7 L.Ed.2d 118 (1961) (upholding affirmative registration statute that exempted women from mandatory jury service).

✯ ✯ ✯

[4] The prohibition of women on juries was derived from the English common law which, according to Blackstone, rightfully excluded women from juries under "the doctrine of *propter defectum* sexus, literally, the 'defect of sex.' " United States v. De Gross, 960 F.2d 1433, 1438 (CA9 1992) (en banc), quoting 2 W. Blackstone, Commentaries [FN4] In this country, supporters of the exclusion of women from juries tended to couch their objections in terms of the ostensible need to protect women from the ugliness and depravity of trials. Women were thought to be too fragile and virginal to withstand the polluted courtroom atmosphere. See Bailey v. State, 215 Ark. 53, 61, 219 S.W.2d 424, 428 (1949) ("Criminal court trials often involve testimony of the foulest kind, and they sometimes require consideration of indecent conduct, the use of filthy and loathsome words, references to intimate sex relationships, and other elements that would prove humiliating, embarrassing and degrading to a lady");

In re Goodell, 39 Wis. 232, 245-246 (1875) (endorsing statutory ineligibility of women for admission to the bar because "[r]everence for all womanhood would suffer in the public spectacle of women...so engaged"); Bradwell v. State, 16 Wall. 130, 141, 21 L.Ed. 442 (1873) (concurring opinion) ("[T]he civil law, as well as nature herself, has always recognized a wide difference in the respective spheres and destinies of man and woman. Man is, or should be, woman's protector and defender. The natural and proper timidity and delicacy which belongs to the female sex evidently unfits it for many of the occupations of civil life....The paramount destiny and mission of woman are to fulfill the noble and benign offices of wife and mother. This is the law of the Creator"). Cf. Frontiero v. Richardson, 411 U.S. 677, 684, 93 S.Ct. 1764, 1769, 36 L.Ed.2d 583 (1973) (plurality opinion) (This "attitude of 'romantic paternalism'...put women, not on a pedestal, but in a cage").

✳ ✳ ✳

Despite the heightened scrutiny afforded distinctions based on gender, respondent argues that gender discrimination in the **selection** of the petit **jury** should be permitted, though discrimination on the basis of race is not. Respondent suggests that "gender discrimination in this country...has never reached the level of discrimination" against African-Americans, and therefore gender discrimination, unlike racial discrimination, is tolerable in the courtroom. Brief for Respondent 9.

While the prejudicial attitudes toward women in this country have not been identical to those held toward racial minorities, the similarities between the experiences of racial minorities and women, in some contexts, "overpower those differences." Note, Beyond Batson: Eliminating Gender-Based Peremptory Challenges, Harv.L.Rev. (1920, 1921,

1992). As a plurality of this Court observed in <u>Frontiero v. Richardson</u>, 411 U.S., at 685, 93 S.Ct., at 1769-1770:

> "[T]hroughout much of the 19th century the position of women in our society was, in many respects, comparable to that of blacks under the pre-Civil War slave codes. Neither slaves nor women could hold office, serve on juries, or bring suit in their own names, and married women traditionally were denied the legal capacity to hold or convey property or to serve as legal guardians of their own children....And although blacks were guaranteed the right to vote in 1870, women were denied even that right—which is itself 'preservative of other basic civil and political rights'—until adoption of the Nineteenth Amendment half a century later." (Footnote omitted.)

Certainly, with respect to jury service, African-Americans and women share a history of total exclusion, a history which came to an end for women many years after the embarrassing chapter in our history came to an end for African Americans.

[5][6] We need not determine, however, whether women or racial minorities have suffered more at the hands of discriminatory state actors during the decades of our Nation's history. It is necessary only to acknowledge that "our Nation has had a long and unfortunate history of sex discrimination," id., at 684, 93 S.Ct., at 1769, a history which warrants the heightened scrutiny we afford all gender-based classifications today. 9] Discrimination in **jury selection**, whether based on race or on gender, causes harm to the litigants, the community, and the individual jurors who are wrongfully excluded from participation in the judicial process. The litigants are harmed by the risk that the prejudice that motivated the discriminatory **selection** of the **jury** will infect the entire proceedings. See <u>Edmonson</u>, 500 U.S., at 628, 111 S.Ct., at 2087 (discrimination in the courtroom "raises serious questions as to the fairness of the

proceedings conducted there"). The community is harmed by the State's participation in the perpetuation of invidious group stereotypes and the inevitable loss of confidence in our judicial system that state-sanctioned discrimination in the courtroom engenders.

When state actors exercise peremptory challenges in reliance on gender stereotypes, they ratify and reinforce prejudicial views of the relative abilities of men and women. Because these stereotypes have wreaked injustice in so many other spheres of our country's public life, active discrimination by litigants on the basis of gender during **jury selection** "invites cynicism respecting the jury's neutrality and its obligation to adhere to the law." Powers v. Ohio, 499 U.S., at 412, 111 S.Ct., at 1371. The potential for cynicism is particularly acute in cases where gender-related issues are prominent, such as cases involving rape, sexual harassment, or paternity. Discriminatory use of peremptory challenges may create the impression that the judicial system has acquiesced in suppressing full participation by one gender or that the "deck has been stacked" in favor of one side. See id, at 413, 111 S.Ct., at 1372 ("The verdict will not be accepted or understood [as fair] if the jury is chosen by unlawful means at the outset").

[10][11] In recent cases we have emphasized that individual jurors themselves have a right to nondiscriminatory **jury selection** procedures. [FN 12] See Powers, supra, Edmonson, supra, and Georgia v. McCollum, 505 U.S. 42, 112 S.Ct. 2348, 120 L.Ed.2d 33 (1992). Contrary to respondent's suggestion, this right extends to both men and women. See Mississippi Univ. for Women v. Hogan, 458 U.S., at 723, 102 S.Ct., at 3335 (that a state practice "discriminates against males rather than against females does not exempt it from scrutiny or reduce the standard of review"); cf. Brief for Respondent 9 (arguing that men deserve no protection from gender discrimination in jury selection because they are not victims of historical discrimination). All persons, when granted the opportunity to serve on a jury, have the right not to be excluded summarily because of discriminatory

and stereotypical presumptions that reflect and reinforce patterns of historical discrimination. [FN 13] Striking individual jurors on the assumption that they hold particular views simply because of their gender is "practically a brand upon them, affixed by the law, an assertion of their inferiority." Strauder v. West Virginia, 100 U.S. at 308, 25 L.Ed. 664 (1880). It denigrates the dignity of the excluded juror, and, for a woman, reinvokes a history of exclusion from political participation. [FN 14] The message it sends to all those in the courtroom, and all those who may later learn of the discriminatory act, is that certain individuals, for no reason other than gender, are presumed unqualified by state actors to decide important questions upon which reasonable persons could disagree. [FN 15]

☆ ☆ ☆

**1429 *143 IV

[12] Our conclusion that litigants may not strike potential jurors solely on the basis of gender does not imply the elimination of all peremptory challenges. Neither does it conflict with a State's legitimate interest in using such challenges in its effort to secure a fair and impartial jury. Parties still may remove jurors who they feel might be less acceptable than others on the panel; gender simply may not serve as a proxy for bias. Parties may also exercise their peremptory challenges to remove from the venire any group or class of individuals normally subject to "rational basis" review. See Cleburne v. Cleburne Living Center, Inc., 473 U.S., at 439-442, 105 S.Ct., at 3254-3255; Clark v. Jeter, 486 U.S. 456, 461, 108 S.Ct. 1910, 1914, 100 L.Ed.2d 465 (1988). Even strikes based on characteristics that are disproportionately associated with one gender could be appropriate, absent a showing of pretext. [FN 16]

✿ ✿ ✿

V

Equal opportunity to participate in the fair administration of justice is fundamental to our democratic system. [FN 19] It not only furthers the goals of the jury system. It reaffirms the promise of equality under the law—that all citizens, regardless of race, ethnicity, or gender, have the chance to take part directly in our democracy. Powers v. Ohio, 499 U.S., at 407, 111 S.Ct., at 1369 ("Indeed, with the exception of voting, for most citizens the honor and privilege of jury duty is their most significant opportunity to participate in the democratic process"). When persons are excluded from participation in our democratic processes solely because of race or gender, this promise of equality dims, and the integrity of our judicial system is jeopardized.

✿ ✿ ✿

In view of these concerns, the Equal Protection Clause prohibits discrimination in jury selection on the basis of gender, or on the assumption that an individual will be biased in a particular case for no reason other than the fact that the person happens to be a woman or happens to be a man. As with race, the "core guarantee of equal protection, ensuring citizens that their State will not discriminate...would be meaningless were we to approve the exclusion of jurors on the basis of such assumptions, which arise solely from the jurors' [gender]." Batson, 476 U.S., at 97-98, 106 S.Ct., at 1723-1724.

The judgment of the Court of Civil Appeals of Alabama is reversed, and the case is remanded to that court for further proceedings not inconsistent with this opinion.

It is so ordered.

✫ ✫ ✫

G. OPENING STATEMENTS

The formal trial presentation begins with the opening statements made by the parties' attorneys. First, the plaintiff's attorney makes an opening statement, in which he or she attempts to outline the case to be presented and to summarize what will be presented during the presentation of evidence. Next, the defendant's attorney may make an opening statement, in which he or she states the defendant's upcoming evidentiary presentation.

H. PRESENTATION OF EVIDENCE

After the opening statements, the attorney for the plaintiff begins to present evidence for the plaintiff. This presentation of evidence includes both the presentation of witnesses, who will be questioned by the plaintiff's attorney and then questioned by the defendant's attorney, as well as the presentation of any and all relevant physical evidence. When the plaintiff's attorney has finished presenting evidence, the defendant's attorney then has the opportunity to present witnesses and physical evidence on behalf of the defendant. When the defendant's attorney has finished with the presentation of evidence, the plaintiff has an opportunity to present rebuttal evidence; rebuttal evidence is that evidence which responds to or clarifies that which was presented by the defendant. The defense then has one opportunity to present rebuttal evidence of its own.

The role and importance of the attorney in the process needs to be considered. At least, the attendance of the attorney should be required.

✣ ✣ ✣

Case#3-7

Patricia L. v. Steven L.
506 N.Y.S. 2d 198(1986)

PER CURIUM The dispute had its origin in an action for divorce brought by Patricia L. against Steven L. in which both parties sought custody of Steven, then eleven, and Lynn, then six. The custody issue was referred to Family Court, and at 10:00 A.M. on October 7, 1983, the parties were present there for a hearing. Although both parents were represented by counsel, the mother's attorney wasn't in the courtroom when the matter was called. The colloquy between the father's lawyer and the court indicates that this was not the first time the mother's lawyer had been late, and that on the previous hearing date the matter had been marked final against the mother.

...She called (her) lawyer's home and was told by the lawyer that she was just leaving and would be in court shortly. Despite having been informed that the lawyer was on her way, the court, over the mother's protest, proceeded with the hearing, requiring that the mother represent herself if she were to participate at all.

The right to counsel in Family Court custody proceedings is established in Family Court Act section 262.

There can be no doubt that the mother's exercise of her right to counsel was compromised by the Family Court's refusal to wait for the counsel to arrive. Whatever her other shortcomings, the mother's lawyer recognized that her ability to represent her client effectively was completely destroyed by the fact that most of the hearing had been conducted in her absence....(The mother's) attempts at cross-examination and presenting her own case were that of an inexperienced lay person. Palpably, she was unable to match the ability of a competent attorney to expose weaknesses in her opponent's case and present her own case in the most favorable light....

...To require a party to try a custody case without benefit of counsel in order to prevent a delay places the court's interest in moving calendars above the interests of both the children and the parents and gives unacceptable prominence to expediency. Misbehaving or careless lawyers can be punished but the onus for their conduct in child custody cases should be borne by neither the children nor the parents.

☆ ☆ ☆

I. CLOSING ARGUMENTS

At the conclusion of the presentation of evidence, the attorneys for both parties have an opportunity to present their closing arguments. These closing arguments should serve both to summarize that which was presented and also to argue how that evidence should be interpreted and prioritized. Closing argument is the opportunity for counsel to argue the case in its entirety, and to persuade the jury that his client's version of the case is correct.

J. CHARGES TO THE JURY

After the closing statements are made, the judge gives the charges to the jury. These charges to the jury are a set of instructions to the jury members on appropriate law in the particular case, and how it should be applied to the facts in the case. Usually, each attorney prepares a set of instructions to the jury, and the judge uses those sets to begin the jury charge process. The court, of course, may make whatever modifications and changes that it feels are necessary.

K. VERDICT

The jury, after the charges are given to it by the judge, leaves the courtroom and enters into a process of deliberation in an effort to reach a final decision or <u>verdict</u>. The jury in civil trials needs to be convinced by a preponderance of the evidence that one side is more correct than the other. This "preponderance of the evidence" standard simply means that the jury believes that the evidence favors one party. Juries are the determiners of the facts in the case, with the court, in its charges and other rulings, the determiner of law. Once the jury is in its deliberative phase, it has quite complete control over the ultimate outcome of the case.

After the verdict in the trial court, the trial process may continue if the losing party elects to appeal. Appeals to the two levels of higher courts must be based on mistakes in law, not in any perceived error in determining the facts of the case. Further, in civil trials, careful attention must be paid to the cost effectiveness of the appeals process or processes. An appeal to the appeals level and then to the highest court of appeals in a system is time consuming and expensive.

✻ ✻ ✻

CHAPTER SUMMARY

The civil trial process is the crown jewel of the American legal system. It begins with the period of pleadings. The pleadings, formal documents that make the initial arguments in a case, include the complaint, the answer, the countercomplaint, the answer to the countercomplaint, and motions. This initial period is followed by the period of discovery. It is during this stage of the trial that the sides can discover all the information held by the other side. As students, we can consider this time as the time for doing our homework in preparation for the trial. Discovery mechanisms include depositions, interrogatories, demands for documents, and required physical and/or mental examinations.

Following these first two periods comes a time for pretrial conferences. These conferences set the time frames and the structures for the trial.

The trial proper begins with the selection of the jury. Then the opening statements, presentations of evidence, and the closing arguments follow in order. Charges to the jury by the court precede jury deliberations. The verdict follows the deliberations.

Appeals to the next step up the court structure are, in civil trials, an optional next step, presuming a legal justification for the appeal exists, and that the appeal is cost effective in the case. Finally, a second appeals level, the highest court of appeals, would be the elective final step.

CHAPTER THREE
KEY TERMS

Answer
Charges to the Jury
Closing Arguments
Complaint
Defendant
Depositions
Habeas Corpus
Jury

Motions
Per Curium
Plaintiff
Pre-trial Conference
Statute of Limitations
Summons
Venire
Voir Dire

THINK AND WRITE

1. What types of documents or communications should not be accessible in discovery? Why?
2. Who should not sit on a jury? Why should they be excluded?
3. What does an attorney want to accomplish in an opening statement to a jury?
4. What does an attorney want to accomplish in a closing argument to a jury?
5. What are the differences and similarities between <u>Miller-El</u> and <u>Manufacturers Hanover</u>?
6. In <u>Patricia L.</u>, the attorney's efforts were found wanting. Should an attorney's behavior or skill ever be found wanting by a court? If so, when?
7. The trial is the jewel in the crown of the legal system. Discuss.
8. Should limits be placed on access to the court system? If so, when?

PROJECTS

1. Investigate motion practice in your local court.
   A. How can motions be served?
   B. What are the time constraints on motions?
   C. What are the accompanying supporting affidavits required?
2. Research your state's rules on discovery. Research the federal rules on discovery and compare them to your state's rules.
3. What is the procedure for amending a complaint in your state's courts? When is one allowed to amend a complaint?
4. Review and summarize the rules for jury selection in your local court.
5. A. Your client desires representation in a medical malpractice suit in which the alleged malpractice occurred exactly two-and-one-half years ago. Determine whether or not the statute of limitations in your state bars your suit.
   B. Your client desires representation against the U.S. government for an accident caused by a negligently driven U.S. Postal Service truck in which your client and his twelve-year-old daughter were injured. The accident occurred eleven months ago. Is your case time barred by the statute of limitations?

✫ ✫ ✫

ETHICS QUESTIONS

1. During the discovery phase of your client's case, you receive several boxes of documents that you have requested from your adversary. Among the documents received are several items that you clearly did not request, but which are of great help to your case. What

should you do with the extra documents and with the information that you have gathered from them?

2. You have a new job working as a legal assistant in a large personal injury law firm. The firm will pay you a $1,000 for each new client that you can bring to the firm. Is this appropriate?

☆ ☆ ☆

WEBSITES

1. Civil litigation links: http://www.hg.org/litg.html
2. Site of the Federal Rules of Civil Procedure: http://www.wvnb.uscourts.gov/frcp.htm
3. Site of the Class Action and Litigation Resource Center: http://www.classactiorc.com/directory/civil-litigation-process.html
4. American Bar Association litigation site: http://www.abanet.org/litigation/home.htm/

CHAPTER FOUR

FAMILY LAW

Family law encompasses a large and diverse number of subtopics, all of which deal with the most personal and intimate relationships that we have in each of our lives. The law attempts to keep a balance between recognition of our right to individual freedom in our relationships, and society's interests in those relationships. Such diverse topics as divorce, adoption, annulment, child custody, child support, juvenile crimes, child or spousal abuse, and antenuptual agreements all fall with the umbrella of family law. Any discussion of family law, though, surely must begin with the bedrock of personal relationships, marriage.

A. MARRIAGE

Marriage is viewed by the law not just as the intimate social acts between two individuals, but, rather, as a legal act incorporating three parties. Those three participants in marriage are the two individuals being married and the state. The law imposes a variety of requirements, limitations, and restrictions on marriage that reflect the desires and standards of contemporary American society. Most states have the same basic requirements and restrictions on marriage, although some variations occur from state to state.

First, the law requires that the participants to the marriage obtain a marriage license before the ceremony. The license serves a dual purpose for the law. It allows the state to monitor the other requirements by necessitating that the couple comes before a public official and either brings documents or answer questions about the other requirements. It also, like all licenses, serves as an indirect tax on the parties receiving the license. Most states issue licenses through the town clerk's office or through the county clerk's office.

Second, the law mandates that only individuals of <u>adequate age</u> may marry. In all states, that age is eighteen for both parties. One must bring a birth certificate or other acceptable proof of age when applying for the license. States also allow individuals younger than eighteen to marry with proper permissions. In most states, people can marry at sixteen with parental permission. Indeed, some states allow marriage at fourteen, with both parental and judicial permission.

Third, the law in some states requires that <u>blood tests</u> be done prior to the issuing of the license. The blood tests are screening tests for sexually transmitted diseases, such as syphilis. These tests are not tests for AIDS in any states. Those states that require blood tests mandate that the individuals bring a negative test result from a doctor, hospital, or medical laboratory to the clerk issuing the license. Obviously, if a person has a positive test result, then he or she must be treated for the disease and retested before a license will be issued.

Fourth, all states allow only <u>certain individuals</u> to conduct a legal wedding ceremony. All states allow ceremonies to be conducted by members of the clergy; in addition, states allow designated public officials, such as justices of the peace, judges, mayors, and other designated officials, to perform valid marriages. The ceremonies performed by any of these designated individuals must be reported by them to the proper town or county clerk in order for the marriage to be valid.

Fifth, states require that the ceremony be <u>witnessed</u> in order to be valid. In most states, two witnesses to the ceremony are required. These witnesses must sign a statement swearing that they saw the ceremony performed.

Sixth, the law limits the people to whom we may get married in three significant ways. First, marriages are not valid between close members of the same family. This abhorrence of intrafamilial marriages has a long history and is deeply ingrained in our Judeo-Christian ethic. Second, the law in some states does not accept same-sex marriages. Same-sex marriages are currently granted by five states; they are Connecticut, Iowa, Massachusetts, New Hampshire, and Vermont. The District of Columbia also grants same-sex marriages, as does the Coquille Indian tribe in Oregon. Three states, New York, Rhode Island, and Maryland, recognize same-sex marriages but do not perform ceremonies. Thirty states have constitutional amendments that bar recognition of same-sex marriages. The federal government does not recognize same-sex marriages and is prohibited from doing so by the Defense of Marriage Act. However, in July 2010, a federal district court judge in Massachusetts found the Defense of Marriage Act to be unconstitutional; appeals are sure to follow. Third, the law limits the number of people to whom one may be legally married at one time. Individuals who claim more than one spouse have only one partner in the law.

In the next case, a court is asked to assess the administrative requirements that must be present in order to form a legally valid marriage.

✳ ✳ ✳

Case#4-1

Persad v. Balram
187 Misc.2d 711
724 N.Y.S.2d 500 (2001)

GAVRIN, J. The plaintiff commenced this action seeking a declaration that the parties were never married or, in the alternative, for a divorce. * * *On May 22, 1994, the plaintiff and defendant participated in a Hindu marriage or "prayer" ceremony at the home of the defendant's family in Brooklyn, New York. The Hindu prayer ceremony was presided over by Moscan Persad and was attended by 100 to 150 guests.

✻ ✻ ✻

Mr. Persad testified that he is an ordained Hindu priest or "pandit" sanctioned since February 21, 1993, to perform wedding ceremonies.* * *

It was not disputed that the parties lacked a valid marriage license on May 22, 1994. On three separate occasions, once immediately prior to the ceremony, and twice subsequently, (January and April, 1995), the parties began proceedings to obtain a marriage license, but each time it was not properly secured. Each party blamed the other for the failure to obtain the marriage license. It is also not contested that Muscan Persad was not licensed by the City or State of New York to perform marriage ceremonies.

✻ ✻ ✻

Essentially, the plaintiff contends that the marriage is invalid for two reasons: First, the religious ceremony did not comport with the formal legal requirements under the Domestic Relations Law; second, the religious ceremony was merely a custom conducted prior to the parties living together and the parties did not intend to be married until they participated in a civil ceremony.

✷ ✷ ✷

There is an old cliché that goes "if it walks like a duck and quacks like a duck and looks like a duck, it's a duck." This familiar maxim appears perfectly suited to the case at bar, as it conforms to the intent underlying the statutory structure enacted by the Legislature. Essentially, the Domestic Relations Law establishes that where parties participate in a solemn marriage ceremony officiated by a clergyman or magistrate wherein they exchange vows, they are married in the eyes of the law. ✷ ✷ ✷ It is the opinion of this court that this is precisely what occurred in the instant case.

The party's failure to obtain a marriage license does not render their marriage void. Section 25 of the Domestic Relations Law provides that "(n)othing in (Domestic Relations Law article 3) shall be construed to render void by reason of a failure to procure a marriage license any marriage solemnized between persons of full age." Likewise, Moscan Domestic Relations Law section 11-b prior to performing the marriage ceremony did not render the parties marriage void. ✷ ✷ ✷ In New York, a marriage may be solemnized by "(a) clergyman or minister of any religion."✷ ✷ ✷ ✷ ✷ ✷ ✷ ✷

Accordingly, as the plaintiff has not overcome the strong presumption favoring the validity of marriages, ✷ ✷ ✷ ✷ ✷, the marriage is adjudged lawful and the Court directs that a declaration be entered to that effect.

✷ ✷ ✷

LEGAL LIGHT

It was an accepted practice in Babylon four thousand years ago that for a month after the wedding, the bride's father would supply his new son-in-law with all the mead he could drink. Mead is a honey beer. Because the Babylonian calendar is lunar based, this period was called the "honey month," or, today, the honeymoon.

✧ ✧ ✧

B. DIVORCE

Divorce is the legal process by which a valid, legally recognized marriage ends. The rate of divorce in the United States rose over the last half of the twentieth century, until it now stands at over 50 percent. That is, for every one hundred marriages that occur in America in a given year, over fifty divorces occur. While divorce has truly been a growth industry, the law remains steadfast in its commitment to marriage while balancing out the societal need for divorce. Divorce remains a judicial process in our system. The law, as is true of all legal action, requires a civil trial for each divorce. The law of each state sets forth the valid causes of action (or grounds) for divorce in that state. The causes of action differ somewhat from state to state, but the most common causes of action allowed are adultery; imprisonment; abandonment; cruelty; separation; and substance abuse. In truth, many other causes of action for divorce, such as deviant sexual behavior, exist in different states, but the causes that we will examine make up the majority of causes in the majority of states. It is interesting to note that, while it does exist in a small number of states, incompatibility is not frequently validated as a course of action for divorce in most states. Most states take the view that incompatibility as a cause of action for divorce makes divorce too easy a process and reduces divorce to an administrative rather than judicial action. The law has long encouraged couples to stay together rather than to divorce, and, in this light, most states do not want to make divorce too easy an action. On the other hand, divorce laws have responded to the increased societal demand to make divorces easier to obtain than they were for our grandparents.

1. ADULTERY. Adultery, or extramarital sex, has long been a cause of action in virtually all states. Like all causes of action, adultery must be proved in open court by a preponderance of the evidence, making divorce trials based on adultery highly charged. Clearly, adultery divorces reflect the societal norm of monogamy in marriage.

2. IMPRISONMENT. Many states allow the spouse of a convicted criminal to divorce the prisoner on the basis of the <u>imprisonment</u>. Those states that do allow for imprisonment as a cause of action require that the individual imprisoned be incarcerated for at least two years. Suppose Bill, Mary's husband, is convicted of a felony in a state where imprisonment is a cause of action for divorce. The criminal statute in that state calls for a two-year prison term for this crime, and Bill has just been sentenced. Mary wants to divorce Bill on the grounds of imprisonment as his term is for two years. In most states she could not yet do so, as he has not served the statutory time for an imprisonment divorce, nor can Mary guarantee that Bill will serve two years, as convicts in most states, with time off for good behavior or with parole, serve about one-half to two-thirds of their sentence.

3. ABANDONMENT. Abandonment as a cause of action requires that one spouse has unjustifiably departed without consent, and has no intention to return. In most states, the period of abandonment must last one year or more, and must include economic abandonment as well as physical leaving. That is, no economic support can occur. In some states, the term "desertion" is used, rather than "abandonment."

4. CRUELTY. Cruelty is conduct that so endangers the physical or mental well-being of one partner that it is unsafe

for that spouse to continue cohabitation. This cause of action for divorce has long been available for a spouse who is the victim of physical abuse, but, over the last twenty years, has been expanded to include emotional or mental cruelty as well. Most states' courts have an appropriate zero tolerance standard for physical abuse. Any physical blow is an unacceptable level of abuse and establishes a cause of action. For emotional abuse, however, the standards are more variable from state to state. Indeed, the proof required for emotional abuse is more nebulous and variable than for physical abuse. Most states require at least a pattern of abusive behavior over a period of time before the abuse rises to the level of cruelty. Simply calling your spouse a fool during an argument would be an unacceptable threshold for a cruelty standard, as this low a threshold would allow every married couple in America a cause of action for divorce.

5. SEPARATION. Many states have adopted, over the past twenty or so years, a cause of action for divorce based on <u>separation</u>. States typically require that the couple live separate and apart for a statutorily dictated period of time, usually one to one-and-one-half years. As no real negative connotations attach to this cause of action, unlike the other causes of action, this separation divorce is sometimes referred to as a "no-fault" divorce. As a point in fact, it is similar to all other causes of action in that it is established by statute, necessitates a civil trial, and demands that it be proved in a court of law. But, in the highly emotionally charged world of divorce, this separation divorce removes at least one element of possible tension from the proceeding. In those states in which it is available, it is inevitably the most frequently used cause of action for divorce.

6. SUBSTANCE ABUSE. A spouse married to a partner who has a history of <u>substance abuse</u> has a cause of action for divorce in many states. Substance abuse encompasses the use of both illegal drugs and alcohol in most states. The use

must be for an extended period of time, often two or three years, and the period of abuse must be after the marriage has taken place. That is, the person seeking a divorce based on a substance abuse cause of action can only count the time after the wedding, and may not count the time that occurred prior to the marriage.

Whatever the cause of action, the stated intent of the judicial system is to encourage marriage, not divorce. In the following case, perhaps the trial court stretched that noble goal.

✲ ✲ ✲

Case #4-2

Husband W. v. Wife W.
297 A.2d 39 (Del. 1972)

PER CURIAM: In this divorce action...the Trial Court held that the plaintiff failed to sustain his burden of showing that no reasonable possibility of reconciliation existed....

The undisputed evidence shows: the parties had been separated and living apart for almost one and one-half years; recurrent violent quarrels involved the police and the Family Court on numerous occasions to the extent that on October 7, 1970, a Judge of that Court remarked about the frequency of the difficulties and, on December 30, 1970, the same Judge stated "it is obvious that the marriage is finished and they are incompatible"; the defendant put lye in the plaintiff's food; she tried to stab him with an ice pick or knife; she threw a brick through a window in a fit of temper; the plaintiff locked the defendant out of the house on a cold, winter day; he then hit her over the head with a chair, hospitalizing her, and then he presented her with the chair as a souvenir; he hit her over the head with two other chairs on other occasions; he kicked her; he threatened her life with a piece of iron; and he threatened to burn down the house.

In light of that marital history, it is not surprising that…when asked about the likelihood of reconciliation, the plaintiff testified: "No sir, in no way, shape, or form."; and that, in response to the same question, the defendant testified, in the probable understatement of the week: " I don't know if we could (reconcile) or not."

Reversed and remanded with the direction to grant the decree of divorce.

✻ ✻ ✻

LEGAL LIGHT

Some 80 percent of divorced men and 75 percent of divorced women remarry, and the vast majority of these men and women remarry within three years of their divorce. Of all divorces, some 70 percent are initiated by women.

✻ ✻ ✻

C. EQUITABLE DISTRIBUTION

The distribution of property after divorce is an area of family law on which the courts spend a great deal of time. Most states have adopted the statutory standard of equitable distribution for property settlements at divorce. Equitable distribution requires a fair, but not necessarily equal, distribution of property. Equitable distribution recognizes that the marriage is, among other things, an economic partnership.

Equitable distribution statutes, for the most part, do very little to describe the specifics of what is fair and, therefore, equitable. The courts have been left to devise a variety of criteria for equitable distribution. They include age of the spouses, health of the spouses, consideration of any individual holdings, duration of the marriage, standard of living of the parties, tax consequences of any division, and any other facts the court deems relevant. Certainly, the longer the term of the marriage, the more likely the division may be fairly equal, unless some special circumstance associated with the other factors is present.

A significant difference in the change from former standards of property division to the current equitable distribution standard is the elimination of blame as a prime consideration in the division of property. Formerly, an adulterous spouse or an abusive spouse would have that behavior taken into account when property was divided. Under equitable distribution standards, however, fault or blame is not a standard that is to be used. Indeed, while the statutes that create equitable division do not define what it means, they often require specifically that the cause of action for the divorce not be used.

In long-term marriages, those over a year or so in length, virtually all property acquired by the partners or brought by the partners to the marriage is subject to equitable distribution. Some exceptions, however, do exist. The first is an exception for property received by bequest. If either partner receives property through a will or by intestate succession, that property can be excluded from equitable distribution. Second, gifts, other than gifts from one spouse to the other, are often excludable from the division process. Third, if recovery is made in a personal injury lawsuit by one of the spouses, that award is often excluded from the property considerations at the time of the divorce. Of course, different states do have variations on these exceptions. All other property is subject to the provisions of equitable distribution. This includes both real and personal property, and will include such diverse items as pension benefits and professional licenses and practices.

D. CHILD CUSTODY

Child custody arrangements are concerned with the care and keeping of a child or children of a marriage. With whom the child resides, who is responsible for the child, and who makes decisions for the child are the issues decided in child custody awards. Most states have statutorily adopted a standard of child custody that requires the court to do that which is in the "best interest of the child" when making custodial determinations. Child custody arrangements may take many forms, but three basic structures exist as a matter of either law or practice in most jurisdiction. These most frequent custodial arrangements are sole custody, joint custody, and sole physical custody with joint legal custody. Although, again, many variations on these three custodial formats are possible, they are the baselines used in virtually all states.

1. SOLE CUSTODY. Sole custody awards the child to one parent, who is then singly responsible for the care and well-being of that child. The child resides exclusively with that parent, and that parent makes all the decisions for and about that child. Of course, courts may still award some visitation rights to the noncustodial parent, and the noncustodial parent may still be responsible for child support payments, but it is the sole custodian who makes the choices and decision for the child. An advantage of this custodial arrangement is the clear stability it provides for the child.

2. JOINT CUSTODY. Joint custody provides an equal sharing of the physical custody of the child, and an equal sharing of the decision making for the child. In its purest form, the child would reside for six months of the year with one parent and six months of the year with the other. Additionally, during those periods when a parent does not

have physical custody, that parent still has an equal right to make decisions about the child. Obviously, many variations of this type of custody are possible, including one common arrangement in which the child spends the school year with one parent, and summer and winter vacations with the other. Even when the child resides with one parent, the other may be awarded visitation rights. No matter how carefully the courts or the parents may craft joint custody, there is an inherent degree of instability in this type of custody.

3. JOINT LEGAL CUSTODY WITH SOLE PHYSICAL CUSTODY. Joint legal custody with joint physical custody awards the physical possession of the child to one parent, while allowing both parents to be responsible for the decision-making process for the child. There are, commonly, rights for visitation for the noncustodial parent. In some states, this format for custody is grouped under the umbrella of joint custody.

E. CHILD SUPPORT

Child support payments are made from the noncustodial parent to the custodial parent and are intended to provide financial maintenance for the child. The payment of child support to the custodial parent for the benefit of the child has undergone some significant changes over the past decade. These changes have been prompted by two factors. The first is the appalling lack of compliance with child support orders in most states. The number of nonpaying parents reaches over 50 percent in some states. Over the past decade, many states have increased efforts to improve these statistics, with an increased cooperation between states to identify and enforce the support orders. The second factor that has prompted change in the area of child support is recognition of the inconsistency of awards within a given state. The court, historically, had great latitude in determining the support award, and the awards varied greatly. To combat this inconsistency, many states have implemented an award based on a statutory formula. These formulas require the court to award a percentage of the paying parent's income. The percentage awarded increases for each additional child being supported. For instance, Bill and Mary are getting divorced; they have three children, and the court needs to provide child support from Bill to Mary at the time of divorce. In the state in which they live, the legislature has statutorily implemented a scale for child support payments. That scale provides for 15 percent of gross income be paid for one child, 17 percent of gross income for two children, 19 percent of gross income for three children, and 23 percent of gross income for four or more children. In our case, Bill makes $60,000 per year. Multiplying his income by 19 percent, we arrive at a child support payment of $11,400 per year. These payments, in most states, are made monthly, giving us a monthly support amount of $950.

The obligation of the paying parent is at the core of our next case.

✲ ✲ ✲

Case #4-3

<u>Szczygiel v. Szczygiel</u>
581 N.Y.S. 2d 522 (1991)

SEDITA, J. The parties were divorced in 1985 and entered into a binding agreement which was not merged into the judgment.

The agreement provided for a certain amount of child support which was duly paid until 1990. The petitioner's (husband's) illness caused him to take his disability pension from his place of employment, and he was found eligible for social security disability benefits. Fortunately, these two income sources resulted in a comparable income level to the level enjoyed by him prior to his illness and retirement.

In evaluating disability benefits for social security, his two youngest children were also found to be eligible for social security payments. These payments are paid independent of his own, and total more than his contractual support obligation. Due to these payments, the petitioner asserts that he is no longer obligated to make child support payments under his agreement and Judgment of Divorce.

While we are not unsympathetic to the petitioner's medical condition, there is no prima facie showing that it is not possible for him to meet his necessary household expenses. The relative financial circumstances of these parties are roughly comparable to the circumstances at the time they entered into their agreement. The fact that his illness triggered an unexpected benefit from the government does not vitiate his promise under his agreement with respondent.

A leading case in this area of the law is <u>Rubin v. Rubin</u>, 69 N.Y. 2d 702, 512 N.Y.S. 2d 364, 504 N.E. 2d 691. Our Court of Appeals held in this case that an agreement fairly entered into was binding on the parties so long as the needs of the children were being met, even when there was a substantial change in one parent's ability to pay.

✻ ✻ ✻

F. ALIMONY

The traditional concept of <u>alimony</u> was that it was that it was a payment by a divorced husband to his ex-wife for ongoing personal support. Unlike child support, alimony is considered income of the recipient, who must pay taxes on it. The person who pays it may deduct it from his income. These payments were made for the lifetime of the former wife, or until she remarried. More contemporary forms of alimony, often called <u>rehabilitative alimony</u> or maintenance, have evolved over the past fifteen years. First, the current form of alimony is not gender specific. That is either the husband may pay his former wife, or the wife may pay her former husband. Determinations of the flow of the alimony are dependent on the economic roles of the parties in the marriage. If one party was the sole breadwinner of the family and the other party had the sole responsibility for household duties and child rearing, then the alimony could go from the breadwinner to the home provider at the time of divorce. A second significant change that has occurred has been the reduction in the length of alimony payments from a lifetime payment period to a fixed number of years. The intent of traditional alimony was to prevent women from becoming welfare recipients and burdens on the state; it was a form of privatized welfare. At a time when a woman's role was primarily as a wife, this formulation for alimony had validity. Currently, however, women have far more diverse options available to them, providing the impetus to alter alimony. Rehabilitative alimony that lasts for a definite time period while the recipient reconstructs his or her economic life is more reflective of current societal needs. These rehabilitative alimony payments last for a fixed, relatively short period of years, during which time the recipient may reenter the job market, go back to school to upgrade skills, or take advantage of anything that would help him or her to economically recover.

G. ANNULMENT

An annulment is the legal action of voiding, or wiping out completely, a marriage. Marriages are usually not annulled by the court unless they were flawed from the beginning. Divorce terminates a valid marriage, and annulment erases a marriage that can be voided. The three basic grounds for an annulment are <u>non-age</u> of one of the parties, <u>physical incapacity</u> of one of the parties, or <u>fraud</u> by one of the spouses. It is critical to note that each of these grounds must have existed prior to the marriage ceremony. That is, a fraud or physical incapacity that occurs after the marriage ceremony will not give grounds for an annulment.

1. NON-AGE. If one of the parties to a marriage is not of legal marrying age, eighteen years old, then the marriage can be annulled on the grounds of the non-age of one of the participants. An annulment for non-age can be brought to court by the minor, a parent of the minor, a guardian of the minor, or by a court appointed representative of the minor. The annulment cannot, in most states, be brought by the adult party to the marriage, or by a representative of the adult party.

2. PHYSICAL INCAPACITY. If one spouse enters into the marriage lacking the physical capacity to consummate the marriage, then this physical incapacity would be grounds for an annulment. The impotence of the spouse must be related to a physical, not a psychological, cause, and the physical cause must have been present at the time of the marriage ceremony. If the physical incapacity arises after the wedding, then this misfortune is not grounds for an annulment. Also, sterility, or incapacity to conceive, is not a basis for a physical incapacity annulment.

Here is a case discussing incapacity.

✫ ✫ ✫

Case #4-4 Incapacity (Annulment)

Rickards v. Rickards
53 Del. 134, 166 A.2d 425 (1960)

WOLCOTT, Justice.

This is an appeal by the husband from a judgment of the Superior Court of New Castle County granting an annulment of marriage at the suit of the wife, and ordering the conveyance of real estate held by entireties to the wife alone.

The action was based upon 13 Del.C. § 1551, which provides as one ground for annulment of marriages:

'Incurable physical impotency or incapacity for copulation, at the suit of either party; if the party making the application was ignorant of such impotency or incapacity at the time of the marriage.'

The appeal attacks both phases of the judgment—that is, the award of the annulment and the consequent order that the husband convey to the wife the property held in their joint names.

First, the husband argues that the wife failed to prove by 'clear and convincing' evidence incurable physical impotency on his part. Fluharty v. Fluharty, 8 W.W.Harr. 487, 193 A. 838, 840. The husband is, of course, correct in arguing that the plaintiff, in this case the wife, in an action for annulment of marriage necessarily assumes that burden. The trial judge held that the wife had discharged the burden.

It serves no purpose to review the details of the evidence. We have reviewed the record and are satisfied that the ruling below to the effect that the wife had sustained the burden of proving that the husband was sexually impotent, at least as to her, was probably incurable as a "pure form" sexual deviate, and by reason thereof had an incapacity for copulation with the wife, was correct.

We think it also established beyond doubt that the husband's incapacity was entirely due to psychic causes. The evidence is clear that he suffered from no physical defect of a sexually incapacitating nature. We think it apparent that psychogenic causes had made the husband physically unable to copulate, at least with the woman he had married.

The question before us, therefore, is whether 13 Del.C § 1551 permits the annulment of a marriage when the cause of impotency is psychic rather than physical in origin.

The wife argues that the statute, being in the alternative, permits proof of either "incurable physical impotency" or "incapacity for copulation" for any recognized medical reason. This argument was rejected by the Superior Court in S. v. S., 3 Terry 192, 29 A.2d 325, when it held that the second phrase was merely explanatory of the word "impotency," and that the ground of annulment authorized by the statute was incurable physical impotency. If the questions were of first instance in this State we would have some doubt as to the propriety of the construction, but we do not re-examine it for, in the view we take of the case, it is unnecessary to do so. Consequently, we neither approve nor disapprove the rule of S. v. S.

[1] We think this statutory ground for annulment of marriage is an incurable physical inability on the part of one spouse to copulate with the other. This being so, it follows that whether the inability stems from physical or mental defects, provided in either case that the resulting condition is incurable, the requirement of the statute is met.

We think this conclusion inevitable as to the meaning of the statute, and we note that similar statues in other states have been similarly construed. Cf. Tompkins v. Tompkins, 92 N.J.Eq. 113, 111 A. 599; Godfrey v. Shatwell, 38 J.J.Super. 501, 119 A.2d 479; Kaufman v. Kaufman, 82 U.S.App.D.C. 397, 164 F.2d 519; Vanden Berg v. Vanden Berg, Sup., 197 N.Y.S. 641.

[2] The husband does not argue strenuously against the conclusion that impotency under that statute may be the result of psychic causes. The main thrust of his argument is that the wife has failed to establish *incurable* impotency. He cites several authorities but we do not find them to be persuasive.

Thus husband is, of course, correct in maintaining that the asserted impotency must be incurable, but in the case before us we think this fact has been established to a reasonable certainty by the testimony of the psychiatrist who not only had examined him but who for a period of time had had him under treatment. In the opinion of this doctor, the husband "probably" could be classed as incurably physically impotent. It is true that the doctor testified that it was possible to treat the husband's psychic troubles, but the fair import of his testimony is that the possibility of a cure was remote. The trial judge concluded that the doctor's opinion was that the husband was incurably physically impotent. We think conclusion correct from the evidence.

[3] Secondly, the husband argues that, assuming his impotency, still the wife had sufficient knowledge of it at the time of the marriage to preclude its assertion by her as a ground for annulment. The difficulty with argument is that the record does not establish knowledge on the part of the wife. At most, the wife can be said to have been told prior to marriage a veiled hint of past sexual deviation by the husband. She questioned him about it but he passed it off with the explanation that it had happened long ago and no longer troubled him. We consequently agree with the trial judge that there is no evidence that the wife, prior to marriage, had knowledge of the husband's impotency, or of facts sufficient to warn her of its possible existence.

Thirdly, the husband charges that personal habits of cleanliness or lack of cleanliness, on the part of the wife dissipated his sexual desires toward the wife. He argues that, therefore, she cannot obtain annulment for his alleged impotency caused, or at least aggravated, by certain offensive habits of her own.

[4][5][6] The argument is subject to two infirmities. First, it does not appear that it was made to the trial judge, which is a prerequisite to its being made in this court. Second, it rests upon the uncorroborated testimony of the husband alone. In divorce and annulment proceedings, such testimony is not entitled to complete acceptance. Lecates v. Lecates, 8 W.W.Harr. 190, 190 A. 294; Heller v. Heller, supra.

For the foregoing reasons, we affirm that portion of the judgment appealed from granting an annulment, and the resumption by the wife of her name prior to the marriage.

One further matter remains for consideration, viz., the power of the Superior court to compel a conveyance to the wife of real estate held by the parties as tenants by the entireties.

[7] Initially, we observe that the Superior Court has been granted no specific statutory power in this respect. The powers of the court in annulment proceedings thus differ from the powers of the court in divorce proceedings for, by 13 Del.C § 1531, the court is specifically empowered, after the granting of a divorce, to order such division of property as might be equitable. If, following the grant of an annulment, the Superior Court lacks power to order a division of property, or if, having the power, it fails to exercise it, it seems apparent that the dissolution of the marriage would transform by operation of law an estate by the entireties into an estate in common in which each of the former spouses would own an undivided half interest. Townsend v. Townsend, 5 W.W.Harr. 493, 168 A. 67. The husband in this case before us argues for this result, although upon what precise basis is not clear since he apparently concedes the jurisdiction of the Superior court to settle the property rights of the parties in an annulment action.

In any event, we think the authority of the Superior court to settle property rights of the parties in an annulment action has been held to exist by Du Pont v. Du Pont, 7 Terry 592, 87 A.2d 394, 397. In that case the precise question was the power of the Superior Court to award suit money to a wife in the absence of specific statutory authority to do so. We held that the statutory grant to the Superior Court of jurisdiction over annulments (13 Del.C. § 1501) by practical necessity carried with it the inherent powers exercised by the Ecclesiastical Courts of England which had long developed and proclaimed 'rules of procedure and defined those extraordinary incidents to matrimonial jurisdiction which were deemed necessary. * * * to equalize the positions of the contending parties. Those powers, not inappropriate to our judicial system, were conferred upon the Superior Court with the grant of general jurisdiction over annulment.

In the Ecclesiastical Courts a sentence of annulment of marriage, or technically of divorce a *vinculo matrimonii*, pronounced the marriage a nullity *ab initio*. The result was that the wife became *feme sole* and took back her separate property. In addition, adjustments of property between the parties were directed. See Shelford on Marriage and Divorce, 477-479, and cf. Stephens v. Totty, Cro.Eliz. 908, 78 Eng.Rep. 1130; Aughtie v. Aughtie, 1 Phill.Ecc. 201, 161 Eng.Rep. 9671. It follows that the Superior Court has similar powers.

It appears that the house in which the husband now claims an undivided interest was purchased primarily with the money of the wife derived from the sale of a property owned by her prior to the marriage. Likewise, the contract to purchase the property now in dispute was entered into by the wife prior to the marriage, which purchase was completed after the marriage. The husband contributed to the purchase less than $100. The balance of the purchase price, above some $5,800, contributed by the wife in cash, was derived from a mortgage of $10,000 on the property. Title was taken as tenants by the entireties because of the wife's belief that it was required by law. Subsequently, all the mortgage payments were made by the wife, although the husband did personally make some small improvements on the property. We think in all fairness and justice that the property may be regarded substantially as the wife's separate property brought by her to the marriage.

[8] In the light of the facts, the trial judge ordered that the fee to the property be conveyed to the wife after the payment by her to the husband of $450, the value of his contribution, and after she had obtained his release from the bond signed in connection with the mortgage. The settlement of property rights after annulment of marriage is within the discretion of the trial judge and we think his decision in this respect is more than justified by the facts.

The judgment of the Superior Court is affirmed.

166 A.2. 425, 3 Storey 134, 53 Del.134

✵ ✵ ✵

3. FRAUD. <u>Fraud</u>, as a reason for an annulment, requires the intentional misrepresentation of a fact material to the marriage promise that substantially affects the marriage. Such material misrepresentations must be offensive to the core understanding of marriage. In our next case, we shall see an example of and discussion of such an essential misrepresentation.

✫ ✫ ✫

℗   Case #4-5   ⅅ

wife   husb

<u>Wolfe v. Wolfe</u>

76 Ill. 2d 92, 389 N.E. 2d 1143 (1979)

MORAN, J. In 1963, the parties discussed marriage but, when plaintiff informed defendant that she had been previously married and divorced, defendant explained that he, a Roman Catholic, was forbidden by his religion to marry her. In November of that year, however, plaintiff told defendant that she had learned from a friend in Arizona that her former husband had been killed in an auto accident and that she would receive a copy of the death certificate. Under these circumstances, defendant's church considered plaintiff a widow and defendant was free to marry her. Preparatory to marriage, plaintiff underwent conversion to Catholicism, and as a requirement thereof, executed a Sponsa in which she stated, under oath, that her former husband was dead.

Shortly before the couple married, in March of 1965, plaintiff had shown defendant a copy of the purported death certificate of her former husband. A child was born of the marriage in 1966.

In November 1973, the couple separated, and the following month, plaintiff sued for divorce. On May 10,

1974, defendant filed a counterclaim for annulment which alleged that plaintiff had fraudulently induced him to consent to marriage by misrepresenting that her former husband was dead. * * *

The evidence in this case clearly and convincingly showed that plaintiff had perpetrated a fraud upon defendant in order to obtain his consent to the marriage. Although such fraud would render the ordinary contract void, a marriage contract can be voided only if the nature of the fraud itself affects the essentials of the marriage. What constitutes "essentials" of marriage cannot be expressly delineated, for what is essential to one marriage may not be equally significant to another. Whether a fraud goes to the essentials of a marriage must be determined on the basis of the facts in an individual case.

With this background in mind, we turn to the issue before us: Did the fraud, under the circumstances of this case, go to the essentials of the marital relationship, rendering it impossible for the defendant to perform the duties and obligations of his marriage? yes

Sub judice, defendant has established that he is a loyal practitioner of his faith and has lived according to the rules and dictates of his church. In the absence of certain modifying circumstances, which apparently do not exist here, the defendant's religion prohibits marriage with a divorced person whose former spouse is still living. Under the facts of this case we believe that this marriage would not have occurred but for the fraud, executed for the purpose of inducing defendant's consent. Furthermore, since discovering the fraud, <u>defendant is unable to continue marital cohabitation with the plaintiff.</u> It can be seen that this disability is the product of a canon of defendant's religion, placed upon him by his church. This is to be distinguished from a mere subjective personal aversion. * * * * * * * * <u>To deny defendant an annulment would cause the defrauded party to bear the consequences of the deception and allow the deceiver to proceed with impunity.</u>

so, must grant annulment to him

☆ ☆ ☆

We recognize that the parties lived together as husband and wife for several years, and that a child of the marriage exists. Although we consider lengthy marital cohabitation to be a factor mitigating against the granting of an annulment, we do not consider it to be controlling here. Similarly, <u>the existence of a child, although a factor, will not bar an annulment inasmuch as the status of the child, under Illinois law, is unchanged.</u> * * * * * * * * * * *

Based upon the forgoing, we conclude that <u>the defendant is entitled to an annulment.</u> The judgment of the appellate court is, therefore, affirmed.

Judgment affirmed.

☆ ☆ ☆

CHAPTER FOUR
KEY TERMS

Abandonment
Adultery
Alimony
Annulment

Child Custody
Cruelty
Divorce
Equitable Distribution
Imprisonment
Marriage
Rehabilitative Alimony
Separation
Sub Judice
Substance Abuse

☆ ☆ ☆

CHAPTER SUMMARY

Family law serves both the state and society by controlling acceptable family relations and their consequences, both socially and financially. First, the state defines marriage by placing a variety of requirements upon it. The need for a license, the imposition of age requirements, and blood tests, among other things, place thresholds that must be crossed in order for there to be a legally recognized marriage.

Ending marriage is also controlled by the state. Each state recognizes only a limited number of causes of action for divorce. Equitable distribution controls the distribution of assets at the time of divorce. Child custody and child support are state processes that control and monitor these two activities. Alimony, in both its traditional form and the current incarnation of rehabilitative alimony, are state structures for spousal support.

Lastly, annulment is the state-approved invalidation of a marriage. Non-age, physical incapacity and fraud are the three dominant legal justifications for the erasure of a marriage.

☆ ☆ ☆

THINK AND WRITE

1. What changes in the requirements for marriage should happen in the future? Why?
2. Marriage can be viewed as an administrative process. Should divorce also be accomplished through an administrative, rather than judicial, process?
3. What changes in the causes of action for divorce would you like to see happen? Why?
4. We have a divorce rate of slightly more than 50 percent in the United States. Why? Can we improve on this? Should we try?
5. How would you divide property at the time of divorce? What property would you specifically exclude or include?
6. How would you prioritize the three child custody arrangements that were discussed? What are the advantages and disadvantages of each arrangement?
7. Give your views of the child support process and of the amounts awarded. How would you change things?
8. Should the law provide annulments for people? In Wolfe, the court dismisses the length of the marriage and the fact that the couple has a child. Are the court's analysis and decision adequate and acceptable?

✲ ✲ ✲

PROJECTS

1. Locate the divorce statute in your state. What are the specific causes of action allowed by the statute?
2. Your law office does very little divorce work, but has taken on a divorce case for a longtime client. You have been asked to help determine what the possibilities are for spousal support for your client, the wife. While you only have a limited amount of information, you are asked to prepare a memo for the attorney, as best you can. You

do know that your client makes $20,000 per year, that her spouse makes $70,000 per year, and that they have three children, ages seven, nine, and thirteen. Your client has worked only half time since the birth of the first child; she works as a secretary and has an associate's degree in business. The husband has always worked full time, presently as a midlevel manager at a major corporation, and has a master's degree in business. Your client will have physical custody of all three children.

3. The attorney for whom you work wants a memo discussing whether or not a professional degree (in this case, a law degree) is considered property in your state, and whether or not it is subject to equitable distribution.

4. Attend a court session where divorces are heard. Take notes of the disputes and outcomes. How do you feel the divorces were handled and why?

5. For adoption in your state, determine whether or not private placement adoptions are allowed. If so, summarize the process. If not, do you think that they should be allowed?

✿ ✿ ✿

ETHICAL QUESTIONS

1. Your client wants to adopt a child of a different race and ethnicity. Should you alter the advice that you would normally give to prospective adoptive parents?

2. While conducting an interview with your client regarding a child custody dispute, he discloses negative circumstances regarding the mother's behavior towards the child. You do not believe that his story is true. What should you do?

✿ ✿ ✿

RELATED WEBSITES

1. Extensive glossary of family law terms: http://www.divorcelawinfo.com/gloss.htm
2. Information of family law rights: http://family-law.freeadvice.com
3. Information from the Family Law Section of the Florida Bar: http://www.familylawfla.org
4. Family law information and resources: http://www.findlaw.com/01topics/15family

CHAPTER FIVE

CONTRACTS

The segment of the law known as contracts impacts on each of our lives every day. From the purchase of this book to our agreement with our employer to work, many of the promises that we make to each other are forms of contracts. Contracts regulate and add order to the necessary and desired arrangements that give form to our interactions.

A. DEFINITION OF A CONTRACT

A <u>contract</u> is a promise or a set of promises for the breach of which the law gives a remedy, or the performance of which the law in some way recognizes as a duty. Contracts are voluntary promises recognized by the courts, and therefore enforced by the courts. These enforceable promises are entitled to be addressed by the courts and to be redressed by the courts if the promises are not kept. These promises enforced by the courts impose obligations on their makers. One may say that all contracts are promises, but not all promises are contracts.

We must begin by distinguishing those promises that are contracts from those promises that are not. The law requires that several basic elements be present in order for the promises to be contractual. These essential elements, which we will view, are <u>an offer</u>, <u>an acceptance</u>, <u>consideration</u>, <u>competence of the parties</u>, <u>legal purpose</u>, <u>and true consent</u>. All contracts require the existence and identification of these essential elements in order for the contract to be binding and enforceable. The lack of one or more of these essential elements removes our promises from the realm of contracts and places them in a social, not a legal, setting.

1. Offer

An <u>offer</u> is a statement of intent or a proposal made by one party, called the offeror, to another party, called the offeree. The offer is one promise made to do, or not to do, some specific thing in the future. To be valid, the offer must be reasonably definite; that is, it must contain enough information to be clear. This need for clarity doesn't mean that each and every detail need be present, but it does require that the parties be named or be apparent, that the subject matter involved be clear, that the price or consideration be stated, and that the time and place of performance be discernible. Additionally, the offeror must be serious in intent for the offer to be valid. A serious offer must be differentiated from things that may look like offers but are not. These promises that lack seriousness of intent, such that they are not really offers, include statements made in jest, expressions of opinion, advertisements and circulars, auctions, negotiations, agreements to agree in the future, and sham transactions. If I were to offer you a million dollars for a glass of water after playing a hard game of basketball with you, or if your professor were to offer you an A for simply coming to class, these promises are clearly in jest. Lastly, the offer must be communicated to the offeree in such a manner as to inform the offeree of the offer. One cannot agree to an offer without being aware of its existence. Obviously, an offer made to me while I am awake is considerably more binding than the same offer made to me while I sleep.

2. Acceptance

An <u>acceptance</u> is a statement by the offeree that demonstrates assent to the offer. The acceptance, or return promise, should be the mirror image of the offer.

That is, the offeree must not change the terms of the offer. If I offer to sell you my car for a thousand dollars, you cannot accept by saying, "Fine, but I'll give you five hundred dollars." If the acceptance is not unequivocal and complete, then it will not be viewed as an acceptance, but, rather, as a counteroffer. Also, the acceptance must be communicated to the offeror. Silence cannot be construed as acceptance, even if the offer provides for silence as acceptance. Lastly, only the party for whom the offer was intended can accept the offer. No third party can intercede or inject themselves into the exchange of promises being made.

3. Consideration

The third essential element of a contract is the requirement for consideration. <u>Consideration</u> is defined as something of legal value. It requires that the promisor or the promisee receive or lose something that they would not otherwise receive or lose. The money paid for this course or the work that you do has legal value and would be considered as adequate support for the promises that one may make. Legal value is not synonymous with economic value. Legal value certainly includes those items that have economic worth, but also includes refraining from doing something that we would have a right to do.

4. Competence

The competence of the parties making the promises is an additional essential element of a contract. The evaluation of the parties' <u>competence</u> focuses on whether or not they have the capacity to understand the promises that are being made, and that these promises have a binding quality, with consequences associated with them. Individuals who are insane, for example, lack, in most cases, legal competence. They do not have the requisite capacity to understand that which they are undertaking in a contract. Also, minors are presumed in most cases to lack legal capacity.

5. Legal Purpose

The courts will only enforce those contracts that have, at their core, promises that have <u>legal purpose</u>. Those agreements to do something that is criminal in nature, or deal with a criminal activity or the product of a criminal enterprise, are not enforceable by the courts as they lack legal purpose. As examples, gambling contracts in areas where gambling is not legal, or a contract for the sale of stolen goods, would not be enforceable by the courts as they lack legality of purpose.

6. True Consent

The final piece of the agreement that needs to be present in order to have a contract is the <u>true consent</u> of the parties. This requires an actual comprehension of the material elements of the contract at hand. Material elements are those contract terms that are critical to the transaction. True consent is different from the competence of the parties in that competence evaluates the capacity or innate ability to understand, while true consent presumes this ability and questions whether or not the parties actually understand. This true consent is often referred to as a need for a meeting of the minds of the parties; it may be viewed as a need for the parties to be on basically the same wavelength as one another. Two general areas may defeat true consent. The first is a mistake in understanding. Mistakes may be either unilateral, made by one party, or bilateral, made by both parties. The mistake, be it unilateral or bilateral, must involve a material element of the contract. The second area that may defeat true consent presumes a requirement of willingness in the consent. Anything that defeats the voluntary quality of the consent would, therefore, negate the true consent required by the courts. Those agreements based on deceit, formed under duress, or formed under undue influence would lack true consent.

All contracts must meet each of the stated essential elements. Indeed, each and every contract evaluation must include an analysis for each and every essential element. Our following case evaluates the presence or lack of consideration.

✵ ✵ ✵

LEGAL LIGHT

Contracts are mainly governed by state law and Common Law. However, in international business, the United States joined the United Nations Convention on Contracts for the International Sale of Goods in 1988, which now controls these types of transactions.

✵ ✵ ✵

CONTRACTS CASE # 5-1

Hamer v. Sidway
124 N.Y. 538, 27 N.E. 256 (1891)

The plaintiff presented a claim to the executor of William E. Story, Sr., for $5,000 and interest. The claim being rejected by the executor, this action was brought. It appears that William E. Story, Sr., was the uncle of William E. Story, 2d; that...on the 20th day of March, 1869, in the presence of family William E. Story, Sr., promised his nephew that if he would refrain from drinking, using tobacco, swearing and playing cards or billiards for money until he became twenty-one years of age he would pay him a sum of $5,000. The nephew assented thereto and fully performed the conditions inducing the promise.

PARKER, J. The question which provoked the most discussion by counsel on this appeal, and which lies at the foundation of plaintiff's asserted right of recovery, is whether by virtue of a contract defendant's testator William E. Story, Sr., became indebted to his nephew, William E. Story, 2d, on his twenty-first birthday in the sum of five thousand dollars.

The defendant contends that the contract was without consideration to support it, and, therefore, invalid. He asserts that the promisee by refraining from the use of liquor and tobacco was not harmed but benefited; that that which he did was best for him to do independently of his uncle's promise, and insists that it follows that unless the promisor was benefited, the contract was without consideration.

"In general, a waiver of any legal right at the request of the other party is sufficient consideration for a promise." (Parson's on Contracts, 444)

"Any damage, or suspension, or forbearance of a right will be sufficient to sustain a promise." (Kent, vol.2, 465, 12th ed.)

Pollock, on his work on Contracts, page 166, says: "The second branch of this judicial description is really the most important one. Consideration means not so much that one party is profiting as that the other abandons some legal right in the present or limits his legal freedom of action in the future as an inducement for the promise of the first."

Now, applying this rule to the facts before us, the promisee used tobacco, occasionally drank liquor, and he had a legal right to do so. That right he abandoned for a period of years upon the strength of the promise of the testator that for such forbearance he would give him $5,000. We need not speculate on the effort which they have been required to give up the use of those stimulants. It is sufficient that he restricted his lawful freedom of action, within certain prescribed limits upon the faith of his uncle's agreement, and now, having fully performed the conditions imposed, it is of no moment whether such performance actually proved a benefit to the promisor.

☆ ☆ ☆

B. BREACH OF CONTRACT

A breach of contract is a failure to perform or a failure to perform as required. Breaches of contracts may involve either a full or partial failure to perform one's promise as required. In a full breach, one party fails to perform any part of the contractual promise made. In a partial breach, only part of the promise is not performed. If you contract to mow the neighbor's lawn, and you fail to do so, then you are in full breach. If, however, you mow the front lawn but not the back lawn, you are in partial breach. Additionally, a breach of contract may arise not from a failure to perform all or part of the contract, but may arise from a performance that is inadequate. A contract for the delivery of a ton of tomatoes from a farmer to a market would certainly be breached upon the delivery of a ton of rotten, fetid fruit.

A special type of breach of contract allowed by the court is an anticipatory breach. An anticipatory breach is a breach of contract that occurs prior to the required performance of a promise. It occurs when one party clearly states unwillingness or an inability to perform as required by the contract. Anticipatory breach allows the nonbreaching party to institute a lawsuit without having to wait for the time of the contract. It is an attempt by the law to be time efficient, something for which the law is not famous. Should the farmer in our previous example inform the manager of the market that no delivery of tomatoes would be made next month, as had been agreed upon, the market manager would not have to sit and wait out the month before starting a suit.

C. REMEDIES FOR BREACH

Once a determination has been made that a contract has been breached, some relief, or compensation, must be provided to the nonbreaching party. These redresses for the nonbreaching party are referred to as the remedies for breach and are the means used by the courts to compensate for the injury caused by the failure to perform. The function of contract remedies is not to punish the breaching party but to relieve the nonbreaching party from any losses suffered. The thrust of remedies for breach is to give the injured party the benefit of the original bargain. There are four common types of remedies available to nonbreaching parties: damages, and the associated topics of mitigation and liquidated damages; rescission and restitution; specific performance; and reformation.

1. Damages

Damages are intended to pay the nonbreaching party for all injuries incurred by the breach. The court attempts to place the nonbreaching party in the position that he would have been in had there been no breach. Damages are divided into four categories. These four types of damages are compensatory damages, consequential damages, nominal damages, and punitive damages.

a. Compensatory Damages

Compensatory damages replace the direct losses suffered and are intended to put the nonbreaching party precisely in the position he was in before the breach. For instance, Mr. Smith and Mr. Jones enter into a contract in which Mr. Smith sells his bicycle to Mr. Jones for fifty dollars. Mr. Jones gives Mr. Smith the fifty dollars; Mr. Smith, however, doesn't give the bicycle to Mr. Jones. In fact, he gives the bike to his nephew as a present. Mr. Jones could sue Mr. Smith for breach of contract and expect to recover fifty dollars as compensatory damages. Please notice that the purpose of compensatory damages is firmly rooted in the economics of the contract and not in the morality of the breach. Mr. Smith has breached a contractual promise, not robbed and plundered. He need not be flogged or otherwise punished for his breach.

b. Consequential Damages

Consequential damages, sometimes called special damages, are foreseeable damages that result from the

breach of the contract but which are caused by special circumstances outside the direct terms of the bargain. For example, we will again look at Mr. Smith's failure to deliver the bicycle to Mr. Jones. Let us presume that Mr. Jones intended to use the bicycle to make deliveries and that Mr. Smith knew of the intended use. The breach of the contract caused Mr. Jones to lose a day of deliveries, as he had to go to the sporting goods store to look for a new bike. As a result, Mr. Jones lost five dollars in delivery fees. Certainly, this additional loss was not suffered as a direct consequence of Mr. Smith's breaching the contract, but was foreseeable as a damage caused by special circumstances outside the contract itself. This additional loss would be viewed as a consequential damage resulting from the breach, and, as such, would be recoverable by Mr. Jones.

c. Nominal Damages

Nominal damages are those damages awarded when there has been a breach of contract but no discernible loss has been suffered. It is an opportunity for the court to recognize a breach of contract even though economic loss is discernible or measurable. Nominal damage awards are usually one dollar. Obviously, litigants do not enter into lawsuits with the intention of collecting nominal damages. Occasionally, however, a litigant will misjudge or be unable to clearly demonstrate the damages resulting from a breach of contract; the court may then end up in awarding only nominal damages.

d. Punitive Damages

Punitive damages are those awards given when it is the intent of the court to punish the breaching party. As the purpose of contract damages is to recompense for loss, not to punish, punitive damages are not awarded in most contract actions. In order to recover punitive damages, the litigant must show that the wrongdoing was of a systematic and continuous nature, that the wrongdoing was aimed at the public in general, and that the wrongoing was aggravated by an evil motive or intent. Courts hope that punitive damages will discourage others from similar conduct in the future. If, for example, you and other litigants, in a class action suit against a car dealer who sold all of you automobiles that he knew were defective, proved that the contracts were filled with fraud and deceit, the court would consider punitive damages for such a fraudulent series of sales contracts.

2. Mitigation of Damages

In all contract breaches where damages may be awarded, the courts will always look to see that the nonbreaching party has attempted to mitigate, or lessen, the damages suffered. Under this doctrine of mitigation, the injured party has an affirmative obligation to try to minimize the amount of damages that he has suffered. This need to mitigate the amount of damages flows from the basis for damages found in the field of economics. If the need to mitigate did not exist, there would be the potential for waste, and that would not be prudent economics. Let us imagine that we had a contract to deliver a ton of apples from our farm to a cider maker upstate. If, upon our attempt to deliver the apples, the cider maker refused delivery, that would leave us with a ton of apples on our truck, warming in the noonday sun. At this point, it occurs to us that the cider maker has breached the contract, and we can sue for damages. But, if the law simply allowed us to sue at this point, we would be wasting a ton of perfectly good apples. We are instead required to attempt to mitigate our damages. In this problem, we are required to attempt to sell our apples by any reasonable means available to us. If we could sell our fruit to a neighboring grocery for less money than our original contract price, then we would be allowed to sue for the difference as damages. But, the apples would not have gone to waste, and the cider maker would not have to pay the full amount for the breach of contract, also a form of nonwaste.

3. Liquidated Damages and Penalties

Liquidated damages are amounts that are predetermined by the contracting parties that would satisfy them in case of a breach of the contract. They are an agreement to limit and to settle damages in the event of a breach. A liquidated-damages clause in a contract saves the court the time and expense of evaluating and balancing losses; after all, the parties themselves agreed in advance to the amount of the damages. Liquidated-damages clauses also benefit the parties to the contract. The parties know the extent of their losses, should the need arise for a breach. Liquidated damages have to be proportionate to the loss; that is, they must seem reasonable. Liquidated damages provisions of contracts are enforceable by the courts.

Here is a case on liquidated damages.

☆ ☆ ☆

CASE #5-2 LIQUIDATED DAMAGES

HEGNER v. REED
2 A.D.3d 683(2003)

In August 2001 the plaintiffs Isabel Hegner and Bettina Koster (hereinafter the buyers) and the defendants Cornelia De Groat Reed and Julia Toal Reed (hereinafter the sellers) entered into a contract for the purchase of a home in Sagaponack for $1,300,000. Upon execution of the contract the buyers deposited 10% of the purchase price, or $130,000, with the sellers' attorney, the defendant-escrowee, Miles Anderson. The closing date was originally set for October 15, 2001. The contract contained a default provision which stated in pertinent part as follows:

"If Purchaser defaults hereunder, Seller's sole remedy shall be to receive and retain the Down payment as **liquidated** damages, it being agreed that Seller's damages in case of Purchaser's *willful* default might be impossible to ascertain and the Downpayment constitutes a fair and reasonable amount of damages under the circumstances and is not a penalty." [emphasis in original]

The buyers alleged that the events of September 11, 2001, caused them economic hardship and shortly thereafter they sought rescission of the contract and refund of their down payment. However, the sellers refused and then set a "time of the essence" closing date for November 13, 2001. On the morning of the closing, the buyers appeared at the house to conduct a walk through inspection and discovered that the premises were not in "broom clean" or vacant condition. The buyers alleged that this was a violation of the contract, and neither they nor any representative on their behalf appeared for the closing. The buyers then brought this action for return of the down payment, and both sides moved for summary judgment. The Supreme Court decided that although the buyers had anticipatorily breached the contract, the $130,000 down payment "[did] not reflect a reasonable measure of the [sellers'] actual damages." Instead, the Supreme Court decided that the sellers should retain only $35,000 of the deposit and that the balance, $95,000, less some costs and expenses, should be refunded to the buyers. This was error.

*The Supreme Court correctly concluded that, under all of the facts and circumstances of this case, the buyers anticipatorily breached the contract since they "evinced an intent[ion] to abandon the contract" (Savitsky v. Sukenik, 240 A.D.2d 557, 559; see Petrizzo v. Pinks, 154 A.D.2d 521; Cooper v. Bosse, 85 A.D.2d 616). However, since the sellers thereafter set a time of the essence closing date, they chose to ignore the breach and treat the contract as still valid (see Inter-Power of N. Y. v. Niagara Mohawk Power Corp., 259 A.D.2d 932; Savitsky v. Sukenik, supra; see also Dub v. 47 E. 74th Street Corp., 204 A.D.2d 145). Accordingly, the buyers were then obligated to perform the contract or forfeit their deposit.

Moreover, even assuming that the sellers were in breach of the contract on the day of the closing because the premises were not vacant, this alleged defect was curable within a reasonable time and thus the buyers were obligated to tender performance and permit the sellers the opportunity to cure (see llemar Corp. v. Krochmal, 44 N.Y.2d 702; Cohen v. Kranz, 12 N.Y.2d 242; R.C.P.S. Accocs. v. Karam Developers, 258 A.D.2d 510). The buyers' failure to do so bars them from recovering their deposit (see Cohen v. Kranz, supra at 246).

Finally, the sellers were entitled to retain the entire $130,000 down payment as **liquidated** damages in accordance with the terms of the contract. Contrary to the Supreme Court's conclusion, the sellers' retention of the entire down payment constitutes neither unjust enrichment nor an "unenforceable penalty" (see Ittleson v.. Barnett, 304 A.D.2d 526; see also Maxton Bldrs. v. Lo Galbo, 68 N.Y.2d 373).

☆ ☆ ☆

Penalties, on the other hand, are both punitive and wasteful and are, therefore, not enforceable by the courts. If a clause that is called a liquidated-damage provision calls for a clearly excessive amount to be paid upon a breach, then it is really a penalty. If, in the preceding example, the farmer and the cider maker had a contract that called for five million dollars in liquidated damages should one of the parties fail to perform, then it would seen as a penalty, and would be unenforceable. Again, the intent of contract damages is not to be punitive or wasteful. Penalties are both punitive and wasteful, and are, therefore, not enforceable as part of a contract.

4. Rescission and Restitution

Rescission is the act of placing the parties to a contract in the same position they were in prior to making the bargain. Rescission is most commonly available when there was a defect in the bargaining positions of the parties to the contract through no fault of the party claiming the right to the rescission. Fraud on the part of one party would afford the nonbreaching party to negate the contract by rescission. Also, contracts formed under duress and contracts where the consideration has been destroyed are both candidates for rescission. The party rescinding the contract must give prompt notice of the rescission. Restitution, or the return of any consideration previously conveyed, must be made in order to complete the rescission. Ideally, the exact property conveyed as consideration will be returned, in precisely the same condition in which it was received. If the conveyed property has already been used, making it impossible to return, then restitution must be made with money. Suppose we had a contract with Clarence the Clown to perform at our daughter's birthday party. We had paid Clarence his fee of one hundred dollars several days prior to the party. Unfortunately, Clarence trips and falls the day before the party, breaking his ankle and requiring him to be hospitalized. We would then be required to notify Clarence of our rescission of the contract, citing Clarence's inability to deliver his consideration, the performance. We would be entitled to restitution of the one hundred dollars already paid.

5. Specific Performance

Specific performance as a contract remedy for breach requires the breaching party to carry through on its promise. As specific performance gives the nonbreaching party exactly that for which it had bargained, this remedy is very appealing to the injured party. Specific performance, however, is not a common remedy for contract breach. The law prefers the contract breach be remedied with money, rather than forcing people to do something that they do not want to do. The remedy of specific performance is available only in very special circumstances when money damages are not an adequate remedy. In order to successfully seek specific performance as a remedy, the plaintiffs must demonstrate two things. First, they must demonstrate that the party seeking the specific performance has clean hands. "Clean hands" means that the party suing must be guilty of no wrongdoing or unjust or unfair conduct with regard to the matter involved in the litigation. Second, they must demonstrate that the item involved in the contract is unique. For instance, each piece of real estate is considered unique and, therefore, subject to the remedy of specific performance if involved in a breach of contract action. Similarly, pieces of art or collectible stamps and coins would be examples of unique items.

6. Reformation

Reformation is the rewriting of a contract, or some part thereof, to reflect the true intentions of the parties when some mistake has prevented their true intentions from being accurately expressed in the original contract. Reformation, like specific performance, is only used in special circumstances and is an unusual remedy. If we were to enter into a personal service contract with a famous actor, we could imagine that the contract contains the wrong dates of a performance that he is required to give. Using this remedy of reformation, the courts could reform the contract so that the parties could agree on the dates for the performance. Notice that this allows the contractual promises to be fulfilled.

7. Election of Remedies

Having now viewed the possible remedies available to an injured party in a contract breach, we can see that, on occasion, more than one remedy might be available to the nonbreaching party. If the injured party does have more than one remedy available to him, then he must elect, or choose, which remedy to pursue. This need to elect a remedy prevents a double recovery by a plaintiff. For example, if one purchased a work of art from an art gallery, and the piece, although paid for, was never delivered, one has the remedy of specific performance available, and one has the remedy of damages available. Clearly these remedies would overlap and would, therefore, be inconsistent with one another. The plaintiff would be required to elect, or chose, which remedy to pursue.

Our next two cases provide somewhat unusual views of the promises that we keep in contracts.

* * *

CONTRACTS CASE #5-3

Peevyhouse v. Garland Coal & Mining Co.
382 P.2d 109 (1962)

JACKSON,J. In the trial court, plaintiffs Willie and Lucille Peevyhouse sued the defendant, Garland Coal & Mining Co., for damages for breach of contract. Judgment was for plaintiffs in an amount considerably less than was sued for. Plaintiffs appeal and defendants cross-appeal.

Briefly stated, the facts are as follows: plaintiffs owned a farm containing coal deposits, and, in November, 1954, leased the premises to defendant for a period of five years for coal mining purposes.... In addition to the usual covenants found in a coal mining lease, defendant specifically agreed to perform certain restorative and remedial work at the end of the lease period. It is unnecessary to set out the details of the work to be done, other than to say that it would involve the moving of many thousands of cubic yards of dirt, at a cost estimated by expert witnesses at about $29,000.00....

It (the jury) returned a verdict for plaintiffs for $5,000.00— only a fraction of the "cost of real performance" but more than the total value of the farm even after the work is done.

On appeal, the issue is sharply drawn. Plaintiffs contend that the true measure of damages in this case is what it will cost plaintiffs to obtain performance of the work that was not done because of defendant's default. Defendant argues that the measure of damages is the cost of performance "limited, however, to the total difference in the market value before and after the work was performed."...

The explanation may be found in the fact that the situations presented are artificial ones. It is highly unlikely that the ordinary property owner would agree to pay $29,000.00 (or its equivalent) for the construction of "improvements" upon his property that would increase its value only about three hundred dollars. The result is that we are asked to apply principles of law theoretically based upon reason and reality to a situation that is basically unreasonable and unrealistic.

...The American Law Institute's Restatement of the Law, Contracts, Volume 1, Sections 346(1)(a)(i) and (ii) submits the proposition that the cost of performance is the proper measure of damages "if this is possible and does not involve unreasonable economic waste"; and that the diminution of value caused by the breach is the proper measure "if construction and completion in accordance with the contract would involve unreasonable economic waste."...

Under the most liberal view of the evidence herein, the diminution in value resulting to the premises because of non-performance of the remedial work was $300.00. After a careful search of the record, we have found no evidence of a higher figure, and plaintiffs do not argue in their briefs that a higher diminution in value was sustained. It thus appears that the judgment was clearly excessive, and that the amount for which the judgment should have been rendered is definitely and satisfactorily shown by the record....

We are of the opinion that the judgment of the trial court for plaintiffs should be, and it is hereby, modified and reduced to the sum of $300.00, and as so modified it is affirmed.

☆ ☆ ☆

CONTRACTS CASE #5-4

Lester v. Pickwick International, Inc.
528 F.Supp. 1011 (1981)

NEAHER, J. Plaintiffs in this diversity action seek rescission, restitution and damages stemming from alleged fraudulent misrepresentations relating to an agreement entered into by plaintiff Sumner Lester...with defendant Pickwick International, Inc. Pursuant to the 1977 agreement, Pickwick had paid the sum of $300,000. to Lester, the parties terminated a 1974 license agreement under which Pickwick had been paying Lester substantial royalties, and Pickwick purchased the master recordings (except for four) which had previously been delivered under the license agreement. Defendant received the exclusive right to manufacture and sell records derived from the masters and dispose of all existing inventory. In addition, Lester expressly released Pickwick from any claims arising out of the subject matter of the license agreement or "the manufacture, sale or distribution of records thereunder."

Since the complaint appears to be predicated on breaches of the 1974 license agreement and the manufacture and sale of records from master recordings delivered thereunder, the release in the 1977 agreement would, if effective, proscribe the present action. Yet plaintiffs allege that Lester was fraudulently induced to enter the latter agreement, claiming that he relied on misrepresentations concerning the manufacture and sale of (discount) records derived from the master recordings.

The law is clear that a contract may be voidable when an agreement is induced by "a promise...made with a preconceived and undisclosed intention of not performing it" Sabo v. Delman, 3 N.Y.2d 155. Such a promise constitutes "a misrepresentation of a material existing fact" so that, to sustain a claim for rescission, a plaintiff need only prove the additional elements of justifiable reliance and injury.

However, the law is equally clear that plaintiffs must establish by clear and convincing evidence the requisite elements of fraud, and that the inference of fraud must be unequivocal. Because the pretrial depositions and affidavits submitted on the instant motion show that plaintiffs cannot possibly present clear and convincing evidence of the requisite element of justifiable reliance, summary judgment for the defendant is appropriate.

✵ ✵ ✵

LEGAL LIGHT

Contracts have been around since people started doing business. This is a translation from a clay tablet from the last days of the Sumerian empire, around 2000 BC.

Sini-Ishtar, the son of Ilu-eribu, and Apil-Ili, his brother, have bought one third Shar of land with a house constructed, next to the house of Sini-Ishtar, and next to the house of Minani; one third Shar of arable land next to the house of Sini-Ishtar, which fronts on the street, from Minani, the son of Migrat-Sin. They have paid four and a half shekels of silver, the price agreed. Never shall further claim be made on account of the house of Minani. By the King they swore. (The names of fourteen witnesses and a scribe follow) Month Tebet, year of the great wall of Karra-Shamash.

✲ ✲ ✲

D. SETTLEMENT OF CLAIMS

Prior to any judicial, or court-based, decision for damages in a lawsuit, the parties may settle their dispute in two ways. These two methods for settling claims against a party who supposedly breached a contract are an accord and satisfaction, and a release.

1. Accord and Satisfaction

An accord and satisfaction is available for the purpose of compromising an existing claim for injury resulting from a breach of contract, provided that the claim is unliquidated, or unresolved as to the amount of the debt. Such a claim, where the amount is honestly in dispute, can be satisfied by offering a lesser amount, if the lesser amount is accepted. The lesser amount must be clearly marked as payment in full for the debt, to prevent it from being confused with a partial payment. The accord and satisfaction explains that the lesser amount is being taken to fully satisfy a disputed amount.

2. Release

A release is the giving up of a right or claim by a person which bars any further recovery. If, for example, we had a right to sue an individual who breached a contract that he had with us, we might decide to accept an amount of money less than that which we are owed and execute a release for that amount. This differs from an accord and satisfaction in that the accord and satisfaction compromises an amount in dispute and a release satisfies a claim against a party. A release, like a contract, must be supported by consideration.

E. ASSIGNMENT OF CONTRACTS AND DELEGATION OF CONTRACTS

Assignments of contracts and delegation of contracts both involve the transfer of some responsibilities from existing contracts to a third party not an original party to the contract.

1. Assignment of Contracts

The assignment of a contract refers to the transfer of a right or benefit from one contract party to a third individual who was not an original contract party. The party to the original contract who is assigning his rights is referred to as the assignor; the person to whom he is assigning the rights is called the assignee. Assignments of rights often occur as security for credit, as an outright sale of the rights, or as a gift. Debt collection agencies often buy the rights to collect a sum owed to a contract party. The contract party sells his rights to collect for a sum much less than is owed, as this is certain money. The collection agency then attempts to collect the money owed, knowing that they will only collect on a small portion of the rights that they buy, but they will, hopefully, collect on enough of the assigned rights to make the business profitable.

2. Delegation of Contracts

A delegation refers to the transfer of a duty or obligation from an original contract party to another person not a party to the original contract. In a delegation, the original party to the contract still remains responsible for the obligation should the new party not perform. If the teacher, who is responsible for cleaning his room at the end of each day, delegates the responsibility to clean the room to a student, who accepted in the hopes of gaining extra credit, the teacher would remain responsible for the obligation to leave the room clean should the student fail to meet the obligation.

F. STATUTE OF FRAUDS

The statute of frauds is the common name for an English law, passed in 1677, which has been adopted in almost every state that prevents enforcement of certain contracts if they are not in writing. The purpose of the statute of frauds is to lessen fraudulent claims and to avoid the temptation for perjured testimony by requiring that a document be produced so that proof will be easier in case of a dispute.

A variety of contracts must, according to the statute of frauds, be put in writing. The writing need not take any particular form, and a series of notes or notations may add up to a sufficient writing. The following are the most common types of contracts that must be in writing. First, all contracts for the sale of real estate must be in writing. This includes the creation or transfer of any interest in the real property, such as an easement, as well as the purchase of the property. Second, leases must be in writing. This requirement only applies to those leases whose term is longer than one year. Third, surety contracts must be in writing. A surety contract is a contract which guarantees the payment of a debt owed by someone else. Fourth, contracts whose term cannot be performed within one year of their formation must be written. The one-year period begins to run the day after the contract is made. Fifth, contracts for the sale of goods are covered by the statute of frauds if the goods are priced at five hundred dollars or more. Sixth, those contracts made in consideration of marriage must be written. As arranged and paid-for marriages are, thankfully, rare in contemporary America, this requirement applies more often to prenuptial agreements. Seventh, promises made by the executor or administrator of an estate to pay the debts of the deceased must be in writing.

* * *

CHAPTER FIVE
KEY TERMS

Acceptance
Accord and Satisfaction
Breach of Contract
Compensatory Damages
Consequential Damages
Consideration
Contract
Election of Remedies
Liquidated Damages
Mitigation of Damages
Nominal Damages
Offer
Punitive Damages
Reformation
Release.
Rescission
Restitution
Specific Performance
Statute of Frauds

☆ ☆ ☆

CHAPTER SUMMARY

Contracts are those types of promises that the law recognizes and enforces. They contain an offer, an acceptance, consideration, are for a legal purpose, and the parties are competent and give true consent. Without even one of these essential elements, that which may appear to be a contract is not a legal contract.

If one of the promises of a contract is not kept, then the contract has been breached. Contract breaches can be full, partial, or anticipatory. Courts remedy breaches by awarding damages, through a rescission and restitution, by reformation, or by specific performance. Damages are the most common remedy by far, and come in four types: compensatory, consequential, nominal, and punitive. An additional consideration for the breach of contract is the need for the nonbreaching party to mitigate the overall damages of the breaching party in order to minimize economic waste.

Additionally, contract claims may be settled by the agreement of the contract parties. These settlements may produce either an accord and satisfaction, or a release.

THINK AND WRITE

1. Please provide examples of contract breaches in which rescission and restitution may be an appropriate remedy.
2. Please give examples of contract breaches in which specific performance may be an appropriate remedy.
3. Draft a contract between you and Picasso for the sale of a painting. Label the essential elements of the contract.
4. What does Peevyhouse tell us about contract damages? Does this concept seem appropriate to you? Why or why not?
5. What damages may be recovered for breach of contract? Provide examples of each type.
6. Distinguish between assignment and delegation. Provide examples.

PROJECTS

1. Obtain a blank copy of a contract of sale of an automobile. Read, review, and summarize the contract. What improvements would you like to make?
2. Keep a list of the arrangements that you make over the next three days that are contracts.
3. You have entered into a contract with your neighbor's son to sell him your car for $4,000. The day after the sale, the son, who is sixteen years old, returns the car and asks for the return of his money because he has changed his mind. As a minor, can he get his cash back in your state?
4. Obtain a blank copy of a contract of sale of real estate. Compare it to a contract of sale for goods. How are they similar and how are they different?
5. Three types of third-party contracts exist. The third partiers are known as donee beneficiaries, creditor beneficiaries, and incidental beneficiaries. Define each and give two examples of each.

✼ ✼ ✼

ETHICS QUESTIONS

1. You are aware of a number of defects, none of which can be categorized as material to the agreement, in the car that you are selling. Are you personally or legally bound to disclose some or all of the defects? Two of the problems are wiper blades and a fuel pump that will have to be replaced soon.
2. You have entered into an agreement to buy a house. Shortly before you execute the formal contract of purchase, you learn that a friend of yours wants to buy the house and is willing to pay the seller $50,000 more

than you are willing to pay. Should you disclose this to the seller?

✵ ✵ ✵

RELATED WEBSITES

1. Information relating to contracts law: http://www.findlaw.com/01topics/07contracts/
2. Articles and resources relating to contracts: http://meetingsnet.com/law_contracts
3. Law links relating to contracts, including some links relating to foreign contracts law: http://catalaw.com/topics/contract.shtml
4. Government contracts: http://www.law.gwu.edu/facweb/sschooner/links.html

CHAPTER SIX

TORTS

The word "tort" comes to us from the Norman French word for "wrong." It has come to mean those private or civil wrongs done by individuals that injure other individuals. Torts are recognitions by the law that certain obligations are imposed on people in a society not to inure or harm other members of society. If some injury or damage is caused by a breach of this obligation, then the law recognizes that some compensation should be made to the injured party. The field of tort law defines those incidents that should be recognized as breaches of the obligations that we owe one another, and describes what compensation is appropriate.

The field of torts can be divided into four categories: negligence, intentional torts, strict liability, and product liability. Various levels of expectations of behavior exist for these four areas, but all are involved in the evaluation of behavior that causes injury. For almost all torts, however, only behavior that is below expected behavior is tortious. That is, not all injuries are recompensable in the law. The only real exception to this, as we shall see, is those injuries sustained in the limited field of strict liability.

A. NEGLIGENCE

The tort area of <u>negligence</u> gives relief to people injured by individuals who act in an unreasonable manner. It regulates the omission of that care which allows us to exist safely in society. Negligence lacks the moral culpability present in criminal law, but recognizes that we can and do act in substandard ways that may cause damage to others. Medical malpractice, automobile accidents, and slip-and-fall cases are but a few of the common types of negligence cases that our legal system recognizes. Every negligence case has, at its core, the evaluation of behavior referred to as the reasonable man, or reasonable person, standard. That is, has the defendant acted as a reasonable person would have acted in a given situation? If he has acted as a reasonable person, then no negligence is present. If he has not acted as a reasonable person would have acted, and someone is injured as a result of his unreasonable behavior, then negligence exists, and the injured party is entitled to be compensated for the damages. A simple example of negligence would be an auto accident in which one party went through a red light. Clearly, this person has fallen below the reasonable person standard and has caused damages to another party. The driver of the car that went through the red light would be responsible for the damages he had caused.

An orderly way of assessing whether a tort of negligence is present may be done through a series of questions that one may ask. First, is a duty of care owed? Second, if so, to whom is it owed? Third, what is the duty owed? Fourth, has the duty of care been breached? Last, has someone been injured as a result of this breach of the duty? The duty of care owed is, of course, to act as a reasonable person would act in the given circumstance. Looking at our auto accident example above, how would these questions help us analyze the problem? First, is a duty of care owed when you drive a car? Clearly, one has a responsibility when one drives a car. To whom does one owe this duty? The driver owes a duty of care to other people on the road, both people in other cars and pedestrians. What is the duty owed? The duty owed is to act as a reasonable person would act when driving. Specifically, one should drive safely and obey the laws of the road, including stopping at red lights. Has the duty been breached? Yes, in our example the driver has gone through a red light, falling below an acceptable standard of action. Last, has there been an injury as a result of the substandard behavior. Again, yes, as our driver has hit another car when going through the red light, causing damage to the other car.

Here, in our next case, we see the birth of contemporary negligence.

✫ ✫ ✫

TORTS CASE #6-1

Devlin v. Smith
80 N.Y. 470 (1882)

RAPALLO,J. Defendant Smith entered into a contract with the supervisors of the county of Kings, by which he agreed to paint the inside of the dome of the court-house. Smith was not a scaffold builder, and knew nothing of that business. He entered into a contract with defendant Stevenson, who was an experienced scaffold-builder, and had been previously employed by Smith, to build the necessary scaffold. Instead of fastening the walkway by lashing it was nailed in place. The scaffold was ninety feet in height.

Devlin was a workman in Smith's employ. He was working on the curve of the dome of the courthouse, and sitting on a plank of the walkway which was nailed in place, when the piece gave way and broke. Devlin was precipitated to the floor below and so injured that he died soon after.

...Witnesses accustomed to working with scaffolds testified that the scaffold should be fastened by lashing with ropes, instead of by nailing...(as) the springing of the planks when walked upon was liable to break nails...

The defendant Smith claims that no negligence on his part was shown. He was a painter...(who) did not undertake to build the scaffold in question himself...

If any person was at fault in the matter, it was Stevenson. It is contended, however, that even if through his negligence the scaffold was defective, he is not liable in this action because...he owed no duty to the deceased, his obligation and duty being only to Smith, with whom he contracted.

Stevenson undertook to build a scaffold ninety feet in height, for the express purpose of enabling the workmen of Smith to stand upon it to paint the interior of the dome. Any defect or negligence in its construction, which should cause it to give way, would naturally result in these men being precipitated from that great height. A stronger case where misfortune to third persons not parties to the contract would be a natural and necessary consequence of the builder's negligence can hardly be supposed...

We think there should be a new trial as to the defendant Stevenson, and that it will be for the jury to determine whether the death of plaintiff's intestate was caused by negligence on the part of Stevenson in the construction of the scaffold.

LEGAL LIGHT

In England, the right to a jury trial in a tort action was eliminated in 1966. The only tort exempted from this was an action for defamation of character.

B. INTENTIONAL TORTS

Intentional torts are those wrongs that are willful and cause damage. It is the deliberate infliction of harm or damage to another. If, for example, the person sitting next to you in class was to take your text and hit you over the head with it, he would be responsible for an intentional tort. He would have caused willful damage to your head and would have to recompense you for these damages. Notice, intentional torts may correspond to criminal behavior. In our example, the person sitting next to you has committed a battery, and would be liable in criminal court for this behavior. Criminal law, however, punishes on behalf of society and for social order, which doesn't get your medical bills paid. The civil law, specifically intentional torts, allows for individuals to be compensated for injuries deliberately caused them.

In our next case, we can see the need for damages in an intentional tort.

✳ ✳ ✳

TORTS CASE #6-2

Tischler v. Dimenna
609 N.Y.S.2d 1002 (1994)

LEFKOWITZ, J. During the period February, 1980 until the summer of 1989 plaintiff and Robert Lawson, now deceased, engaged in unprotected sexual intercourse. Beginning in the summer of 1989 the parties made sporadic use of condoms. Plaintiff and Mr. Lawson lived together for several years and contemplated marriage.

Plaintiff alleges in her complaint that prior to his death, Robert Lawson contracted "HIV (AIDS) Virus, that eventually caused his death and failed to advise plaintiff at any time during their relationship". Decedent is survived by a daughter. Plaintiff sues the estate (of which Phyllis Dimenna is executrix) for $100,000 damages for intentional tort and negligence. Defendant denies the allegations and asserts an affirmative defense of culpable conduct and assumption of risk.

As of February, 1993, plaintiff has been tested three times for the HIV virus with negative results....

Defendant moves for summary judgment dismissing the complaint on two grounds: (1) that plaintiff has not suffered a physical injury and absent a verifiable precipitating event the claim is not cognizable; and (2) the only proof of sexual conduct between plaintiff and the decedent is her word and such testimony would be barred...

Plaintiff vigorously opposes the motion through her counsel's affidavit, claiming that the law supports an AIDS-phobia claim where, as here, there exists an indicia of legitimacy and, further, that on a motion for summary judgment, the Court may consider evidence that might ultimately be barred by statute at trial.

The law of tortious wrongs, intentional and negligent, recognizes claims for sexually transmitted diseases. The usual principles underlying causes of action apply, to wit: defendant must have owed a duty to the plaintiff that was breached and proximately caused the condition complained of. The duty has been found in the relationship between the parties where the defendant knew or should have known that he had a communicable disease....

Plaintiff has made the requisite showing in opposition to the motion for summary judgment to establish prima facie her claim of emotional distress for the fear of contracting AIDS. The law recognizes that the decedent owed a duty to the plaintiff not to intentionally or negligently inflict emotional distress. The plaintiff has proven probable exposure to the disease. Whether defendant did knowingly or negligently expose plaintiff are questions for the jury. Similarly, plaintiff's knowledge, actual or constructive, of decedent's condition and his liaison with another man as well as participating in unprotected sexual activity are for the triers of the facts on damages. Additionally, as in other cases in where probabilities must be weighed, the issue of the reasonableness of the plaintiff's fear and for what period of time that fear is compensable are questions for the jury after hearing testimony...

※ ※ ※

C. STRICT LIABILITY

Strict liability imposes responsibility on parties, regardless of their actions, when certain entities are involved. This area of torts, unlike the ones we have previously viewed, does not focus on behavior, but, rather, imposes an absolute liability on individuals who possess dangerous instrumentalities. Historically, the Common Law imposes strict liability on owners of wild animals or gunpowder. If a person possessed a cheetah for a pet, then the owner was responsible for damages that the animal caused, no matter how those damages were caused. If the cheetah was kept in a cage, in the basement, behind a locked door, and with warning signs on the premises, a burglar who broke in and was injured by the animal would be entitled to compensation under a strict liability tort cause of action. No amount of due care or precaution can shield the owner. No analysis of responsibility for behavior is needed, only the requisite ownership.

This form of tort liability is more properly viewed as a scheme of insurance, rather than a traditional concept of law. The owner of the object really assumes the role of an insurance company, guaranteeing that any injuries or damages will be paid. Similarly, your insurance company doesn't care whether you or a friend is responsible for an injury that you have, it simply pays the medical benefits due you. The law viewed items in this category of torts as being so dangerous that they had a will of their own and could injure no matter what precautions were taken. Certainly a wild animal may indiscriminately bite someone without provocation and no matter what precautions the owner takes. In like fashion, when gunpowder was a highly unstable compound, it could just explode, no matter what precautions the owner or handlers took. In order to provide for those injured, the law provides a form of enforced insurance. This structure is much different from the traditional function of the law, which is to evaluate behavior and assign responsibility based on that behavior.

D. PRODUCT LIABILITY

Product liability defines the limits of responsibility of makers of products that are placed in the stream of commerce when those products injure people. It has evolved from strict liability, in that it places a much higher level of accountability on manufacturers than negligence, but has only rarely imposed absolute liability on manufacturers. Product liability makes manufacturers responsible for injuries caused by products when those products are being used in a foreseeable fashion and an injury results. If, for instance, you sit on a chair, and it collapses, then the maker of the chair would be liable if you were injured. Notice that this concept removes from the consumer the responsibility to prove that the chair was somehow defective, a difficult task. Product liability, like absolute liability, makes the manufacturer the insurer of its products; this cost is passed on to the consumer as part of the price.

The limit of product liability, which differentiates it from absolute liability, is the foreseeability of use of the product. Suppose, in the above example, you stand on the chair to screw in a light bulb and the chair breaks, injuring you. This use of the chair is a readily foreseeable one, and the maker would be liable. Suppose now that you use the chair as a weapon against the person seated next to you, who has somehow offended you. Beating your neighbor over the head with the chair, while certainly a possible use of the chair, is not really a readily foreseeable use of the item. Your neighbor would not be successful in suing the manufacturer of the chair, even though the chair certainly did injure him.

Our next three cases demonstrate the use of products liability. The first, Torgesen, provides a glimpse of the beginning of product liability; the next two cases demonstrate contemporary themes in product liability.

☆ ☆ ☆

TORTS CASE #6-3

Torgesen v. Schultz
192 N.Y. 156, 84 N.E. 956 (1908)

BARTLETT, J. The plaintiff has suffered the loss of an eye by reason of the explosion of a siphon bottle of aerated water filled and put upon the market by the defendant corporation. The siphon had been charged at a pressure of 125 pounds to the square inch. The plaintiff was a domestic servant and on July 1, 1901, between one and two o'clock in the afternoon she received at her employer's house in the city of New York two siphons which had been filled with water by the defendant and which had been purchased from a druggist who had purchased them from the defendant. The day was very hot, the registered temperature at the weather bureau being as follows: 1 p.m., 95 degrees; 2 p.m., 96 degrees; 3 p.m., 96 degrees; 4 p.m., 96 degrees...Upon receiving the siphons the plaintiff took them to a room on the third story, where they remained until between 7 and 8 o'clock in the evening, when she carried them down stairs and placed them in a standing position in a pan containing ice. As she turned away, one of the siphons exploded, with the result stated....(A lengthy description of the testing of the siphon bottles was presented by the bottler's experts. These tests included a test subjecting them to pressure, and a test subjecting them to severe temperature changes. Experts testified that the defendant tested the bottles more completely than any other bottler in the business.)

The plaintiff also called as an expert witness an instructor in Physics at Columbia University, who described a series of experiments which he had made on a number of siphon bottles of aerated water sold by the defendant. These experiments were conducted by subjecting the bottles to conditions designed to reproduce approximately those which existed at the time when the explosion occurred by which the plaintiff was injured. Out of seventy-one bottles which were thus tested, five exploded, and all of those explosions occurred within half a minute after the bottles were placed in contact with ice. It furthermore appeared that when the bottles came back to the defendant, after having once been distributed to its customers, they were not tested again, and that the defendant had no means of determining how many times the bottles were sent out after they had been filled and after they had been returned for filling, although they were probably sent out a large number of times....

It may very well be that the defendant, if put to its proof on the subject, may establish the adequacy of its test and that nothing further can reasonably be required to be done to assure the safety of those making use of their charged siphons as against explosions of the character which injured the plaintiff, but upon the evidence as it stood at the close of her case I think there was enough to entitle the plaintiff to have the question of the defendant's negligence submitted to the jury.

The judgment should be reversed and a new trial granted...

✳ ✳ ✳

CASE #6-4 PRODUCTS LIABILITY

McENEANEY v. HAYWOOD
179 Misc.2d 1035, 687 N.Y.S2d 547 (1999)

✳ ✳ ✳

In this action seeking damages for strict products liability, breach of warranty, negligence and failure to warn, the court dismissed the complaint on the ground that plaintiff failed to sustain her burden of proof under the line of "second impact" or "second collision" cases in which there was an allegation of a design defect. In addition, prior to the commencement of the trial, the court had precluded plaintiff from introducing evidence on the issue of late deployment of the air bag.

Both plaintiff and her sister, who was a passenger in the car rented from Avis (PV Holding Corp.) and driven by plaintiff, testified that there was a minor impact with a car that had come from their right at an intersection. Neither of the people in the car was hurt as a result of that impact and the damage to the rented car was "minor." Both sisters testified that after about 20 seconds, they heard a hissing type of noise and the air bag began to inflate slowly. Plaintiff, whose hands were still on the steering wheel, testified that some type of gas, or acid, began spewing out of the lower half of the steering wheel as the bag inflated partially and slowly and that it burned her hands and face. Defendant, PV Holding Corp., produced its expert who testified that the air bag could not deploy in that manner. He stated that the air bag was folded by hand after it was manufactured.

[1][2][3][4][5] A motion by defendant to dismiss at the close of a plaintiffs case should not be granted unless by no rational process could a jury find in favor of the plaintiff. It should not be granted simply because there are inconsistencies in the proof or questions of witnesses'

credibility. Where there are varying inferences to be drawn from the evidence, the jury must resolve them (<u>O'Neil v.. Port Authority of New York & New Jersey</u>, 111 A.D.2d 375, 489 N.Y.S.2d 585). It is not the trial court's function to weigh evidence (<u>Hyung Y Choi v. Mann</u>, 104 A.D.2d 354, 478 N.Y.S.2d 686). This was not the type of case where plaintiff failed to show any negligence and proximate cause (see, <u>Calandriello v. New York Racing Association</u>, 203 A.D.2d 503, 611 N.Y.S.2d 247). It was a case where plaintiff and her sister both testified that the air bag deployed some seconds after the initial impact and then did not function properly. That defendant's expert testified that it was "impossible" for the air bag to deploy that way presented an issue of fact for a jury's determination.

* * * In <u>Halloran v. Virginia Chemicals, Inc.</u>, 41 N.Y.2d 386, 388, 393 N.Y.S.2d 341, 361 N.E.2d 991, the court stated:

"In a products liability case it is now established that, if plaintiff has proven that the product has not performed as intended and excluded all causes of the accident not attributable to defendant, the fact finder may, even if the particular defect has not been proven, infer that the accident could only have occurred due to *some defect in the product or its packaging* [citing authority; emphasis added]."

✫ ✫ ✫

In the case at bar, both plaintiff and her sister stated that the impact between the two cars was minor and that they did not sustain any injury as a result of that collision. Both sisters testified that some seconds after the impact, they heard a "hissing" noise and plaintiff began screaming because the bag was coming slowly out of the bottom half of the steering wheel and that some "acid" or chemical was being sprayed on her hands and face. The fact that defendant produced an expert witness who testified that the bag could not deploy in that fashion does not remove this issue from the consideration of the jury and should not prevent them from being able to infer that the bag deployed improperly because of either the way it was manufactured or the way it was installed. Defendant's expert stated that the air bag was installed after being folded by hand, that it was a manual act. It is entirely within the realm of the trier of fact to be able to conclude that the air bag did not perform as intended when it came out slowly and sprayed a hot acid or chemical on plaintiff's hands.

[9] It is the conclusion reached herein, that this was not a "second impact/collision" case because plaintiff's injuries were not caused by the first impact. Had the sensors worked properly, the minor-type impact should not have caused the air bag to deploy. It should not have deployed slowly, leaking or spraying acid or chemicals on plaintiff's hands. Whether the injuries to plaintiff I were the result of this chemical or acid, or the result of a burn from a sudden inflation, is also an issue for the trier of fact. Plaintiff is claiming that her injuries were caused by the improper deployment of the air bag and that they were not caused by the first impact. This alone would distinguish it from the cases cited by defendant in support of its claim that this is a second impact case. In addition, when looking at the second impact cases, one is struck by, the fact that it was the first impact which propelled plaintiff into, under or over some other item which caused the injury. In the case at bar, plaintiff is not claiming a defective design, is not claiming that the impact with the car caused any damage and is claiming that while sitting in the car, the air bag began to slowly deploy, spraying her hands and face with some burning element.

[10] As to the issue whether plaintiff should be able to introduce evidence of late deployment of the air bag, suffice it to say that the court erred in its holding that since plaintiff was an interested witness, her testimony alone would not be sufficient to support this claim. In addition to her testimony

ultimately coming in, it should be noted that defendant's employee, Mr. Fagan, interviewed plaintiff shortly after the accident and defendant could not account for the missing reports labeled one and two, since the report in evidence had a number "3" on top. Therefore plaintiff should have been permitted to present her proof on the issue of late deployment of the air bag.

✲ ✲ ✲

CASE #6-5 Products Liability

GEBO v. BLACK CLAWSON COMPANY, ET AL.
92 N.Y.2d 387, 703 N.E.2d 1234 (1998)

SMITH, Judge.

Defendant, the prior owner of an embossing machine, built into the machine a protective guarding system for its own use, not for purposes of market sale. We bold that in the circumstances presented defendant, as a "casual manufacturer," cannot be held liable to the plaintiff-user in strict products liability or negligent design but is under a duty to provide plaintiff adequate warnings, a duty that was discharged here.

Plaintiff, Scott Gebo, an employee of Knowlton Specialty Papers, was injured on October 24, 1990, while operating a combination saturator/dryer line and paper embossing unit. Plaintiff's hand became caught in the unit's "nip" point—the point at which two high-speed spinning rollers meet. As a result, he suffered the loss of four of his fingers; Knowlton Specialty acquired the paper mill and its contents some three and a half years prior to the accident. The unit itself had originally been purchased by defendant, Filtration Sciences, more than two decades earlier, in 1966, from third-party plaintiff Black Clawson Company. [FN1]

Over the years, defendant made numerous changes to the embossing unit, including the addition of a saturator/ dryer line, and the design and installation of a protective guarding system.

* * *

The guarding system was intended to provide protection to the unit's operator from the dangers of the high-speed nip point. The system itself contained a guard panel, which, when raised, served to protect the operator from the nip point. On October 24, 1990, the system failed, allowing the unit to operate with the guard panel down and nip point exposed. Investigation revealed that the system's failure was caused by a build-up of resin on the unit and safety system. A natural byproduct of the paper manufacturing process, the resin would, left unattended, eventually envelop the system's microswitch, causing it to malfunction, and allowing the unit to continue operating even with the guard panel down and nip point exposed. Moreover, while the unit did have an emergency shut-off switch, the switch was located high above the hood of the dryer line, neither readily visible nor accessible for use in an emergency.

Plaintiff commenced this personal injury action alleging claims in strict products liability, negligent design, failure to provide adequate warnings and breach of warranty. Under those theories, plaintiff claimed that defendant was liable for its design, manufacture, location, installation, warnings, maintenance and sale of the saturator/dryer line, embossing unit and safety guarding system. Plaintiff further alleged that defendant was liable for its failure to provide the unit with an available emergency shut-down switch and for the negligent positioning of the microswitch in a place where it would become covered with resin and malfunction. Thus, plaintiff claimed that the embossing unit was unsafe for its intended use by the operator.

Following discovery, defendant moved for dismissal, arguing that it could not be held liable in strict products liability, negligence, and breach of warranty or for the failure to provide adequate warnings. Although defendant admitted to its design, assembly and installation of the guarding system, it claimed that it had done so for its own use, and not with the intent of market sale. Defendant claimed that it was not regularly engaged in the manufacture or sale of anything other than paper, and, at most, it could be considered only a "casual/occasional" seller in the marketplace. Therefore, defendant argued that it could not be required to answer claims in strict products liability or negligence.

Supreme Court agreed, granted the motion for summary judgment, and dismissed all claims. The court agreed that defendant was neither a manufacturer nor a regular seller of paper mills, mill-associated fixtures or manufacturing equipment, but had engages in a one-time bulk sale of its mill and equipment. Therefore, the court concluded, defendant could not be liable in strict products liability or negligence. In dismissing the claims in negligence, the court ruled that "more than one casual sale of an item 'manufactured' or 'assembled' by a business for its own use and not for sale to the public is required to maintain a negligence claim against it." The court further found that the same considerations that undermined plaintiff's claims in strict products liability and negligence also barred plaintiff's claim for failure to provide adequate warnings. While defendant had a duty to warn of known defects which were not obvious or readily discernible, the court concluded that prior to plaintiff's accident, his employer had been aware of the unit's resin-related problems and had failed to take any steps to counteract plaintiff's exposure to the danger. Thus, there was no causal connection between Filtration Sciences' failure to provide plaintiff adequate warnings and plaintiff's injury, making summary judgment proper [FN2]

✵ ✵ ✵

On appeal, the Appellate Division affirmed the grant of summary judgment for the reasons states by Supreme Court (244 A.D2d 870, 668 N.Y.S.2d 110). We granted leave to appeal and now affirm.

[1][2][3] Under New York law, it is well settled that a manufacturer may be held liable for placing into the stream of commerce a defective product which causes injury. A product may be defective by reason of a manufacturing flaw, an improper design, or a failure to provide adequate warnings for the products use (Liriano v. Hobart Corp., 92 N.Y.2d 232, 677 N.Y.S.2d 764, 700 N.E.2d 303). Where a defective product is sold by a seller, dealer or distributor engaged in its normal course of business, the burden of strict liability has been imposed (see, Stiles v. Batavio Atomic Horeshoes, 81 N.Y.2d 950, 597 N.Y.S.2d 666, 613 N.E.2d 572; Velez v. Craine & Clark Lbr. Corp., 33 N.Y.2d 117, 350 N.Y.S.2d 617, 305 N.E.2d 750). Similarly, the manufacturer of a defective product engaged in its normal course of business may also be held strictly liable for injuries caused by a product, regardless of privity, foreseeability or the exercise of due care (see, Voss v. Black & Decker Mfg. Co., 59 N.Y.2d 102, 463 N.Y.S.2d 398, 450 N.E.2d 204; Codling v. Paglia, 32 N.Y.2d 330, 345 N/Y.S2d 461, 298 N.E.2d 622).

We next apply these principles to the "casual manufacturer." Central to our decision today is the affirmed finding, supported by the record, that Filtration Sciences built the protective guarding system for its own use, not to sell or transfer to another. We leave for another day the task of defining the precise outer boundary of casual manufacturer status.

[4] The decision to impose strict liability rests largely upon matters of public policy (see, Sukljian v. Charles Ross & Son Co., 69 N.Y.2d 89, 94-95, 511 N.Y.S.2d 821, 502 N.E.2d 1358; Victorson v. Bock Laundry Mach. Co., 37 N.Y.2d 395, 401 373 N.Y.S.2d 39, 335 N.E.2d 275). In the past, we have discussed

some of the policy considerations which favor the imposition of strict liability upon manufacturers, stating:

> "Given the increased complexity of modem products and modem production methods, most often only the manufacturer 'can fairly be said to know and to understand when an article is suitably designed and safely made for its intended purpose'; by the same token, the manufacturer most often 'alone has the practical opportunity, as well as a considerable incentive, to turn out useful, attractive, but safe products' " (Sukljian v. Ross & Son Co., 69 N.Y.2d 89, at 95, 511 N.Y.S.2d 821, 502 N.E.2d 1358 [citing cases]).

In Sukljian v. Ross & Son Co. (supra), we recognized that not every seller of goods is properly subject to the imposition of strict liability. There, we concluded that in contrast to the strict duties and liabilities imposed upon manufacturers and sellers in the normal course of business, a much more limited duty is imposed upon casual sellers. For those casual sellers, there exists only a duty to "warn the person to whom the product is supplied of known defects that are not obvious or readily discernible" (id., at 97, 511 N.Y.S.2d 821, 503 N.E.2d 1358). Inasmuch as the casual seller "is not part of the regular commercial network for that product" (id.), no greater duties are imposed.

[5] Our decision in Sukljian to withhold the imposition of strict liability upon casual sellers was based upon the conclusion that those considerations which justify the imposition of strict liability upon manufacturers and sellers in the normal course of business "lack applicability in the case of a party who is not engaged in the sale of the product in issue as a regular part of its business" (id. at 95, 511 N.Y.S.2d 821, 503 N.E.2d 1358). In the case at bar, plaintiff claims that because defendant designed, assembled, installed and sold the modified embossing unit, defendant must be held to the same standard as a product manufacturer. We disagree. Filtration Sciences' single act of design and

assembly does not without more make it equivalent to a product manufacturer. We agree with both Supreme Court and the Appellate Division that at most defendant was subject to the same limited duty as a casual seller (Sukljian v. Ross & Son Co., 69 N.Y.2d 89, at 97, 511 N.Y.S.2d 821, 503 N.E.2d 1358).

[6] In Sukljian we also rejected a claim that the casual seller should be held liable for negligence (69 N.Y.2d 89, at 97, 511 N.Y.S.2d 821, 503 N.E.2d 1358). There we noted that any determination of negligence should begin with the policy issue of whether a duty was owed. We concluded that "the duty of a casual or occasional seller would be to warn the person to whom the product is supplied of known defects that are not obvious or readily discernible" (69 N.Y.2d 89, at 97, 511 N.Y.S.2d 821, 503 N.E.2d 1358). We reach that same conclusion here for the casual manufacturer.

[7] Manufacturers and sellers in the normal course of business are liable for injuries caused by ordinary negligence, and are therefore under a duty to exercise reasonable care so as to avoid the occurrence of injuries by any product which can reasonably be expected to be dangerous if negligently manufactured or sold (see, Codling v. Paglia, 32 N.Y.2d 330, 345 N/Y.S2d 461, 298 N.E.2d 622, supra; MacPherson v. Buick Motor Co., 217 N.Y. 382, 111 N.E. 1050; Restatement [Second] of Torts, § 395, comment a, at 326). The justification for the imposition of ordinary principles of negligence liability upon manufacturers:

"rests upon the responsibility assumed by the manufacturer toward the consuming public, which arises not of contract, but out of the relation resulting form the purchase of the product by the consumer; upon the foreseeability of harm if proper care is not used; upon the representation of safety implied in the act of putting the product on the market; and upon the economic benefit derived by the manufacturer from the sale and subsequent use of the chattel" (Restatement [Second] of Torts § 395, comment b, at 326-327).

[8] In the instant case, it cannot be said that the policy considerations which serve to justify the imposition of ordinary negligence liability upon the manufacturer and the seller in the normal course of business apply with equal weight and force to defendant. As a casual manufacturer, Filtration Sciences cannot be said to have derived from the one-time bulk sale of its paper mill and embossing unit. Furthermore, as the purchaser of a product from a casual manufacturer, Knowlton Specialty Papers cannot be said to have held the same type of consumer expectations that Filtration Sciences would continue to stand behind its goods. Defendant was and direct commercial participant in the paper manufacturing market. Plaintiff's injuries, however, did not arise from defendant's activities within the paper market. They instead arose from the one-time bulk sale of its mill and manufacturing equipment, events which were not foreseeable at the time the guarding system was designed. Therefore, plaintiff's negligence claims against defendant were properly rejected.

[9] As a casual manufacturer, although Filtration Sciences could have been held to answer for failure to provide adequate warnings to the product's user, and is under a duty to warn of known defects in its product which are not obvious or readily discernible, we conclude that such a duty was discharged here. As Supreme Court noted, there exists a wealth of uncontroverted evidence. In this case the Knowlton Specialty Papers, both the long-time owner of the embossing unit and plaintiff's employer at the time of the accident, was aware of the very problems which led to plaintiff's injuries. It is also undisputed in this case the Knowlton's awareness of the problems was widespread among its supervisors and employees. In fact, in a meeting which occurred just days prior to plaintiff's accident, Knowlton's safety committee specifically addressed the problems being caused by the resin. Knowlton failed, however, to take any additional defensive actions. We agree with Supreme Court that any causal connection between negligent acts or omissions of Filtration Sciences,

in its alleged failure to provide plaintiff adequate warnings and the injuries which later resulted was sufficiently negated. Additionally, by the existence of these very same factors, the danger, at a minimum, was "readily discernible" (Sukljian v. Ross & Son Co., 69 N.Y.2d 89, at 97, 511 N.Y.S.2d 821, 503 N.E.2d 1358).

Accordingly, the order of the Appellate Division should be affirmed, with costs.

KAYE, C.J., and BELLACOSA, LEVINE, CIPARICK and WESLERY, JJ., concur.

✳ ✳ ✳

E. DAMAGES

Torts damages attempt to make the injured party whole again. The limits of these damages depend upon a causal link between the action or entity that is at the basis of the suit and the damages allegedly sustained. Once a causal link has been established, then the limit on damages is their foreseeability.

A causal link, or definitive cause-and-effect connection, must be established between the damage and that which has allegedly caused the injury. In our example of negligence, wherein a driver went through a red light and struck another car, the action of going through the light caused the accident, which resulted in damages to the car that was hit and to the driver of the car. There exists a causal link between the negligent act and the damages.

There is also a need that the damages be a foreseeable result of the action that caused them. Certainly, in our auto accident negligence tort, damages to the car, medical injuries, and lost wages due to the injuries are all foreseeable consequences of the accident.

The final consideration in assessing damages is the intent to make the injured party whole. The courts attempt to provide the defendant with the amount of money that would fully compensate the injured party for each of his damages. While attempting to make the plaintiff whole again, however, the courts are, of course, limited to providing money for each and every damage and injury. If one has lost a limb as the result of our auto accident, then the arm cannot be replaced by the court. The only way the court has to make the party whole again is with financial compensation.

✵ ✵ ✵

LEGAL LIGHT

In Great Britain, medical damages are not awarded to personal injury victims who have national health insurance, and almost everybody does. Additional general damages for pain and suffering are set by a Judicial Studies Board: damages for a broken arm or leg are about ten thousand pounds sterling (roughly nineteen thousand dollars). Punitive damages are only allowed in police misconduct, fraud, or intentional torts.

✵ ✵ ✵

CHAPTER SIX
KEY TERMS

Causal Link
Duty of Care
Intentional Tort
Negligence
Product Liability
Reasonable Care
Strict Liability
Torts

* * *

CHAPTER SUMMARY

Torts are those civil wrongs, excluding contract breaches, which the law recognizes are appropriate for judicial remedy. Torts help make people whole again for noncriminal injuries and damages. Torts are divided into four areas. Negligence, the largest area, compensates people injured by the unreasonable actions of others. Intentional torts compensate people injured by the deliberately harmful actions of others. Strict liability compensates people injured by the owners of certain inherently dangerous objects when those objects cause harm. Product liability compensates people injured by products that are put into the stream of commerce; it makes the maker responsible for injuries.

Damages in torts, unlike those in contracts, are all those losses suffered by individuals when those losses flow directly from one of the four types of torts mentioned previously. These damages are limited by the need for the damages to be reasonable foreseeable. That is, the damages need to seen as reasonable expected to happen, given the behavior of the actor.

* * *

THINK AND WRITE

1. How do contracts damages differ from torts damages? Why should they differ?
2. If a doctor misdiagnoses your flu as a cold, do you have a legal recourse in negligence?
3. How does the standard of reasonable care change when a nurse practitioner treats a patient in the hospital versus when a doctor treats the same patient?

4. In tobacco litigation, why have people had difficulty in successfully suing the cigarette makers?
5. How do negligence and intentional torts differ?
6. How do negligence and products liability differ?
7. If your town requires a three-foot fence around your swimming pool, have you met the standard of care required of homeowners?
8. What impact do warning signs have on negligence litigation?

PROJECTS

1. Research whether your state is a comparative negligence or contributory negligence state. How do the two differ?
2. Contact your insurance agent and/or review your insurance policies. Does your car insurance policy provide for legal representation if you are sued? Does your homeowner's (or rental) policy provide coverage for legal costs?
3. Bring to class two or three newspaper articles that have incidents in them that might lead to a tort action. Be prepared to explain them to your classmates.
4. Both assault and battery are torts. What are the defenses to these torts in your state?
5. False imprisonment is, generally, defined as the deliberate confinement or restraint of a person without justification. However, many states allow for this type of restraint by a merchant who suspects someone of shoplifting. Does your state allow this type of restraint? How vigorously may the merchant be to restrain the individual? Do you approve?

✹ ✹ ✹

ETHICS QUESTIONS

1. Advertising by lawyers for clients in the media is a relatively recent change in American law. Recent events regarding potential liability over the drug Vioxx have prompted a barrage of television and newspaper ads soliciting clients. Given that these suits, taken on a contingency fee basis, may bring enormous profits to some law firms, what are the ethical responsibilities of the firms advertising? Should we allow these ads?
2. A client of ours has had surgery to repair a broken leg that was injured in an auto accident. Our client was struck by a car while crossing the street. Liability clearly rests with the auto driver. Our client, however, has had a longstanding deformity in the injured leg, which is resolved in the surgery. Should we disclose this benefit to the defendant's attorney? Should it make any difference?

RELATED WEBSITES

1. Information and sites on torts: http://www.hg.org/torts. html
2. Various references and articles on torts: http://www. cato.org/legalissues/torts.html
3. Articles and books on torts: http://jurist.law.pitt.edu/sg_ torts.htm
4. Website of the American Trial Lawyers Association: http:// www.atlanet.org

CHAPTER SEVEN

REAL PROPERTY

The ownership of real property has a long and important history in our legal system. In our Constitution, the phrase "life, liberty, and the pursuit of happiness" was, until the final drafts of the document "life, liberty, and property." Ownership of real estate represents a higher degree of comfort, security, and accomplishment than any other item we can own. For most Americans, "the American dream" can be defined as ownership of a comfortable three-bedroom home in the suburbs, complete with white picket fence. Indeed, even the education you are currently absorbing serves not only to enrich your lives, as you will be a more knowledgeable person, but it will also enrich your life as a more employable person so that you may buy that house.

A. PHYSICAL ELEMENTS

The ownership of real property is viewed in the law as the ownership of the divisible parts of the real estate. These parts of the whole that make up what we routinely think of as owning real estate are <u>airspace</u>, <u>riparian rights</u>, <u>crops and timber</u>, <u>minerals</u>, <u>oil and gas</u>, and <u>fixtures</u>. The owner of the real estate may divest herself of one or more of these parts and still maintain ownership of the rest; conversely, one may own or be able to use only one of these parts of real estate without being able to use the others.

1. Airspace

The airspace over real property is considered part of the land itself. An owner of real property owns the airspace as far above the property as can be reasonable to the normal use of real estate. This precludes you, as the owner of the real property, from suing an airline that flies a plane over your property at 30,000 feet; but, if the same airline flies helicopters over your property repeatedly at 75 feet, then they are trespassing and subject to suit. Telephone lines, cable lines, and electric lines running over your property are common uses of the airspace associated with real property.

2. Riparian Rights

Riparian rights are those rights associated with the use of water that exists on real property. If you a piece of land that has a stream on it, you own the stream on it, but your use of the stream is limited by the uses or potential uses of other landowners upon whose land the stream travels. For example, if there is a stream on a piece of farmland that you own, you can certainly dig an irrigation canal to carry that water to another part of the property. If, however, you divert so much water that you significantly reduce the water flow to your downstream neighbors, such that they don't have sufficient water for their needs, you have taken too much water. You can take as much water as you want, but you cannot negatively impact on the other owners' rights.

The following case deals with riparian rights.

☆ ☆ ☆

CASE #7-1 RIPARIAN RIGHTS

PARSONS v. WHITTAKER
1996 WL 33360266 (Mich.App.)
[UNPUBLISHED]

PER CURIAM.

*1 In docket number 170274, plaintiffs appeal as of right the October 12, 1993, order granting defendant's motion for summary disposition of Count II of its countercomplaint. In docket number 171456, plaintiffs appeal as of right the trial court's December 10, 1993, order denying plaintiffs' motion for sanctions. The appeals were consolidated by order of this Court. We affirm.

Plaintiffs, defendant, and several others own property surrounding an artificial lake that was created when a gravel pit filled with water. Deeds acquired by each of the parties granted the respective parties a portion of the lake bed. Plaintiffs' property, which they purchased in 1991, includes property on both sides of the lake. Plaintiffs were granted an easement over a portion of property now owned by defendant that provided access to the rear of plaintiffs' property. Apparently, a dispute developed between the parties when defendant attempted to maintain a locked gate at the entrance to the easement.

During March through July 1992, plaintiffs erected a forty-eight foot bridge to provide access to the rear portion of their property on the far side of the lake. The bridge was erected across a shallow portion of the lake that is approximately twenty-four inches deep. The bottom of the bridge was thirty-eight inches above the surface of the water. Plaintiffs also erected an earthen embankment. The area of the embankment was partially filled in with existing gravel, and cement blocks, gravel, and limestone were added to make the embankment more suitable for walking.

Plaintiffs filed a verified trespass complaint on October 27, 1992. They alleged that defendant's locking of the gated entrance to the easement constituted a trespass, and they sought a restraining order enjoining defendant from obstructing plaintiffs' use of the easement.

On November 25, 1992, defendant filed an answer and a countercomplaint for declaratory and injunctive relief In the second count of the countercomplaint, defendant alleged that plaintiffs' bridge interfered with the rights of defendant and the other riparian owners to use the surface of the lake for recreational purposes, as well as with the natural flow and water quality of the lake. Defendant sought an injunction requiring plaintiffs to remove the bridge and restraining them from interfering with the rights of defendant and others to use the entire surface of the lake.

Plaintiffs filed a motion for summary disposition with respect to their complaint and defendant's countercomplaint pursuant to MCR 2.116(C)(8) and (10). On September 13, 1993, the trial court issued a judgment wherein it held that plaintiffs and their guests and invitees were entitled to unrestricted ingress and egress to their property. The court also issued an injunction that barred interference with the use of the easement. A decision regarding Count II of the countercomplaint was reserved.

On October 12, 1993, the trial court granted defendant's motion for a temporary restraining order and permanent injunction and required plaintiffs to restore the lake to its original condition. The court found that the lake abutted the property of several landowners and that no single party could assert riparian rights over the bottom land or surface waters. In an order dated December 10, 1993, the trial court denied plaintiffs' motion for sanctions under MCR 2.114.

*2 Plaintiffs first argue that the trial court erred as a matter of law in concluding that all of the land that abutted the lake had riparian rights. There are no reported Michigan decisions addressing whether riparian rights arise in connection with an artificial lake where the rights are alleged to stem from shore ownership. The general common law rule is that land abutting on an artificial watercourse has no riparian rights. The rationale for this rule is that:

The natural corporeal right in question is possessed by riparian owners of land on natural channels of water courses only. *Such right does not exist in the water flowing in an artificial channel.* The right of those owning land bordering upon or through which artificial channels pass, to the use of the water flowing therein, is not a natural right, nor a corporeal right, but an incorporeal right, which can be acquired only by grant, express or implied, or by prescription. (Emphasis in original.) *[Thompson, infra at 679]*

The common law rule has generally applied to artificial channels or watercourses that are designed to connect to a natural body of water. In that context, the land abutting the artificial watercourse does not have riparian rights, because those rights belong to the landowners whose property abuts the natural body of water. See, e.g., Publix Supermarket, Inc v. Pearson, 315 So2d 98 (Fla App 1975). Here, the artificial lake exists independently of any natural body of water. Therefore, the land abutting the artificial lake is the only land that could possibly have riparian rights. Thus, plaintiffs' reliance on the common law, Hess v. West Bloomfield Twp., 439 Mich. 550, 561; 486 NW2d 628 (1992), and Thompson v. Enz, 379 Mich. 667; 154 NW2d 473 (1967), is not persuasive. Not only are the facts of Hess and Thompson distinguishable, but in those cases the Courts were not confronted with the task of deciding whether riparian rights attach to land abutting an independently existing artificial lake. Thus, the Court's failure to expand the common law in those cases does not establish that riparian rights may *never* exist in artificial bodies of water.

☆ ☆ ☆

The question, therefore, becomes whether plaintiffs' maintenance of the bridge interfered with the reasonable use of the waters by other riparian owners:

[U]se of the water by riparian owners is governed by principles of reasonableness. Thus, where there are several riparian owners on an inland lake, they may use the surface of the whole lake for boating, swimming fishing, and other similar riparian rights, as long as they do not interfere with the reasonable use of the waters by other riparian owners. (Citations Omitted.) [West Michigan Dock & Market Corp v. Lakeland Investments, 210 Mich.App 512- 513.; 534 NW2d 212 (1995).]

See also Burt v. Munger, 314 Mich. 659, 665; 23 NW2d 117 (1946) (riparian owners generally may construct a dock to facilitate use and enjoyment of a lake, but they may not invade the rights of other riparian owners with respect to the lake).

✳ ✳ ✳

Here, the lake is approximately eight acres in area. Plaintiffs' sole purpose in constructing the bridge was to facilitate access to the rear portion of their property. Clearly, a forty-eight foot bridge that is only thirty-eight inches above the surface of the water will interfere with recreational use of the lake. The record supports the conclusion that the court properly balanced the benefit that would inure to plaintiffs and the injury to other riparian owners. Plaintiffs still have access to the rear portion of their property via the easement. We cannot say that we would have reached a different result concerning plaintiffs' reasonable use had we been sitting as the trial court. Accordingly, we conclude that the trial court did not err in granting defendant's motion for summary disposition.

Plaintiffs also maintain that the permanent injunction had the effect of destroying their right to access the rear portion of their property. Under the circumstances presented, we disagree. Pursuant to the trial court's order of September 13, 1993, plaintiffs and their guests and invitees are entitled to unrestricted ingress and egress to their property via the easement, and defendant was enjoined from maintaining any obstacle, fixed or permanent, that would block the easement. Consequently, plaintiffs have adequate access to the rear portion of their property despite removal of the bridge.

*4 Next, plaintiffs assert that the trial court erred in denying their motion for reconsideration. We disagree. The new documentary evidence regarding the parties' intent with respect to riparian rights was irrelevant to the legal determination of whether riparian rights exist.

☆ ☆ ☆

3. Crops and Timber

Crops and timber refer to the trees and plants that grow on land. They are, while attached to the land, part of the real estate. When taken down, however, they are considered personal property and, therefore, not part of the land. Suppose we sold our home last week to the Smiths. Just before the actual transfer of the property, we cut down the tree in the front yard, so that we would have firewood for our next home. We would have actually taken a part of the real property with us when we moved, and the Smiths would have opportunity to sue us for the diminished land. On the other hand, the wood that we cut from our front yard last year, and which was stacked in the yard, would be considered personal property, and we could take that with us when we moved.

4. Mineral Rights

The minerals, or minable substances, that exist under the real estate are also a divisible element of the property as a whole. The property owner may separate the minerals from the rest of the property, for example, by mining them, and still retain ownership of the land. Gold, silver, uranium, and coal are but a few of the valuable minerals that may exist and be separated from the land. In the western part of the United States, for instance, ranchers sold the rights to the uranium under their land, while they still owned the land.

5. Oil and Gas

The oil and gas under the land is another divisible part of the land. One may convey the oil or gas under the property without changing the ownership of the other parts of the land. When extracting the oil or gas under the land, you must stay on your own land in order to drill, but you can extract as much of the oil or gas as you can, even if the pool extends under the property of another. Unlike water rights, you don't have to worry about decreasing other owners' rights to the oil and gas.

6. Fixtures

Fixtures are items of personal property that have become part of the real property. The word "fixture" is derived from the term "affixed," or attached, to the land. The law determines whether a piece of personal property has been changed into a fixture by using a two-step test. First, how is the property attached to the land? The more permanent the attachment, the more likely it is to be a fixture. Second, the adaptability to the normal use of real property is evaluated. The more necessary the use, the more likely the item is to be classified as a fixture. As an example, let us consider that we want to protect our car when we park it at our home. If we build an attached garage, it will certainly be considered a fixture. It is attached to both the house and the land and is certainly an adaptation to the normal use of real estate. If, rather than the attached garage, we simply erect a plastic roof on movable poles, the item will not be considered a fixture, as it is not securely affixed to the land.

B. ACQUISITION OF REAL PROPERTY

Real property ownership may be acquired in a number of methods. They are purchase, gift, will or descent, adverse possession, and accretion. Additionally, the government has three more methods for acquiring real estate. They are dedication, escheat, or eminent domain.

1. Purchase

The most common method of acquiring ownership of real estate is by purchase, or buying, the land. The ownership of land is transferred from the buyer to the seller by exchanging the purchase price for the deed transferring ownership. A deed is a written instrument transferring ownership, or title, in real property from the old owner to the new owner. Deeds are used in all forms of transfer, or conveyance, of real property.

2. Gift

Real property may be given as a gift from the owner to any person they desire. The giving of land still requires a deed to complete the transfer of title.

3. Will or Descent

The owner of real property may transfer ownership of the property, upon his death, to any person he desires through a will. The will states the owner desired to pass the property, and the owner's desire is carried out by the executor, who is the person named in the will to be responsible for transferring all assets in the will.

Should the owner of real estate die without a will, then the property passes by descent to the next of kin. People who die without a will are said to have died intestate, and the state statutes that outline the order of the descent are called intestacy statutes. If a land owner dies intestate, the selection of the new owners is not in the control of the deceased, but is dictated solely by the intestacy statute.

4. Adverse Possession

Taking ownership by adverse possession requires that a person live on the property of another for a statutorily mandated time period, such that the person living on the land becomes the new owner. This transfer, unlike the other conveyances, does not require a deed.

5. Accretion

Property that grows due to the gradual accumulation of land by natural causes has grown through accretion. For example, if you own riverfront property, the bank of the river may grow through the depositing of silt. If this happens on your property, the additional land would be yours by accretion.

In addition to the above methods of acquisition of real property, the government and governmental entities have three additional ways to acquire land.

1. EMINENT DOMAIN

Eminent domain is the power of the state to take land for public use. The property taken must be used for the public good, and the state must pay fair value for the property. Courts have been liberal in their interpretation of public good. Roads, hospitals, schools, parks, and utility lines are but a few of the justifications for the public taking of private land. There is the potential for a judicial review of the fair value of the land.

2. ESCHEAT

The property of an individual who dies without beneficiaries or heirs escheats, or reverts, to the state. If, for instance, our client Chuck died intestate, or without a will, his real property would pass to his descendants or heirs by the intestacy statute of his state. Suppose, however, after a diligent search, none of his heirs could be located, or those few that could be found had died before him. The land would then escheat to the state.

3. DEDICATION

A dedication is the gift of land by the owner to the state or a governmental agency, often for a specific purpose. A dedication is really a gift of land to the state by the owner.

As an example, if we have a client who is developing a large piece of land into smaller homesites, one of the requirements of the town would be that the homesites have access; that is, they would have to have streets. When the sites are all sold, the streets that have been put in on the developers land would be passed by the developer to the town by dedication, so that the town could maintain them for the residents.

✼ ✼ ✼

LEGAL LIGHT

Neither sellers nor real estate agents are required to tell the buyer whether the home was the sight of a natural death, a suicide, a homicide, or a felony. Further, in most locations, they do not have to voluntarily disclose whether a sex offender lives nearby

✼ ✼ ✼

C. DEEDS

<u>Deeds</u> are the written instrument of transfer of real property from one person to another. The individual who is selling or otherwise conveying the property is called the grantor, and the new owner is called the grantee. Deeds must satisfy several requirements in order to be valid. They must, first, give the name of the grantor and the grantee. Next, the deed must clearly state the grantor's intention to transfer ownership to the grantee. Third, the deed must contain an adequate legal description of the property being transferred. Fourth, the law requires that the grantor sign the deed. In many states, this signature must also be

notarized. Fifth, the deed must be delivered to the grantee. Last, the deed must be recorded. Most states record deeds on a countywide basis in a special location, usually a land office or recorder's office. A fee is required to record the deed.

Several types of deeds exist. They include <u>warranty</u> or <u>grant deeds</u>, <u>quitclaim deeds</u>, <u>trust deeds</u>, and <u>correction deeds</u>.

1. Warranty or Grant Deeds

<u>Warranty</u> or <u>grant deeds</u> provide the new owner with a variety of guarantees or protections against defects or problems with the title or ownership of the property. Warranty deeds may either be general warranty deeds or special warranty deeds. General warranty deeds offer the fullest protections against title defects whether they are known or caused by the grantor or not. Special warranty deeds only protect the new owner if the grantor did something personally to create a title problem. Grant deeds, like the special warranty deeds, only offer a limited protection against problems caused by the grantor, but, unlike the special warranty deed, which states the protections, the grant deed only implies them and leaves to the courts to infer the protection.

2. Quitclaim Deeds

<u>Quitclaim deeds</u> transfer to the grantee only whatever interest in the property held by the grantor, and offer no guarantees that the title being passed is valid or that it has no defects. Quitclaim deeds simply state that they transfer whatever ownership interest is held by the grantor to the grantee, no matter what that interest might be.

3. Trust Deeds

<u>Trust deeds</u>, available in only a limited number of states, are hybrid or combination documents that serve both as a deed and a mortgage. All other deeds provide only for the ownership of the land in the grantee; if the grantee wants

to borrow money using the land as collateral, a separate document, a mortgage, must be used to guarantee the loan. With a trust deed, the ownership is not really with the new owners until the money lent to them to by the property is paid back. The actual legal ownership of the property is held in trust until the loan is fully paid. When the money is paid, the trustee, who is the person administering or in charge of the trust, turns the deed over to the owner, and he has the full title in the property. If the money is not paid back in a timely manner, then the trustee turns the deed over to the lender, and the lender has full title in the property. This mechanism of holding the property in trust eliminates the time-consuming and expensive judicial process of selling the property at a sheriff's sale when the homeowner is delinquent on his home loan, as is required in states that don't allow for trust deeds.

D. TYPES OF OWNERSHIP

The ownership of real property may take on a variety of forms that outline the rights and duties of the owner or owners. The type of ownership of the property is usually detailed in the deed. The most common forms of ownership are <u>sole ownership</u>, <u>joint tenancy</u>, <u>tenancy by the entirety</u>, <u>tenancy in common</u>, and <u>community property</u>. All of these forms of ownership describe how property is owned.

1. Sole Ownership

In <u>sole ownership</u>, a single individual owns the property and has all the rights and obligations associated with the ownership of real estate. The sole owner may convey the property or convey any of the divisible elements of the property, as she sees fit. Further, all the obligations that may apply to the ownership, such as paying the taxes or maintaining the property, are the responsibility of the sole owner. Upon the death of a sole owner, the property will either pass to the beneficiaries of the sole owner as prescribed in her will, or it will pass to her descendants if she dies intestate.

2. Joint Tenancy

In a joint tenancy, there are two or more owners, and the joint tenants, or owners, are said to own an undivided, equal interest in the property, with the right of survivorship. What is meant by an equal, undivided interest in the land is that each owns a total interest in the property, and each may do with the property that which he sees fit. For example, if you and I owned a property as joint tenants, I could cut down the tree in the yard if I wanted, just as you could do the same. The law views our ownership as total to each of us; it is common to say that each joint owner owns 100 percent of the property. The right of survivorship entailed in joint ownership describes what happens when one of the joint tenants dies. If Chuck and Mary own property as joint tenants, and Chuck dies, then Mary becomes the sole owner of the land. Chuck cannot pass the property by will, nor can the land pass to Chuck's descendants if he dies without a will.

3. Tenancy by the Entirety

A tenancy by the entirety is a form of joint tenancy in which the two joint tenants are husband and wife. The tenancy by the entirety differs from a joint tenancy only in that the owners are married. If the owners by tenancy by the entirety divorce, then their ownership of the property becomes a tenancy in common. Not all states recognize tenancy by the entirety.

4. Tenancy in Common

A tenancy in common is a form of ownership between two or more people in which the owners have an undivided interest that may or may not be equal, without the right of survivorship. The owners possess the land proportionately, without distinguishing which part belongs to whom. Let us say that Chuck, Mary, and Tim own a piece of property as tenants in common. If the deed states only that the property is owned as a tenancy in common, then it is presumed that the three individuals own equal shares of the property, or a one-third share each. The deed may state, however, that the shares are unequal; for example one half for Chuck and one quarter each for Mary and Tim, if that are the wishes of the grantees. If, now, one of our three owners dies, then the share of that owner does not simply pass to the other tenants in common, but, rather, becomes part of the deceased's estate. That is, if Chuck dies, his share of the property would either pass to his beneficiaries through his will or, if he died without a will, then it would pass to his heirs through intestate succession.

5. Community Property

Community property ownership is a statutory form of land ownership that exists in only nine states. It provides that a husband and a wife who acquire real estate during their marriage each own equal undivided interests in the land, regardless of whose name appears on the deed. Land that is either inherited or given to one of the spouses, however, is not considered community property.

What happens if you try to create a form of ownership that can't be formed? Our next case demonstrates what would happen in one circumstance.

✻ ✻ ✻

REAL PROPERTY CASE #7-2

Bucci v. Bucci
508 N.Y.S.2d 573 (1986)

BY THE COURT. In 1965, Ralph Bucci, Sr., and the defendant purchased certain real property, taking title as "tenants by the entirety." At the time, Ralph Bucci, Sr. was legally married to another, with whom he had a son, the plaintiff herein. In 1976, after the death of Mr. Bucci's wife, he and the defendant were married. Ralph Bucci, Sr. died intestate in 1978, survived by the plaintiff, the defendant, and a daughter by the defendant. The issue is the ownership of the subject property...

At the time this property was purchased by the decedent and the defendant, a conveyance to two persons who were not legally married "as tenants by the entirety," was deemed to create only a tenancy in common, unless expressly declared to be a joint tenancy. In 1975, this presumption was reversed by statutory amendment so that a joint tenancy was created.... However, this amendment does "not effect dispositions of real property made prior to its effective date". Since the disposition to the decedent and the defendant occurred in 1965, (this amendment) does not apply and the conveyance to them created no more than a tenancy in common. Upon the decedent's death then, in 1978, the defendant remained a tenant in common with the decedent's distributees.

✳ ✳ ✳

LEGAL LIGHT

Of twenty professions studied in California, a real estate agent could qualify to sell homes as a professional agent with as little as forty-eight hours of training. The next lowest was an esthetician or beaulician, who required six hundred hours of training. Next was a police officer, who was required to take 1,120 hours. A hair stylist required 1,500 hours of training, a chiropractor 3,840 hours, and a CPA required 5,980 hours.

✳ ✳ ✳

D. EASEMENTS

An <u>easement</u> is the right to use the real estate of another. It does not confer a right to possess or to own the property, only a privilege to use the property in question in a limited fashion. Four types of easements are recognized by the law. They are an <u>easement by prescription</u>, an <u>easement by implication</u>, an <u>easement by grant</u>, and an <u>easement by necessity</u>. A purchaser of real estate takes possession of the property subject to the easements that exist. That is, if an easement exists, then the easement continues even if the property is transferred. In this way, easements are said to run with the land.

1. Easement by Prescription

An <u>easement by prescription</u> is formed when an individual repeatedly or chronically uses the property of another, without express permission of the owner, for a period of time required by the state's statutes. That is, if one uses someone else's property, over and over, for the mandated period, one acquires a permanent easement to use the property that cannot be ended by the true owner. It is rather similar to an easement by adverse possession, but one does not possess the land, just uses it for one's own purpose. As an example, Harry owns the property next to Ted's property. Harry, being a lazy soul, uses Ted's property to cut through to the bus stop that he uses, which is behind Ted's land. Year after year, Harry walks across Ted's back yard to the bus stop every work day. Ted sells his land after a number of years to Carol, who tries to stop Harry from using her land as a pathway. Harry cannot be stopped at this junction, as he has acquired an easement by prescription to use the land.

2. Easement by Implication

An <u>easement by implication</u> arises when land is subdivided, and the new part reasonably requires that an easement exists for its use. If, for example, we divide a piece of property and sell the new part to a purchaser for the building of a house, and the part that we retain contains a pathway that facilitates reaching the street, then the pathway would be an easement by implication for the new owners to cross our land.

3. Easement by Grant

An <u>easement by grant</u> is an easement that is given, in writing, by the owner to another party. Easements by grant are often given by landowners to utility companies so the utilities may run their wires on or over the land and so that the utility's employees may enter the land to repair the wires when necessary. Easements by grant are typically recorded in the local land office or recorder's office, so that discovering these easements may be accomplished by searching the land records.

4. Easement by Necessity

An <u>easement by necessity</u> arises when a landlocked piece of land requires an easement for access. Landlocked property is that land which is surrounded by other properties and can only be reached by crossing over other peoples' land. Easements by necessity must be strictly and absolutely necessary, and will be described by the courts, not by any of the landowners. If, for example, Paul owned a landlocked piece of property, but he had a grant easement over another property so that he could reach the street, then an easement by necessity would not be required. If, on the other hand, this easement by grant did not exist, and an easement by necessity is warranted, Paul would not be able to pick and choose an easement that suited him; rather, the court would determine an easement based not only on Paul's needs but also on the needs of all the other landowners involved.

Here is a case involving easements.

✻ ✻ ✻

REAL PROPERTY CASE #7-3

Copertino v. Ward
473 N.Y.S.2d 494 (1984)

BY THE COURT. Defendant and his wife are owners of a single-family residence at 26 Birchwood Drive in the Town of New Windsor, New York. To remedy a sewer backup problem, defendant orally contracted with A-1 Sewer Company to replace a section of collapsed pipe located near his feeder line, which connected defendant's house to the municipality's sewer main....(W)orkers from the A-1 Sewer Company, including plaintiff, began to excavate a trench in order to dig up and replace the collapsed pipe. The trench began on defendant's lawn, a short distance from the curb, and extended to the center of Birchwood Drive. No shoring of any kind was used by the contractor to stabilize the walls of the trench. It is undisputed that defendant did not supervise, control, or assist, in any manner, regarding the excavation work. While plaintiff was standing in the portion of the trench located on Birchwood Drive, approximately four to five feet from defendant's property line, the trench caved in and buried plaintiff up to his chest. To recover damages for personal injuries sustained in the accident, plaintiff commenced an action against defendant based on...the Labor Law. Defendant moved to dismiss the complaint, on the ground that he is not an "owner" within the purview of either section (of the Labor Law) because the accident occurred in an excavation on a public street and not on his property.

...The...Labor Law imposed a nondelagable duty on "owners" to provide reasonable and adequate protection and safety to persons employed in construction, excavation, or demolition...However, the section does not define the term "owners."

Defendant, as an easement holder, had a property interest in the excavation site where plaintiff was injured.

Furthermore, defendant contracted with plaintiff's employer, A-1 Sewer Company, to remove the obstruction causing the stoppage of sewer flow in his feeder line. He had the (responsibility) since his property alone would receive the benefit. As a practical matter, defendant had the right to insist that proper safety practices were followed and it is the right to control the work that is significant, not the actual exercise or nonexercise of control. Based on these facts, defendant is an owner...In other words, both the owner of the fee and the grantees of the easement could be found liable...as "owners" of the construction site.

✼ ✼ ✼

E. LIENS

A <u>lien</u> is the use of real property as security for the payment of a debt or to secure performance of some other obligation. Liens are the use of real property as collateral. A lien is a recorded instrument that is recorded in the county land office. Liens are associated or attached to the land itself, and not to the owner of the land. That is, if a property is sold, the new owner acquires not only the land itself, but the liens on the property as well. Liens may be classified as either involuntary liens or voluntary liens. Involuntary liens are ones in which the landowner does not participate in formation. The property is used as security without the express permission of the owner in an involuntary lien. The most common types of involuntary liens are <u>mechanics liens</u> and <u>tax liens</u>. Voluntary liens are ones in which the property owner does participate in formation. The owner must agree to the lien, and sign appropriate documents detailing the lien. The most common type of voluntary lien is the <u>mortgage</u>.

1. Mechanics Liens

Mechanics liens are involuntary liens filed by either contractors who work on the land, or by suppliers of materials that become fixtures on the land. A mechanic, at common law, is an individual who is skilled at working with tools. Mechanics include the bricklayers, carpenters, plumbers, electricians, and the like who work on real property. Statutes in each of the states allow these individuals to secure payment for their work and materials by filing a mechanics lien on the property on which they worked. If you were to put a deck on your house, then both the carpenter who built the deck, and the lumber yard that provided the materials could put a mechanics lien on the property to insure payment. When payment is made, then the lien is to be removed by the individual who first recorded it.

2. Tax Liens

A tax lien is an involuntary lien recorded by an agency of the government to secure payment of a debt to the government. This money owed the government may be directly related to the land, such as a failure to pay real estate taxes, or it may not be directly related to the land, such as if the owner of the land failed to pay their income taxes.

3. Mortgages

A mortgage is a voluntary lien used to secure payment of a debt. Most often today, individuals who buy a house must borrow the money to pay the seller, and, in order to secure the debt, use a mortgage to guarantee payment to the lender. This type of mortgage is often called a purchase money mortgage. Of course, after you own the property, you may borrow money using the land as collateral. These types of mortgages are sometimes referred to as home equity mortgages or as second mortgages. The owner of the land who is borrowing money using a mortgage is called the mortgagor. The lender of the money is called the mortgagee. The vast majority of mortgages are one of the following five types: <u>fixed rate mortgages</u>; <u>adjustable rate mortgages</u>; <u>balloon mortgages</u>; <u>two-step mortgages</u>; and, <u>biweekly mortgages</u>.

a. Fixed Rate Mortgages

<u>Fixed rate mortgages</u> are those mortgage products in which the interest rate remains constant over the life of the loan. Because the interest rate stays constant over the payback period, the payments that are made in a fixed rate mortgage stay the same. Let us say that we borrowed, for example, $100,000 by use of a mortgage from our local bank, in order to buy our home. If the payment period, or term, of the loan was thirty years, and the interest rate of the loan was 10 percent, then our payments would be $878 per month for the next 360 months. The obvious predictability of fixed rate mortgages is appealing to borrowers, as it allows for certain budgeting.

b. Adjustable Rate Mortgage

An <u>adjustable rate mortgage</u> is a mortgage in which the interest rate changes or adjusts at given intervals. Adjustable rate mortgages, called by the acronym ARMs, have payments that change because the interest rate varies. Let us again borrow $100,000, with a thirty-year term, from our local bank to buy our house. This time, however, we borrow using an ARM that calls for adjustments in rate every year. Our initial interest rate is, for our example, 7 percent, making our initial payments $665. ARMs always have lower initial interest rates compared with fixed rate mortgages in a given time period, as lenders offer ARMs at loss leader prices as an enticement. The lender prefers ARMs to fixed rates as it prevents the lender from being locked in to an interest rate that is too low over time. At the end of the period required by the mortgage, here, one year, the interest rate is recomputed and the payments are changed to reflect the new rate. In those ARMs that are offered at a discounted opening rate, the new rate will be higher. If the new interest rate, as computed, jumps to 12 percent at the end of the period, then our payment goes from $665 to $1029 in the second year. To prevent this kind of payment shock, many, but not all, ARMs have caps built in to them. These caps are maximum amounts that the interest rate can change each year and/or for the life of the loan. If our loan had caps of 2 percent a year and 6 percent for its lifetime, the most our rate could rise to in the second year would be 9 percent, and the most our interest rate could ever be for this loan would be 13 percent. One should expect that the rate for the adjustable rate loan will increase for the first few years, at least until the artificially low beginning rate reaches market rates.

c. Balloon Mortgages

Balloon mortgages are fixed rate loans that have payments that are based on a long term but whose real term is relatively short, leaving a large balance for the last payment. Let us suppose we have again borrowed $100,000 at a 10 percent interest rate. We will, for the sake of example, say that this is a 7/30 balloon mortgage. That is, we make payments as if the term was the larger number, here thirty years, but the real term of the loan is the smaller number, here seven years. We would make payments of $878, just as we did for the comparable fixed rate loan, but we would only make those payments for six years and eleven months in our example. The last payment would be for the balance of the loan, here about $97,000. Balloon mortgages, while at first seeming to make little sense, do offer some advantages to both borrower and lender. On the lender's side, the money is locked in to the rate for a lesser time than if it was a thirty-year mortgage, so any changes in rates can be dealt with when the loan comes due, and the money can be lent to the next borrower at a market rate. As the bank's money is not at the same risk of rate changes as it would be in a longer-term mortgage, the lenders offer these mortgages at a slighter lower interest rate than the traditional fixed rate loan. Considering that many homeowners stay in their home a relatively moderate length of time, the lower rate is an advantage to the borrower.

d. Two-Step Mortgages

The two-step mortgage is a hybrid mortgage that combines an adjustable with a fixed rate mortgage. The mortgage starts out as a fixed rate loan, then, at a predetermined time, may be converted to a fixed rate loan, at the option of the borrower, and for the payment of appropriate and predetermined fees and costs.

e. Biweekly Mortgages

Biweekly mortgages are fixed rate loans wherein one makes not a full payment once a month, but, rather, one makes a half-payment once every two weeks. The consequence of this payment schedule is that one makes the equivalent of thirteen monthly payments every year, rather than twelve. For example, if one had a $1,000 payment on the mortgage every month with a traditional payment schedule, one would make twelve monthly payments every year, for a total of $12,000 in mortgage payments for the year. With a biweekly mortgage for the same amount, however, you would make a $500 payment every two weeks. With fifty-two weeks in a year, that would mean twenty-six $500 payments every year, or a total of $13,000 in mortgage payments for the year. The biweekly mortgage is sold to consumers as a method of saving time, and, therefore, interest on the mortgage. It does this, however, by forcing the borrower to prepay by one monthly payment every year.

The following case deals with mortgage issues.

✳ ✳ ✳

REAL PROPERTY CASE #7-4

Basile v. Erhal Holding Corp.
538 N.Y.S.2d 831 (1989)

BY THE COURT. In 1982, the plaintiff, the owner of property located at 244 Morris Avenue in Peekskill, mortgaged the property to the Erhal Holding Corp. in return for a loan at an allegedly usurious rate. The plaintiff instituted this action to declare the mortgage null and void on the ground of usury. On June 2, 1986, and June 6, 1986, while the matter was awaiting trial, the parties entered into a stipulation of settlement in open court whereby the plaintiff agreed to execute a mortgage to Erhal in the sum of $101,303.59 together with a deed "in lieu of foreclosure" which would not be recorded by Erhal as long as the plaintiff fulfilled her obligations under the terms and conditions of the mortgage. The mortgage agreement also included the following provision: "The mortgagor herein has simultaneously executed a deed in lieu of foreclosure which may be recorded by the mortgagee for any default herein."

The plaintiff subsequently defaulted in several mortgage payments and failed to pay the real estate taxes and fire insurance premiums for the demised premises as provided for in the mortgage agreement. As a result of the plaintiff's default, Erhal recorded the deed in lieu of foreclosure in December, 1986. Thereafter, Erhal moved, by order to show cause, for an order declaring that the plaintiff's right of redemption with respect to the property was waived when the mortgage and deed in lieu of foreclosure were executed in June, 1986. The plaintiff cross-moved for an order directing Erhal to accept a check for the sum of $101,303.59 plus interest tendered by the plaintiff and to deliver to the plaintiff a satisfaction of mortgage and a deed for the premises, free and clear of all encumbrances.

In this case, it is clear that the deed in lieu of foreclosure executed by the plaintiff with the $101,303.59 mortgage was not intended as an absolute conveyance or sale of the property by the plaintiff but rather was intended to be security for the plaintiff's $101,303.59 debt to Erhal. As such, the deed constituted a mortgage and the attempted waiver of the plaintiff's right of redemption in the property in the in-court stipulation of settlement as well as the mortgage agreement was ineffective. Erhal's sole remedy is to institute an action in foreclosure. The plaintiff will have a right to redeem the property at any time prior to the actual sale of the premises by tendering to Erhal the principal and interest due on the mortgage.

✲ ✲ ✲

F. ZONING

The freedom of any real property owner to use the land in any manner has come to be restricted by state and local laws. These governmental controls on land use are called zoning. Zoning limits that which can or cannot be built on certain parcels of land, and restricts how it can be built, in order to maintain public safety, value of property, and general welfare of the local residents. The power to restrict land use derives from the state's police power to pass laws to protect the public's health, safety, and general welfare. It is in the general population's best interest to make sure a chemical factory won't be built next to a school, or that a large office complex won't be built in a residential development of homes. State limits on land use cannot be so severe, however, that they can be said to be a confiscation of the owner's land. That is, they cannot so limit the land use as to make the land worthless. If John purchased a piece of property for the purpose of building a development of twenty homes, and the town, trying to restrict development, rezoned the property so that its only use could be as a park, this zoning would be confiscatory. The court would view this action as a taking of the land and would require compensation to the owner for this action, which is the equivalent of a taking by eminent domain. Additionally, the governmental zoning cannot be arbitrary or capricious in nature. Any state action in zoning that can be described as benefiting the general welfare is considered rational by the court. Further, the action of the state cannot be discriminatory. Zoning with a basis in racial, religious, or ethnicity discrimination is clearly unconstitutional.

✻ ✻ ✻

CHAPTER SUMMARY

The law divides property into two large pieces, real property and personal property. Real property is comprised of a number of divisible elements. These physical elements are the airspace, water, crops, minerals, oil, and fixtures that are on, under, or over the land. The laws of real property are extensive and complex and come to us through a thousand years of history.

Real property may be acquired in a number of ways. Individuals may obtain it through purchase, gift, will or descent, adverse possession, or accretion. In addition, governmental entities may acquire real estate through escheat and eminent domain.

Real property ownership comes in a number of forms. A single person may own real estate as the sole owner. More than one person may own real estate as joint owners, owners in common, and owners by the entirety, or as community property.

Liens on real estate are the use of real property as security for a debt or for the performance of some obligation. Liens may be either voluntary or involuntary in nature, depending on whether or not the owner needs to participate in their formation. Involuntary liens include tax liens and mechanics liens. Voluntary liens include various types of mortgages.

Real property law also concerns itself with the right to use property even if one does not own it. The legal right to use real estate of another is called an easement.

Easements are formed by grant, necessity, implication, and prescription.

CHAPTER SEVEN
KEY TERMS

Accretion
Dedication
Easement
Eminent Domain
Escheat
Fixtures
Liens
Mortgage
Quitclaim Deed
Riparian Rights
Trust Deed
Warrant or Grant Deed
Zoning

THINK AND WRITE

1. What kinds of ownership are available to individuals? What are the advantages and disadvantages of each?
2. What kinds of mortgages are available? What are the advantages and disadvantages of each?
3. Please give an example of air rights that are customarily severed from the rest of the real property ownership.
4. What are the differences between a quitclaim deed and a warranty deed?

5. What is the right of survivorship, and when is it part of the rights of ownership?
6. What types of easement exist?
7. When does property escheat to the state?

PROJECTS

1. Research the deed to your house (or any other specific property) at the appropriate recorder's office. Name the previous three owners of the property.
2. Check with your town's zoning board and determine what you would need to do in order to build a deck on the back of your home that would violate the zoning ordinances by being too close to the back property line.
3. Call two or three local banks and research all the closing costs that are required by the bank when a customer closes on a residential property. How do they compare?
4. Call your town tax assessor and determine the tax rate for residential and for commercial properties in your town. Why are they different?
5. Research the federal tax consequences of selling an $800,000 primary residence that has been used as such for the past five years. Assuming the cost basis is $100,000, what might the taxes be for both a married and a single seller?

ETHICS QUESTIONS

1. New York state requires, as part of a residential real estate transaction, that the seller certify that there are

no defects in the major systems of the house. However, failure to execute such a certification results in only a $500 adjustment at closing. Many lawyers in New York recommend to their clients who are selling a house not to complete the certification and risk insuring the buyer against defects, and simply forfeit the $500. What would you do if you were representing a seller in New York?

2. Many beachfront states are struggling with ownership and access questions. Whose rights should be protected, the homeowner whose home is beachfront, or the rest of the population, who have a right to access the ocean?

1. Links to real property law websites: http://www.megalaw. com/top/property.php
2. Summary of U.S. real property laws: http://www. intcounselor.com/real-property.html
3. Index for real property sites: http://www.alllaw.com/ legal_topic_index/real_property
4. Index for various real property sites: www.lectlaw.com/ tlat.htm

CHAPTER EIGHT

WILLS

A <u>will</u> can be described as the statement of an adult which only takes effect on his death, whereby the person describes how his property shall be distributed. A will, as the last statement of a person's life, is treated with great respect by the courts, who, provided the will meets legal requirements, want to ensure that the property is distributed precisely as outlined in the will. Most states provide a separate subject matter jurisdiction court within the trial court level to manage the distribution of property after an individual dies. These courts are called either surrogates courts or probate courts.

Individuals who die and leave a will describing property distribution are said to have died <u>testate</u>, or with a will. Individuals who die without a will are said to have died <u>intestate</u>, or without a will; the property of people who die intestate will be distributed to their descendants by a process defined in state statutes. These statutes are called intestacy statutes.

A. WILLS

Most of the states provide for three types of wills, with particular requirements and limitations for each. The three types of wills recognized in most states are <u>holographic wills</u>, <u>nuncupative wills</u>, and <u>formal written wills</u>. From state to state, the particular requirements of each show some differences, but the basic descriptions are the same.

Certainly, one thing that is a constant from state to state, and is true of all will types, is that the person making the will must have the mental capacity to do so. The required mental capacity for making a will necessitates that the person be eighteen years old and be capable of understanding what he or she is doing.

Before evaluating the three types of wills possible, we must know the terms used in a will. First, and foremost, the person who is leaving his or her property in a will is called, if male, a <u>testator</u>, and, if female, a <u>testatrix</u>. The person who receives property under a will is usually called the <u>beneficiary</u>. If the gift in a will is of real property, then it is called a <u>devise</u>, and, if the gift is of personal property, then it is called a <u>bequest</u>. A person named in a will to take charge of the division of property is called the <u>executor</u>, if male, or the <u>executrix</u>, if female. Additionally, wills may be used to name the person who will raise a child of the testator if the child is left orphaned. This person is called a <u>guardian</u>. Lastly, if money or any other property is left not directly to the beneficiary but to an individual who controls the money on behalf of another, that person who controls the funds is called the <u>trustee</u>.

1. Holographic Wills

<u>Holographic wills</u> are those wills written entirely in the handwriting of the testator. The will can be written on paper, or virtually any other item upon which one may write. The will may be written in ink, indelible marker, or crayon. The state requirements are all established to make the will difficult to alter; for example, the will may not be written in pencil. The will itself can be in an informal style, as long as state requirements are substantially met. As an example, our friend Mary has written her will on the back of a brown paper bag that she has taken home from the supermarket. She has drafted the document using her indelible eyebrow pencil. In most states, this would be a valid holographic will, as long as it was drafted entirely in Mary's own handwriting. In many jurisdictions, it is not even essential that the

holographic will be witnessed, as long as the handwriting can be positively identified as that of the testator.

Here is a dispute involving a holographic will.

✲ ✲ ✲

CASE # 8-1

SCHERER, SCHERER v. DISCEPOLO
No. A100743 (Contra Costa County Super. Ct. No. P0001780)

HAERLE, J.
I.INTRODUCTION

*1This is an appeal from a judgment of the Contra Costa County Superior Court denying probate of a **holographic will** allegedly prepared by the decedent and proffered to the court by the wife from whom he had been estranged and separated for approximately 15 years. The trial court found, substantially from circumstantial evidence, that the will could not possibly have been written by the decedent. Appellant argues that there was no direct evidence that the handwriting on the alleged **holographic will** was not that of the decedent. Finding that the evidence cited by the trial court in its statement of decision constitutes the requisite substantial evidence, we affirm.

II. FACTUAL AND PROCEDURAL BACKGROUND [FN1]

✲ ✲ ✲

The decedent, Robert Scherer, and appellant, Beverly Scherer, were married in 1963 and separated in 1985. In

1996, a judgment of legal separation was entered by the Contra Costa County appellant. Notwithstanding their separation, however, decedent and appellant remained equal shareholders and managers of a small business in Richmond, S & L Machine Shop, Inc.

In 1988, decedent met and established a relationship with the respondent, Gwendolyn Discepolo. That relationship, which the trial court found to be "the functional equivalent of a marriage," lasted until decedent's death on November 7, 2000.

On October 17, 1998, a little more than two years before his death, decedent executed a formal, witnessed will leaving everything to respondent and naming his and appellant's daughter, Robin Kinney, as the contingent beneficiary.

In 1999, decedent was diagnosed as having ALS or Lou Gehrig's disease. This disease attacks and destroys the muscles of the body, and exactly that happened to decedent. Dr. Yuen So of the Stanford University Medical Center examined decedent several times in 1999 and 2000. As of late 1999, according to Dr. So, decedent was almost totally wheelchair-bound, as it was impossible for him to bear weight. Three days before the proffered **holographic will** was allegedly executed, Dr. So examined decedent again. At that time, according to Dr. So, decedent was unable to rise from the wheelchair, and had no movement in his right leg and only feeble movement in his left leg.

Five other witnesses, including respondent, confirmed that, starting in late 1999, decedent was almost entirely wheelchair-bound.

Appellant testified that, on January 31, 2000, decedent came to her home and, using a walker and with some assistance from her, walked up her walkway and back stairs, entered her kitchen, and then and there executed the **holographic will** at issue. That purported will left all his assets to her.

On August 22, 2000, decedent filed two civil actions against appellant in Contra Costa Superior Court. The first asked for damages on behalf of S & L Machine, Inc., for alleged diversion by appellant of corporate funds. The second sought involuntary dissolution of the corporation. These two actions were, apparently, later dismissed without prejudice.

*2 On September 12, 2000, decedent filed, also in Contra Costa County Superior Court a petition to dissolve his marriage to appellant.

In September and October 2000, decedent sought the counsel of two attorneys regarding his 1998 will. The first attorney referred him to the second (who is respondent's attorney in this litigation) who suggested that, in lieu of a will, decedent execute a living trust to avoid the time and expense of probate. Legal descriptions of real property and other work related to this goal were being undertaken when decedent died on November 7, 2000.

On December 12, 2000, respondent filed a petition to probate decedent's will of October 1998. On January 5, 2001, appellant filed a petition to probate the alleged **holographic will** of January 31, 2000. On February 9, 2001, respondent filed a contest of the alleged **holographic will**.

The case was tried in two court days before the Honorable David Flynn in June 2002. The court first issued a tentative statement of decision and then, on August 27, 2002, a final statement of decision in respondent's favor, i.e., sustaining the contest, refusing to admit the alleged **holographic will** into probate. A judgment to this effect was entered on October 2, 2002. Appellant filed a notice of appeal on October 23, 2002.

II. DISCUSSION

Appellant argues there was no substantial evidence to sustain the trial court's statement of decision and judgment rejecting the proffered **holographic will** of January 2000. More specifically, she contends that, whereas she testified personally and directly regarding the preparation and execution of that document, respondent presented no direct evidence (e.g., a handwriting expert) that the document was not prepared by the decedent. Her attorney sums up this argument thusly in appellant's reply brief: "The presentation of circumstantial evidence, even if relevant, does not rise to the level of necessary proof in the absence of direct evidence of the validity of the handwriting."

That is not, however, the law in California. At least five times, our Supreme Court has made clear that circumstantial evidence may well overcome direct evidence and, additionally, that it can and does constitute the necessary "substantial evidence" for purposes of securing an affirmance of a trial court's factual findings on appeal.

The first such holding, or at least the first such that our research has uncovered, was in Parsons v. Easton (1921) 184 Cal. 764, 769 (Parsons), a negligence case in which the court declared flatly: "Direct testimony may be contradicted by circumstantial evidence and the contradiction may be so strong that it will justify a disbelief of the testimony."

✻ ✻ ✻

In another negligence case, Gray v. Southern Pacific Co. (1944) 23 Cal.2d 632, 641, the court, citing Parsons, expanded on this theme: "[The jury] could reject positive testimony and accept circumstantial evidence as proof of the facts, as it is elementary that direct evidence may be disbelieved and contrary circumstantial evidence relied upon to support a verdict or finding." And in Scott v. Burke (1952) 39 Cal.2d 388, 398, the court was even more emphatic: "[C]ircumstantial evidence may outweigh, in convincing force, both the strongest of disputable presumptions…and direct evidence as well. [Citations.]" (See also Bruce v. Ullery (1962) 58 Cal.2d 702, 711.)

*3 Most recently, the court summed up the point thusly: "[T]he fact that evidence is 'circumstantial' does not mean that it cannot be 'substantial.' Relevant circumstantial evidence is admissible in California. (Evid.Code, § 351.) Moreover, the jury is entitled to accept persuasive circumstantial evidence even where contradicted by direct testimony. [Citations.]" (Hasson v. Ford Motor Corp. (1997) 19 Cal.3d 530, 548, overruled on other grounds in Soule v. General Motors Corp. (1994) 8 Cal.4th 548, 572-580.)

These holdings apply, of course, whether the finding being attacked is made by a jury or, as here, by a trial court sitting without one.

Further, we agree with the trial court that the evidence was very substantial that the decedent neither could have or would have gone along to appellant's house, made his way with a walker up a walkway and steps (with or without her help in so doing), go into her kitchen and write out and sign the document in question. On the physical side of things was the testimony of Dr. So and several others that, from the fall of 1999 onward (indeed increasingly as 2000 wore on) decedent was, in effect, "wheelchair-bound." Indeed, Dr. So, who examined decedent three days before the purported events of January 31, 2000, opined as to decedent's physical ability to perform as appellant testified he did on that date: "I think it's impossible for him to do that on his own.... [H]e was wheelchair-bound and he was wheelchair-bound for a reason. He couldn't walk, even with a walker." On cross-examination, appellant's counsel was unable to get Dr. So to alter his opinion.

Additionally, numerous witnesses testified to the fact that ramps were constructed to get decedent into his vehicle (and for other purposes), that the vehicle was equipped with hands-only controls, and that decedent was often lifted into the vehicle (and elsewhere) by friends and co-workers. These witnesses also testified that, once he became wholly or substantially "wheelchair-bound," decedent seldom if ever used his walker (the device by which appellant claimed he made it up her walkway and into her house in January 2000). [FN2]

FN2. To be sure, appellant introduced testimony, mostly from family members, that decedent was able, at some points of time in 2000, to get around via his walker alone, i.e., without his wheelchair. But the converse was, as the trial court pointed out in its statement of decision, testified to by numerous witnesses not "shown to have reason to have any bias in favor of" respondent.

There was also substantial evidence that it was extremely unlikely that, as of 2000, decedent wanted to leave all his assets to his estranged wife and nothing to his "constant companion" and daughter. As noted above, shortly before his death in November 2000, decedent (1) filed two lawsuits against his wife basically accusing her of misusing corporate assets, (2) filed a dissolution action, (3) talked to two attorneys about his October 1998 will, (4) was in the process of converting his property disposition to a living trust in favor of respondent, and (5) told his (and appellant's) daughter the day before he died to "make sure my mom didn't get any more money than she already had."

Clearly, the trial court also had problems with the credibility of the version of events testified to by appellant, especially regarding her "delay in coming forth with the alleged instrument." Her testimony was that, although the document was supposedly executed by decedent in her kitchen on January 31, 2000, she had "forgotten about" it until New Year's Day of 2001, almost two months after decedent's death. She testified that she had carried the document around in her purse, oblivious to its importance, and discovered it only while "cleaning out her purse" on New Year's Day, pursuant to a New Year's "resolution." [FN3] But the trial court had an opportunity to examine the document in its original form and noted in its statement of decision that it did "not show nearly the wear and tear that would be expected if it were, as the proponent claimed, carried about in a purse for eleven months."

FN3. She also testified that she did not know the document was "any kind of a will" until talking to her lawyer a few days after discovering it.

*4 There is one other source of substantial support for the trial court's findings on the credibility issue, although one not specifically cited by it. The daughter of the decedent and appellant, Robin Kinney, testified that, after the death of her father, respondent gave her a copy of the October 1998 will and she, in turn, told her mother (appellant) and other family members about it. The general consensus among her family, she testified, was that the 1998 will was not genuine, i.e., they "did not believe this will." After participating in many intra-family conversations along these lines, Kinney told respondent: " 'Well, don't be surprised if they try to do something. Just kind of be on the lookout if something happens. Just to let you know that they just don't believe this." She concluded by telling respondent that she, Kinney, "wouldn't be surprised if...another will came about." Finally in this connection, Kinney testified that, during the two weeks before her appearance in court, she had received telephone calls from unidentified members of her family asking her to change her planned testimony.

We have no difficulty whatsoever in concluding that the findings and judgment of the trial court are supported by substantial evidence.

II. DISPOSITION

The judgment is affirmed.

✳ ✳ ✳

2. Nuncupative Wills

Nuncupative wills are oral deathbed statements that distribute the property of the testator. Nuncupative wills are generally only valid when made during the final illness of the testator. Many states do not allow for nuncupative wills, except for state residents who are members of the armed forces on active duty; some states do, however, allow for more liberal uses of nuncupative wills. Nuncupative wills are only valid for the bequest of personal property, not for the devise of real estate. That is, the testator can distribute any property except real estate through the nuncupative will. Nuncupative wills must be made in the presence of the statutorily required number of disinterested witnesses. Usually, this number is either two or three persons. The need for disinterested witnesses is obvious; should the parties hearing the will be beneficiaries, the temptation to elaborate the amounts left to them would be too tempting. A typical nuncupative will is a hospital deathbed statement made before sufficient medical personnel as witnesses.

3. Formal Written Wills

Formal written wills are those documents prepared by someone other than the testator, properly signed by the testator, and then witnessed by the statutorily required number of persons. States place a variety of witnessing and notarization requirements on formal written wills in order for them to be valid. Some states require two witnesses, while other states require three witnesses. Some states require that the testator's signature be notarized, and some states require the witnesses' signatures be notarized as well. Formal written wills are those wills usually prepared by an attorney and signed by the testator. They are what we normally think of when we think of a will. Formal written wills are one of the more cost-effective pieces of legal work that most consumers can have done. They provide for a smooth and orderly transition of property, done as the testator wishes.

B. GIFTS BY WILL

Under all three will types we have seen, three categories of gifts can be made. The three categories of gifts under a will, which all transfer property to the beneficiaries, are specific gifts, general gifts, and residual gifts. As we have mentioned before, if the gift is of real property, then it is named a devise, and if it is of personal property, then it is named a bequest.

1. Specific Gifts
Specific gifts are the giving of particular, individual gifts to a beneficiary. Should, for example, you want to leave your diamond engagement ring to your Auntie Mame, this would be a specific bequest, as it would be the giving of a distinguishable item to the beneficiary. Should you not own the diamond engagement ring when you die, then Auntie Mame would get nothing.

2. General Gifts
General gifts are gifts of fungible items, rather than distinguishable items, to a beneficiary. Fungible items are things which are of a class and indistinguishable from one another. For our discussion, the most common fungible item is money. One cannot distinguish one dollar bill from another. If you were left a dollar, it wouldn't matter to you which particular dollar you received. An example of a general bequest in a will would be the leaving of $15,000 to each of my three brothers, Tom, Dick, and Harry. Let us suppose, however, the testator's estate only had a total of $15,000 available. This money would be apportioned to each of the brothers, so that each would receive $5,000. This pro-rating of general bequests in a will because of insufficient funds is called abatement. However, if the testator would like to ensure that one beneficiary receiving a general bequest will not have that gift abated, he may do so.

3. Residual Gifts

Residual gifts are accomplished through the use residual clauses in wills which divide all the property remaining after the specific gifts and general gifts are made. Residual clauses apportion the remaining estate, eliminating the need to list each and every piece of property that is owned by the testator. The residual clause also eliminates the need to revise the will when the testator accumulates new items or new money. As an example, a residual clause might provide that, after other gifts and expenses, the remaining assets will be divided equally between Charles and Diane, the two children of the testator. This would mean that, after the other gifts and expenses, that Charles and Diane would each receive 50 percent of the remaining amount. That which remains after the other gifts and expenses is called the residual estate or residuary.

The next case illustrates the latitude courts attempt to give to testators.

☆ ☆ ☆

WILLS CASE #8-2

Matter of Johnson

460 N.Y.S.2d 932 (1983)

MOLLEN,J. The issue presented in this appeal is whether the Equal Protection Clause of the Fourteenth Amendment is violated when a Surrogate reforms the provisions of a will so as to give effect to a testamentary bequest which discriminates on the basis of sex.

In 1978 Edwin Irving Johnson died. His will created a gender-based scholarship fund to be administered by the Croton-Harmon Union Free School District for the benefit of its needy and deserving male high school graduates.

The school district declined to award the scholarships on a gender-restricted basis, proposing instead to make the selections without regard to sex. In a proceeding to construe the will so as to permit gender-neutral scholarship awards, the Surrogate refused to delete the sex restriction. Instead, he decreed that the school district be replaced by a private trustee who was willing and able to administer the fund and award the scholarships as directed in the will. The appellant and amici curiae now contend that the Surrogate's decree, which clears the way for the scholarships to be awarded on a discriminatory basis, is...violative of the constitutional guarantee of Equal Protection...

Although charitable in nature, however, the trust Mr. Johnson created was clearly vulnerable to an equal protection challenge. By naming the Croton-Harmon Union Free School District, a public agency, as trustee to receive, invest, administer and dispense scholarship funds and to select scholarship recipients, the bequest required substantial state involvement, thereby triggering the guaranties of the Fourteenth Amendment. And, those guaranties would plainly be violated by the award of scholarships pursuant to the bequest's sex-based discriminatory restriction because it had no substantial relation to the goal of promoting higher education.

Accordingly, we conclude that the Surrogate was correct in determining that it was appropriate to reform the trust. We turn, then, to the question of whether the reformation he made was proper.

...It is indeed fundamental that one may dispose of his property as one wishes, including to select beneficiaries such as a favored religious institution, a fraternal organization, or a group which performs good work for a limited segment of society. And the right, of course, is not necessarily limited to the disposition of property to groups or causes which society views as worthy. The right to dispose of property may be exercised as well in a manner that indulges one's own personal bigotry and irrational prejudices....

Nevertheless, it is both the genius and the strength of our system that rights, no matter how important, are rarely, if ever, absolute. So it is with the right freely to dispose of one's property. The Surrogate is precluded from reforming the trust in such a way that has the immediate objective and ultimate effect of enforcing its discriminatory provision.

LEGAL LIGHT

According to a study by PNC Advisors reported in the April 2005 issue of *Worth* magazine, 43 percent of individuals with at least $10 million in investable assets have not executed wills. However, only 30 percent of individuals with investable assets between $500,000 and $1,000,000 have not prepared wills.

The survey also studied the reasons why these individuals have not prepared wills. Some 56 percent indicated that they had procrastinated making a will, while 12 percent admitted to not wanting to confront their own mortality.

C. REVOCATION OF WILLS AND CHANGES IN WILLS

Wills may be revoked or changed in a variety of ways. First, the testator may deliberately make will changes by a physical act, by writing a new will, or by adding a codicil to an existing will. Second, the law may force changes in will terms whether they are intended by the testator or not.

Those three occasions when the law mandates changes are when the testator <u>marries</u>, <u>divorces</u>, or has <u>after-born children</u>.

1. Physical Act

A testator may revoke a will by the <u>intentional destruction</u> of the existing will. The testator may burn or tear up a will, and, by doing so, will make its terms null and void. In some states, the testator may partially revoke a will by crossing out or otherwise obliterating a portion of the document. This would nullify only those portions so crossed out.

2. Write a New Will

A second intentional act of a testator that would revoke an existing will is to <u>write and sign a new will</u>. The second will, if it clearly states that it is meant to replace a previous will, accomplishes the revocation of the earlier will. If a second will does not clearly state that it is revoking all previous wills, then the multiple wills are read as one, with the terms of the second will taking precedence over the first in cases of conflict. To insure that conflicting will terms or multiple wills do not create expensive legal conflicts for the beneficiaries, it is not uncommon, when writing a new will, to both state that it revokes all previous wills and also physically destroy any previous wills.

3. Codicils

A <u>codicil</u> is a separate written document that amends an existing will. It is normally used to change a part of a previous will and avoids the necessity of writing a whole new will. Codicils must be executed and witnessed in the same fashion as a will. Codicils are used primarily to update a will. Let us suppose that a testator's lengthy will needs to be changed because the beneficiary of a specific bequest has died. Rather than write an entire new will, it is more cost effective and less time consuming to add a codicil to the existing will, amending the one term that needs to be changed.

4. Marriage

When the testator of a will <u>marries</u> after writing a will, the law requires a change in the distribution of property, whether the testator changes the will or not. Spouses have, by statute, the right to elect either that which has been given them in their spouse's will or a defined fraction of the deceased spouse's estate. That defined fraction is either one-third or one-half, depending on the state involved and the number of children of the marriage. The right to elect against the will, that is to take a fraction of the estate rather than that which is given by will, also may be taken if a spouse writes a will while married and doesn't provide for the spouse. In effect, this precludes a spouse from disinheriting, or not leaving a sufficient part of an estate to the other spouse. All states allow great freedom to leave or not leave an estate to anyone a testator desires, but states feel a need to protect spouses with the statutory right of election. Testators may choose not to leave any part of an estate to their children, parents, or other relatives, but a spouse will receive the required share of the estate, even if the testator specifically states that he does not want this to happen. The one instance where a spouse will not receive the elective share is when a valid prenuptial agreement includes the renouncing, or giving up, of the spousal right of election.

5. Divorce

When the testator of a will <u>divorces</u>, then that portion of the will which provides for a portion of the estate to be passed to the spouse will be revoked. Suppose a will called for one-half of an estate to go to a wife, and the remaining one-half to be equally divided between the two children of the marriage. If the couple divorced and then the testator died, the now-former wife would receive nothing and the children would divide the entire estate equally. The law presumes that the testator would not want to leave the ex-spouse any part of the estate. Divorce also ends the spousal right of election discussed in the previous section. The law also treats an annulment the same way it treats a divorce for the purposes of wills. If a testator actually wants to leave a portion of the estate to an ex-spouse, then the will must be redone or amended to specifically provide for this to happen.

6. After-Born Children

After-born children are those children born after a will has been written. The law presumes that after-born children are entitled to a portion of the estate, if it seems as though the testator would have provided for them. The most common demonstration that the testator wanted to provide for an after-born child is a will in which the children living at the time the will was written are provided for in an equitable manner. Let us say that the testator gave equal shares to each of his three children born prior to the writing of the will. If the testator has two after-born children, then it will presume they are to share in the estate as well. In many states, the share for after-born children is that which they would have received had there been no will.

The next case illustrates the types of disputes that wills may precipitate.

✲ ✲ ✲

WILLS CASE #8-3

Matter of Hedges
473 N.Y.S.2d 529 (1984)

BY THE COURT. In a contested probate proceeding, proponents and the Presbyterian Church Society of Bridgehampton appeal from stated portions of a decree of the Surrogate's Court, Suffolk County, dated March 14,

1983, which, (1) upon a jury verdict, denied probate of a certain codicil signed by the testatrix on March 14, 1978....

On August 24, 1977, on the eve of her 102d birthday, Nellie Hedges executed a Last Will and Testament in which she bequeathed her residence to her long-time friend Halsey Brower. Less than seven months later, on March 14, 1978, she signed a codicil to the will, revoking this bequest and leaving the residence to her church, the Presbyterian Church Society of Bridgehampton. After Hedges's death on June 9, 1981, Louise Hildreth and Frederick Hagerman, named as executors, offered the will and codicil for probate. Brower filed objections to the probate of the codicil, alleging lack of due execution, lack of testamentary capacity and undue influence. A jury trial was held and the jury found in favor of the objectant on each of the stated grounds.

With respect to the issue of due execution, the jury determined that the testatrix did not "declare" the instrument to be her codicil. At trial, however, each of the three subscribing witnesses to the codicil, one of whom was the testatrix' attorney, testified that the testatrix read the document, acknowledged it to be her codicil, and signed it, and that each of them affixed his or her signature to the instrument.... [T]here is no room for doubt that the statutory requirement of declaration was complied with here.

The jury's determination that the testatrix did not possess the necessary testamentary capacity at the time she executed the codicil is also unsupported by the record.... No evidence was offered, however, to contradict the testimony of the subscribing witnesses which established at the time the codicil was executed the testatrix was of sound mind and capable of understanding the nature of her action. It has long been recognized that old age, physical weakness and senile dementia are not necessarily inconsistent with testamentary capacity as long as the testatrix was acting rationally and intelligently at the time the codicil was prepared and executed....

Finally, the jury found that the execution of the codicil was procured by the undue influence of the proponents, the subscribing witnesses, the testatrix's attorney (also a subscribing witness) and/or the pastor of the devisee church. At the outset, we note that the record is completely devoid of any evidence as to improper conduct...

In light of the foregoing, the Surrogate should have directed a verdict for proponents on all three issues, and it was error for him not to grant their motion to set aside the verdict.

✳ ✳ ✳

LEGAL LIGHT

A former chief justice of the Supreme Court, Warren Burger, left a self-written (holographic) will. The document had only 176 words and left his entire estate to his two children. He failed, however, to express any powers for his executors, and made no plan or provisions for estate taxes. These failings cost his estate thousands of dollars.

✳ ✳ ✳

D. INTESTACY STATUTES

If an individual dies without a will, then he or she is said to have died intestate. Provisions for the passing on of the deceased's property have been made in each of the states by means of an intestacy statute, or a law that describes the distribution of property of owners who die without a will. As the lines for descent are established by statute in each of the states, there are variations in that order. However, all the states provide for spouses and children to receive a share or shares of the estate of an intestate. Only if no spouse or child is alive will the state look for other individuals to receive property. In most states, if no spouse or child remains to take the estate, then the possessions will pass, in order, to the deceased's lineal descendants. Lineal descendants include grandchildren, siblings, and parents. In most states, the order of descent has self-limiting features. That is, when a level of descendants is reached where a person is still living, the distribution of property will go only to that level. For example, Willie dies intestate, at the age of ninety. He has outlived his spouse, and had one child. His child predeceased him by five years. In the state in which Willie lives, if no spouse or child survives, grandchildren and then siblings are next in line. Willie has two grandchildren, who are still living, and one younger brother, who is also still alive. As the grandchildren are next in line, they would take the possessions, even though his brother still remains; when a level of descent has existing heirs, the property is distributed in that level. If no lineal descendants survive the deceased, then the intestacy statutes distribute the property to collateral descendants. Collateral descendants include cousins, aunts, uncles, nieces, and nephews.

If no lineal descendants or collateral descendants of intestate decedents remain, then property ownership will be taken by the state, by virtue of statute. This reversion to the state is called an escheat. The concept of escheat comes to us from the feudal law, when property that had no descendant to own it reverted to the feudal lord.

E. TRUSTS

A trust is an arrangement where the legal rights of ownership of property are divided into two parts and the two parts are given to two different persons. One of the persons, the trustee, has the control of the property, and that person manages the property held in trust for the benefit of the second party, the beneficiary of the trust. If, for example, Charles dies and leaves his money to his minor grandson in trust, then the trustee named in the will would manage the money and the grandson would receive the profits.

F. ESTATE ADMINISTRATION

The surrogate or probate courts do not independently gather the assets of the deceased and distribute them to the beneficiaries or heirs. Those tasks of <u>estate administration</u> or management of the assets fall to the representative of the deceased. That representative is an executor, in the case of a person who dies testate, or an administrator, in the case of a person who dies intestate.

Executors are named in the will by the testator to manage the distribution of the property in the estate.

Administrators are appointed by the court to do those tasks for individuals who die intestate. While the courts have the ultimate authority over the estate, and the estate administrator or executor must report to the court, it is the administrator or executor that carries out the distribution of the property. To make sure that the estate is handled in an honest and efficient fashion by the executor or administrator, most states require that a bond, or form of insurance, be obtained by the estate executor prior to beginning work on the estate.

The first duty of both executors and administrators is to gather or collect the assets of the estate. This includes determining the value of the assets, often by having them professionally appraised. Next, the estate administrator must pay all the creditors of the deceased and his estate. These payments include the bills of the deceased and the taxes due on the estate itself. Then the estate administrator must distribute the assets, as required by either the will or by the intestate succession statute. Lastly, the executor or administrator must give to the court a full accounting of the distribution.

Our last will case deals with the fees available to executors.

✩ ✩ ✩

WILLS CASE #8-4

Will of Grant
600 N.Y.S.2d 423 (1993)

ROTH, SURROGATE.   The executors of the estate of Delaney Thorn Grant seek an advance payment of their commissions computed in accordance with the will rather than pursuant to (statute). Implicit in the application is whether a clause determining the compensation of the fiduciary is contrary to public policy.

By the express terms of his will, Mr. Grant provided that his executors, the Bank of New York and Donald E. McNicol, shall be allowed commissions on specifically bequeathed personal property and upon assets passing outside the will but comprising part of his gross taxable estate. Thus the will departs from the statutory scheme only with respect to the nature of the assets considered commissionable. If the computation were to be made only on the assets traditionally included, the executors would be entitled to commissions on assets of only $20,000. Under the specific provisions of Mr. Grant's will, his executors are entitled to commissions on assets of $2.4 million.

A cornerstone of the law of wills is respect for the wishes of the testator. He or she has the undisputed right to direct the devolution of his or her property, a right which is embodied in the statutory provisions governing testamentary dispositions. It follows that the testator may attach conditions to his or her bequests and that these conditions will be honored, as long as compliance does not violate public policy.

Finally, it is observed that the statutory commissions are, of necessity, merely estimates of appropriate compensation. Such commissions are not necessarily fair in every case, but the law has tried to achieve overall fairness in the majority of cases....

Mr. Grant, in his will, recognized this reality. Absent fraud or undue influence, no public policy consideration justifies judicial interference with a testator's freedom to decide how he wishes to compensate his fiduciaries. A contrary rule would deprive testators of the right to obtain fiduciaries if their choice.

✲ ✲ ✲

G. ESTATE TAXES

The federal government assesses a tax on the taxable estate of a deceased. The tax is levied on the gross estate, less the debts of the deceased and less the costs of administration of the estate. These taxes are paid by the executor or the administrator prior to the distribution of the estate, and do not depend on the type of gift or the identity of the recipient. However, gifts to a surviving spouse have some exemptions built into the federal tax code.

State inheritance taxes are imposed by many states. State inheritance tax, as opposed to the federal tax, is dependent not only on the size of the estate but on the relationship of the beneficiary or heir to the deceased. The surviving spouse and children of the deceased have the largest exemptions from the state tax, as well as having the lowest rate on that part of the estate upon which they must pay taxes. The rates are higher for other recipients, and the exemptions for other recipients are much lower.

✲ ✲ ✲

CHAPTER EIGHT
KEY TERMS

Administrator
Beneficiary
Bequest
Devise
Executor
Heir
Holographic Will
Intestate
Nuncupative Will
Trust Beneficiary
Trust
Trustee

✫ ✫ ✫

CHAPTER SUMMARY

Wills are the legally recognized statements of how an individual's property is to be passed after one's death. States recognize three basic types of wills. The first are nuncupative wills. These are oral deathbed statements as to how property is to be passed. These wills are not valid as to real property, only personal property. The second type is holographic wills. These are wills written entirely in the handwriting of the person who is passing on their property. The last type is formal written wills. These are the documents that one obtains from a lawyer and are the wills with which we are most familiar.

Property may be passed in wills in three ways. First, one may pass a specific item to a specific person through a specific bequest. Second, one may pass fungible items to a particular person through a general bequest. Third, after the specific bequests and general bequests are distributed, the balance of the estate may be passed in a residual bequest.

Wills may be revoked, in whole or part, by the testator by destroying the will, by writing a new will, or by a codicil. The law revokes wills, in whole or part, when the testator marries, divorces, or has after-born children.

Individuals who die without a will are said to have dies intestate. Each state has an intestacy statute that describes how property is to be passed from decedents who die intestate. If no relative can be found, then the property escheats to the state.

✲ ✲ ✲

THINK AND WRITE

1. What are the three will types?
2. Distinguish between heirs and beneficiaries.
3. Describe a trust.
4. What types of bequests can be made in a formal written will?
5. A husband leaves his estate to "his wife" in his will, not using her name. When he dies, he is married to a different woman than the one he was married to when he made the will. Suggest what could happen and why.

✲ ✲ ✲

PROJECTS

1. Draft (or obtain from a form book) an appropriate financial questionnaire for clients who come to your office for a will.

2. Create your own family tree. If you die intestate, who would inherit your property? Who would be next in line? And next?
3. What factors would determine whether a client should create a testamentary or *inter vivos* trust.
4. What are the tax rates and tax exemptions currently in place at the federal level and in your state?
5. Contact local paralegals. What are the responsibilities that paralegals have in the area of estates and estate administration?

ETHICAL QUESTIONS

1. In a number of states, children born out of wedlock are the heirs, for the purposes of intestacy, of their mother but not their father if he has not acknowledged them, or if paternity has not been established. Is this stance ethically appropriate?
2. Your aged cousin has told you she plans to destroy her will in order to disinherit the beneficiaries in this will. Immediately upon telling you, she has a heart attack and dies. Her will is in her hand. Should you destroy it?

WEBSITES

1. Information regarding wills: http://www.nolo.com/lawcenter/ency/index.cfm/ep_ency.html
2. Site links for estate planning: http://www.estateplanninglinks.com

3. American Bar Association site concerning wills and estate plans: http://www.abanet.org/rppt/public/home.html/#estateplanning
4. Site of the *Journal of Wealth Management for Estate Planning Professionals*: http://www.trustsandestates.com

CHAPTER NINE

CRIMINAL LAW

Criminal law regulates behaviors that are offensive to the society as a whole. Most wrongful behavior is governed by private law, which covers that behavior that injures another individual; some behavior, though, is so harmful that it is deemed threatening and harmful to society and is regulated by criminal law. Criminal law in America is founded on the principle that without a law, there can be no crime. That is, we rely on our legislative bodies to establish criminal codes that outline precisely those acts for which society will exact punishment. The American Law Institute, in 1956, drafted and published the *Model Penal Code and Commentaries*, which, in its original and updated forms, has served as a standard example for the criminal codes of the various states. However, every state is free to adapt this model, and there are many variations in the state codes. Each state, however, has drawn heavily from this model, which, of course, draws heavily upon our English Common Law roots.

The criminal statutes provide for laws that have two major components. The laws contain an actus reus and a mens rea for the particular crime detailed.

✲ ✲ ✲

CRIMINAL LAW CASE #9-1

People v. Dowd
530 N.Y.S.2d 733 (1988)

COOPERMAN, J. Defendant stands convicted after a jury trial of Robbery in the First Degree, Robbery in the Second Degree, Attempted Robbery in the First Degree, and Attempted Robbery in the Second Degree.

The court imposed the minimum sentence authorized by law...and stayed the execution thereof upon defendant's application (of appeal). The Court recognizes that the legislature has latitude in determining which ills of society require criminal sanctions, and in imposing, as it reasonably views them, punishments, and even mandatory ones, appropriate to each....

However, notwithstanding the power of the Legislature to make laws, it is inherent in the judicial branch of government to determine whether the Legislature has contravened a constitutional problem. The court in Weems said, in that respect and for that purpose "the legislative power is brought to the judgment of a power superior to it for an instant."...

Accordingly, defendant's motion to set aside his sentence as a violation of his constitutional right against cruel and unusual punishment is granted without opposition.

✵ ✵ ✵

A. ACTUS REUS

The <u>actus reus</u> is the act or action that is prohibited by the law. Each crime contains a particular overt act that is an integral part of the law. The law has long felt that some physical element was a necessary part of the crime.

Thoughts cannot constitute the actus reus of a crime, as thoughts can do no harm and may simply be one's fantasy. Also, thoughts are difficult to prove and, as the criminal law require proof beyond a reasonable doubt, thoughts would be unprovable to this level. This level of proof of an action helps to prevent abuses by the state of the power and authority of the state. The actus reus needs to be a demonstrable prohibited act that has consequences that society finds unacceptable for the public good and order.

Here is a case that concerns actus reus of crimes.

✲ ✲ ✲

CASE #9-2 Actus Reus

UNITED STATES v. JONES

No. CR. 02-527 June 10, 2003

PADOVA, J. *1 Defendant Brandon Jones was convicted by a jury on one count of carjacking, in violation of 18 U.S.C. § 2119, on February 14, 2003. At the end of the Government's case-in-chief, Defendant moved for judgment of acquittal before submission to the jury under Federal Rule of Criminal Procedure 29(a). The Court reserved decision on the Motion at the time, pursuant to Federal Rule of Criminal Procedure 29(b). Defendant has now renewed that Motion and has filed a similar motion under Federal Rule of Criminal Procedure 29(c) for Judgment of Acquittal after jury discharge. For the reasons that follow, the Court denies both Motions in all respects.

I. Background

Shortly after midnight on April 29, 2002, Defendant carjacked Lorena Edwards, a lone woman, at the Coastal Gas Station located at the corner of Stenton Avenue and Tulpehocken Street in Philadelphia. The victim unlocked her green 1996 Jeep Cherokee with her remote and entered it through her driver's side door after she returned from the gas station where she purchased cigarettes. At the same time, Defendant entered her vehicle through the passenger-side door. He immediately told the victim, "I have a gun, don't look around, just drive." (N.T. 2/10/2003 at 38.) Defendant had his hand shoved in the side of his puffy jacket, which was bulging towards her, and motioned as if he were holding a gun. (N.T. 2/10/2003 at 39.) The victim testified that she did not see a gun, but that she followed Defendant's demands. When the victim reached to put her seatbelt on, Defendant grilled her as to what she was doing and told her, "Don't worry about your seatbelt, just drive." (N.T. 2/10/2003 at 38.)

Defendant forced the victim to drive him to an ATM machine at Cedarbrook Mall, located at the corners of Cheltenham Avenue and Easton Road in Wyncote, just across the northern border with Philadelphia. They arrived at the ATM machine at approximately 12:30 a.m. Throughout the victim's forced ride with Defendant, he repeatedly told her in a loud and threatening manner that he would shoot her if she looked at him. (N.T. 2/10/2003 at 43, 47.) Defendant also stole $6.00 from the victim's person and $1.00 from her purse. After rifling through her car and purse, he also took her house keys, identifying information, including her daughter's social security card, and some cigarettes.

Defendant told the victim to park the vehicle by the ATM machine and then ordered her to withdraw money from the machine. Defendant also threatened her, "If you try to run or if you try to signal for help I'm going to run you down." (N.T. 2/10/2003 at 46, 47.) The victim testified that she thought the car was still running when she went to the ATM machine to attempt to withdraw money. (N.T. 2/11/2003 at 65-66.) She testified that she did not run while at the ATM machine because she "didn't think [she] could outrun a bullet...or the vehicle." (N.T. 2/11/2003 at 38.) She testified that during the drive, Defendant repeatedly threatened to shoot her, so that when she was at the ATM machine, she was "extremely scared" and kept looking over her shoulder to see what

Defendant was doing or whether "he was moving the car or training the gun on me." (N.T. 2/10/2003 at 47.) The victim accessed through the ATM machine a bank account oat Sovereign Bank which had almost no funds. She reported her lack of success to Defendant who ordered her back into the vehicle. At this point, Defendant had possession of her purse, including her house keys and grilled her as to which door each key opened. She also testified that Defendant moved to the driver's side of the vehicle after she returned from the ATM and showed him the receipt that showed she had no money. (N.T. 2/11/2003 at 38.)

Defendant eventually ordered the victim to get out of her car and told her to "Go in the back door, your husband is home. Walk home normal." (N.T. 2/10/2003 at 50.) He took social security cards, including her daughter's, which he identified as such, and told her, "I know who you are and I know where you're at." (N.T. 2/10/2003 at 49-50.) He again threatened her, "Don't call the police, don't flag down a car. If you do, I'm going to shoot you; I'm going to run you down. I know where you're at, I'm going to come to your house, there's gonna be an upset." (N.T. 2/10/2003 at 54.) Defendant then abandoned the victim in the parking lot near the ATM machine and drove away in her vehicle.

*2 After being carjacked, the victim ran to the nearby residence of the mother of her daughter's friend and reported the incident to the police. Philadelphia Police Officer William Helsel responded, at which point the victim described the defendant and her stolen vehicle. At about 12:50 a.m. the police issued a bulletin about the carjacking. At about 1:30 a.m., about an hour after Defendant left the victim in the parking lot near the ATM machine, Philadelphia Police Sergeant Shawn Wilson, after having heard the police bulletin, spotted Defendant driving the victim's vehicle on Wister Avenue in Philadelphia. This location is near both the scene of the carjacking and Defendant's home. When Sergeant Wilson activated the dome lights of his police cruiser, Defendant fled, disregarding traffic lights and stop signs, and led Sergeant Wilson on a high-speed chase for more than two miles. Defendant lost control of the victim's vehicle at Wadsworth and Mansfield Street I Philadelphia, crashing it, flipping it several times, and totaling it. Sergeant Wilson then apprehended and arrested Defendant.

During Defendant's arrest, Sergeant Wilson recovered from Defendant's person some of the items that Defendant had stolen from the victim, including her car keys, her daughter's social security card, money, and her cigarettes. He did not recover a gun. The victim testified that other items from her vehicle, including a camera and tool kit, were never recovered. (N.T. 2/10/2003 at 108-09.)

✲ ✲ ✲

*3 Defendant was convicted of carjacking as charged in Count 1 of the Indictment. In order to sustain hits burden of proof of the crime of carjacking, the Government had to prove that Defendant: (1) with intent to cause death or serious bodily harm; (2) took a motor vehicle; (3) that had been transported, shipped or received in interstate or foreign commerce; (4) from the person or presence of another; (5) by force and violence or intimidation. <u>United States v. Applewhaite</u>, 195 F.3d 679, 684-85 (3d Cir.1999) (citing <u>United States v. Lake</u>, 150 F.3d 269, 272 (3d Cir.1998)); 18 U.S.C. § 2119.

✲ ✲ ✲

Defendant argues that there is insufficient evidence to show conditional intent to use the vehicle as a weapon because the threat to run the victim down had no nexus to the "taking" of the vehicle, which he argues occurred at the moment he entered the victim's passenger door and commandeered her to drive. He argues that the statement

"I'm going to run you down" was not uttered until after the "taking," when the victim was about to retrieve money from the ATM machine. The Court finds that the "taking" did not occur only at the moment Defendant entered the victim's vehicle, but occurred during the entire carjacking incident under the facts in this case. In so holding, the Court finds persuasive the reasoning in United States v. Hicks, 103 F.3d, 843-44 (9th Cir.1996) and the concurring opinion in United States v. Lebron-Cepeda, No.01-1650, No.00-2293, 2003 U.S. App. LEXIS 6052, at *28-29 (1st Cir. Mar.31.2003).

In Hicks, the defendants confronted one of the two carjacking victims with a gun, ordered the victims out of the car, locked them in the trunk of the car, drove to another site, released the victims from the trunk and separated them, beat the male victim to death, left his body in a pile of gravel, repeatedly raped the female victim, forced her back into the trunk, hit her in the head with a large piece of asphalt, left her on the roadside, and then drove away in the vehicle, eventually abandoning it. 103 F.3d at 839-40. One defendant argued that the evidence about the murder, rape and assault was improperly admitted because it was not relevant to the carjacking. Id. at 842-43. The court did not examine the conditional intent issue, but held that "the vehicle was not taken from the person or presence of both victims until [the female victim] was dumped along the side of the road. [FN3]" Id. at 843. The court reasoned:

✲ ✲ ✲

[FN4] The deeds are entirely committed in the usually brief and frequently instantaneous period of time that it takes to initiate and complete the **actus reus**: the demand (in the case of an attempted carjacking) or the taking (in the case of a successful carjacking) of the subject vehicle. They are, in other words, crimes in which the typical **actus**

reus is aptly thought to occur at a "moment" in time and not over a period of time.

✧ ✧ ✧

Id. at 31. The carjacking in <u>Holloway</u> was of that nature, and thus, reasoned Judge Howard:

> It is not surprising that the <u>Holloway</u> majority opinion would use the phrase "the moment the defendant demanded or took control over the driver's automobile" to describe the point in time at which the fact finder should assess the mens rea of defendants who have committed this kind of carjacking. After all, the defendant's mens rea is to be measured when he commits the **actus rea.**

Id. at 31-32 (citing 18 U.S.C § 2119 (stating that the proscribed taking or attempted taking must be committed "with" the specified intent) and <u>Holloway</u>, 526 U.S. at 8 ("The statute's mens rea component thus modifies the action of 'taking' the motor vehicle.")). Judge Howard continued:

> [I] do not find anything in <u>Holloway </u>to suggest that the majority in that case intended the phrase also to have prescriptive significance in those carjacking cases where the defendant kidnaps the vehicle's occupants and thus commits the **actus reus** not in a 'moment' but rather over an extended period of time.

Id. at 32 (citing <u>Ramirez-Burgos</u>, 313 F.3d at 30 n.9; other citations omitted). Judge Howard noted that, in <u>Holloway</u>, "there was no issue as to when the assailant's intent is properly measured because only one possibility presented itself under the case facts: the 'moment' at which the vehicle was commandeered (which was the moment at which the **actus reus** was concluded)". *Id.* at 33. <u>Holloway</u>

did not address the temporal limits of a carjacking. *Id.* (citing Ramirez-Burgos, 313 F.3d at 30 n. 9). Judge Howard concluded: "There is [n]o reason to suppose that, in those cases where the carjacking occurs over a period of time, Holloway circumscribes the factfinder's entitlement to assess appellants' mens rea at any point during the commission of the **actus reus**." *Id.* at 34. This logical reading of Holloway permits sustaining convictions where the jury could have found that, at some point in time, defendants engage in conduct constituting part of the **actus reus** proscribed by 18 U.S.C. § 2119 with the specified mens rea. *Id.* at 35. In the instant case, to demand that the intent exist only at the first moment Defendant commandeered the car is illogical since he commandeered the car for more than twenty minutes, and the victim could have resisted at any time during such commandeering.

ORDER

AND NOW, this 10th day of June 2003, upon consideration of Defendant's Motion for Judgment of Acquittal made at trial pursuant to Federal Rule of Criminal Procedure 29(a) and Motion for Judgment of Acquittal pursuant to Federal Rule of Criminal Procedure 29(a) and Motion for Judgment of Acquittal pursuant to Federal Rule of Criminal Procedure 29(c) (Doc. No. 73), all related responses and pleadings thereto, and the hearing held before the Court on June 4, 2003, IT IS HEREBY ORDERED that the Motions are DENIED.

2003 WL 21362798 (E.D.Pa.)

☆ ☆ ☆

B. MENS REA

The mens rea is the culpable state of mind required by the statute. The law reflects the societal decision that one must have decided to commit the crime and distinguishes that decision and consequent action from those accidents that may have caused damage. The criminal must have the intent to commit a crime in order to satisfy the mens rea portion of the criminal statute.

One of four levels of legal intent has been used in most states' statutes for the crimes defined in the code. The first of the four possible intents is purposely causing a specific result. If, for instance, Charles bought a gun in order to kill Peter, and then kills Peter with the gun, Charles has purposely killed Peter. Purposely committing an act means that you intend to accomplish a specific result. The second level of criminal intent is called knowingly, which means that one knows that a specific act will almost certainly bring about a specific result, but without specifically intending that result. If, for example, you blow up your professor's office in order to destroy your test results, you did not specifically intend to harm your professor. You did know, however, that the teacher would be in his office, and should know that the person could be harmed or killed. The third level of wrongful state of mind is recklessness. To act with recklessness means to know that a substantial and unjustifiable risk exists when you commit a particular act, and the act might cause a particular harm, even if the harm isn't specifically intended. If you drive your car at a speed of 80 miles per hour through a crowded city, you might not intend to harm anyone, but you have acted recklessly, and when you do hit a pedestrian, you knew that there was a great risk of this happening. The fourth intent that the law prescribes for some crimes is called negligence. To act negligently is to thoughtlessly or carelessly create a significant, unjustifiable risk, without realizing that the risk has been created, but such that a reasonable person would have known that the risk would create a harm. If, for instance, you toss a lighted cigarette out your car window and cause a forest fire, you have probably satisfied the requirement for criminal negligence. Although you did not intend the result, or even to cause any harm, you should have known that the act could do damage.

One of these four levels of criminal intent makes up each criminal statute at either the state or federal level of criminal code. Those crimes that are the most serious have the intent of "purposely" as the requisite mens rea. The severity of the crime lessens with "knowingly," lessens further with "recklessly," and is at it its lowest point with "negligently." The severity of the punishment decreases with the severity of the crime.

Here is a case that deals with the criminal intent.

✫ ✫ ✫

CASE #9-3 Mens Rea

SHAWN v. (ANONYMOUS)
2004 WL 201690 (N.Y.A.D. 2 Dept.)

MYRIAM J. ALTMAN, J.P., GABRIEL M. KRAUSMAN, STEPHEN G. CRANE, and BARRY A. COZIER, JJ.

*1 In a juvenile delinquency proceeding pursuant to Family Court Act article 3, the appeals are from (1) a fact-finding order of the Family Court, Queens County (Lubow, J.), dated March 19, 2003, made after a hearing, finding that the appellant committed acts which, if committed by an adult, would have constituted the crimes of robbery in the second degree, grand larceny in the fourth degree, and criminal possession of stolen property in the fifth degree, and (2) an order of disposition of the same court dated May 7, 2003, which, upon the fact-finding order, adjudicated the appellant to be a juvenile delinquent and, inter alia, placed him on probation for a period of 12 months.

ORDERED that the appeal from the fact-finding order is dismissed, without costs or disbursements, as that order was superseded by the order of disposition; and it is further,

ORDERED that the order of disposition is reversed, on the law, without costs or disbursements, the fact-finding order is vacated, and the proceeding is dismissed.

The appellant contends that the evidence was legally insufficient to establish, beyond a reasonable doubt, that he intended to deprive the complainant of her property. We agree.

[1] The complainant testified that on May 17, 2001, she was approached by Erika W., Fatima T., and the appellant upon exiting a city bus. While Fatima held the complainant's hands, Erika punched her in the stomach, and Fatima threw the complainant on her side. The appellant, meanwhile, was standing to the complainant's side, laughing and "egging Erika on" to take the complainant's bookbag and throw it in a nearby ditch, which was approximately three-feet deep and protected by a gate the height of the complainant's waist. Erika then removed the complainant's bookbag and eyeglasses from her person, placed the glasses inside the bookbag, and put the bookbag in the ditch. Erika, Fatima, and the appellant then ran away. The complainant could still see her bookbag in the ditch after the appellant and the others had left, but made no immediate attempt to retrieve it because the ditch was muddy and she did not want to fall in. Instead, the complainant ran to her home, which was about a block away. Later that day, the complainant's bookbag was left with the security guard of her apartment building by a girl named Denia.

Viewing the evidence in the light most favorable to the presentment agency (cf. People v. Contes, 60 N.Y.2d 620, 467 N.Y.S.2d 349, 454 N.E.2d 932), we find that it was legally insufficient to establish that the appellant had the requisite intent to steal the complainant's bookbag and eyeglasses (see People v. Parker, 96 A.D.2d 1063, 1065, 466 N.Y.S.2d 700).

The appellant cannot be found to have committed acts which, if committed by an adult, would have constituted the crimes of robbery in the second degree, grand larceny in the fourth degree, and criminal possession of stolen property in the fifth degree, unless the presentment agency established, beyond a reasonable doubt, that the complainant's bookbag and eyeglasses were in fact stolen (see Penal Law §§ 155.05, 155.30[5], 160.00, 160.10, 165.40). Pursuant to Penal Law § 155.05(1), "[a] person steals property and commits larceny when, with *intent to deprive* another of property [that person] wrongfully takes, obtains or withholds such property from an owner thereof" (emphasis supplied). In turn, to "deprive" another of property means, inter alia, "to dispose of the property in such manner or under such circumstances as to render it *unlikely* that an owner will recover such property" (Penal Law § 155.00[3][6] [emphasis supplied]).

[2] Here, there was no evidence that Erika, Fatima, and the appellant intended to dispose of the book bag and the eyeglasses in such a manner as to make it unlikely that the complainant would recover them. At most, they intended to cause the temporary loss of the complainant's property "in an attempt to humiliate and inconvenience [her]" (People v. Parker, supra; see People v. Garland, 125 A.D.2d 328, 329, 508 N.Y.S.2d 605). The **mens rea** element of larceny is simply not satisfied by an intent to temporarily take property without the owner's permission (see People v. Jennings, 69 N.Y.2d 103, 119, 512 N.Y.S.2d 652, 504 N.E.2d 1079). Absent legally sufficient evidence of the appellant's larcenous intent, the order of disposition must be reversed, the fact-finding order vacated, and the petition dismissed.

In light of our determination, we need not address the appellant's remaining contentions.

✳ ✳ ✳

C. CATEGORIES OF CRIMES

States categorize crimes on their level of severity, with most states having three levels of crimes. These three levels are <u>felonies</u>, <u>misdemeanors</u>, and <u>infractions</u>.

Felonies are those most serious of crimes and are punishable either by death or by imprisonment for one year or longer. Felonies may be referred to as either capital crimes, those punishable by death, or noncapital crimes, those punishable by prison only. Many states have further refined the classification of felonies into class groupings.

Misdemeanors are crimes in which the penalty is either a fine or imprisonment for less than one year or both. Misdemeanors are lesser degree crimes and, as such, have less severe penalties attached.

Infractions, sometimes called violations, are punishable only by fines. Infractions do not carry the sense of moral wrong that felonies and misdemeanors carry. Disturbing the peace is one example of an infraction in most states.

LEGAL LIGHT

The average elapsed time from sentencing to execution in a capital case is ten years and ten months. The average elapsed time an innocent inmate spends on death row before being freed is seven years and six months.

D. CONSTITUTIONAL GUARANTEES

Our county's Founding Fathers considered the position of the accused criminal with great care in writing the U.S. Constitution. In evaluating the potential for abuse of the criminal process by the state to coerce individuals, and when considering the great disparity between the resources of the accused and the resources of the state, the writers of the Constitution included a variety of protections to the accused criminal to insure that the accused would benefit from our basic criminal presumption that we are innocent until proved guilty in a court of law. These Constitutional guarantees are not provided to any plaintiff or defendant in the civil law.

Double jeopardy is prohibited by the Fifth Amendment, and precludes an individual from being tried more than once for the same crime. Without such a guarantee, the number of prosecutions of an individual by the state could be endless. Given the disparate resources between the state and the defendant, the need to protect individuals from this potential abuse is apparent.

The Fourth Amendment protects citizens from unreasonable searches and seizures. Further, it requires that probable cause be present prior to a court issuing an order for a search or seizure of a person or thing. The potential for police abuse is no more threatening than in their exercise of searches and arrests. To have one's home invaded, without justification, is certainly an invasion of our right to privacy, and borders on the type of behavior commonly used in police states to insure a passive and uninvolved population.

The Sixth Amendment guarantees the accused the right to the assistance of counsel for his defense. Given the complexities of the legal system, and the disparity between the state and the accused, this right is an important part of the Constitutional guarantees afforded the defendant. This counsel must be effective, but may be refused by individuals who wish to represent themselves.

✵ ✵ ✵

CASE #9-4 RIGHT TO COUNSEL

SCOTT v. GREINER
2004 WL 180045 (E.D.N.Y.)

MEMORANDUM AND ORDER
GLEESON, J.

*1 Clarence Scott petitions for a writ of habeas corpus, challenging his convictions in state court for criminal possession of crack cocaine. On January 23, 2004, I held oral argument, in which Scott participated by telephone conference. The petition is denied for the reasons set forth below.

BACKGROUND

The People's evidence at trial established that, at around 12:20 a.m. on January 1, 1998, in the vicinity of South Road, Jamaica Queens, three plain-clothed police officers patrolling the area in an unmarked car heard gunshots at a nearby housing project. While investigating this area, they observed Scott in a courtyard next to the housing project. When one of the officers exited the car to ask Scott if he could speak with him (to ascertain whether or not he could provide any information about the gunshots), Scott ran away from the officer. While in flight, he discarded a brown bag. This brown bag contained 333 vials of crack cocaine. Scott testified that he went out shortly before midnight to buy wine. He further testified that he ran because he thought he was being accosted by a man with a gun, and he never possessed or dropped any bag filled with drugs.

Scott was charged with criminal possession of a controlled substance in the first and third degrees. After deliberations, the jury convicted him of both offenses. Scott was sentenced to concurrent prison terms of from fifteen years to life and from four and a half to nine years imprisonment. The judgment of conviction was entered on February 18, 1999.

In January of 1999, Scott, through counsel, appealed his conviction to the Appellate Division. Appellate counsel claimed that Scott's conviction could not be sustained because his trial counsel was ineffective for the following reasons: (a) he elicited and opened the door to prior convictions, including one for drug possession, which had been excluded by the court's Sandoval [FN 1] ruling; (b) he failed to object to extensive irrelevant and prejudicial expert testimony about drug packaging; (c) he repeatedly had difficulty moving items into evidence; and (d) he delivered a bizarre summation that failed to address his criminal history. The Appellate Division rejected these arguments and affirmed Scott's conviction on June 26, 2000. *See* People v. Scott, 273 A.D.2d 488, 711 N.Y.S.2d 890 (2d Dep't 2000). It held that "the defendant received the effective assistance of counsel." *Id*. On August 4, 2000, the New York Court of Appeals denied Scott's application for leave to appeal his conviction. People v. Scott, 95 N.Y.2d 871, 715 N.Y.S.2d 226, 738 N.E.2d 374 (2000).

☆ ☆ ☆

On May 14, 2001, Scott, proceeding *pro se*, filed a petition for a writ of error coram nobis, alleging ineffective assistance of appellate counsel. In particular, he maintained that appellate counsel was deficient because she failed to argue that trial counsel was also ineffective based on his failure to properly request a Dunaway [FN2] hearing. The Appellate Division, Second Department, denied the writ on October 15, 2001, stating that Scott "has failed to establish that he was denied the effective assistance of appellate counsel." People v. Scott, 287 A.D.2d 583, 731 N.Y.S.2d 670 (2d Dep't 2001).

☆ ☆ ☆

*2 On December 18, 2001, Scott filed a *pro se* motion in the state Supreme Court to vacate his judgment of conviction pursuant to N.Y.Crim. Proc. Law § 440.10. He asserted that he was denied his right to effective assistance of trial counsel when counsel failed to accurately marshal facts in his omnibus motion seeking a *Dunaway* hearing to determine whether he was unlawfully seized, searched and arrested. The state Supreme Court rejected Scott's arguments as procedurally barred. *See* <u>People v. Scott</u>, Indict. No. N10218/98, slip. op. (N.Y. Sup.Ct., Queens County, January 2, 2002) ("Defendant's claim is procedurally barred since it is based upon matters in the record which could have been raised on direct appeal. In any event, defendant was afforded meaningful representation since counsel employed a trial strategy that any reasonably competent attorney might well have pursued.") (citations omitted).

✧ ✧ ✧

d. *The Summation*

Scott also objects to his counsel's summation as "bizarre" and as lacking in a recitation of his criminal history. (Pet. at 5(A).) In the appellate brief on direct appeal, his appellate counsel highlighted several problematic remarks in the summation, including the following: (1) the summation began with a quote from "The Night Before Christmas" (Tr. at 504-505); (2) the court admonished counsel for wearing Scott's jacket from the incident, despite repeated warnings not to "demonstrate" (Tr. at 507-08); and (3) counsel argued that the police should have tested the bag in which the crack was found for DNA evidence and relatedly remarked that "If you had a dress and you had semen on it" then you would test it, referring to Monica Lewinsky (Tr. at 518-520). (See App. Br. at 34-35.)

*8 I have reviewed defense counsel's summation. In addition to the problems recited by Scott's appellate counsel, the transcript reveals that defense counsel made some inappropriate state (referring to the location in question as a "ghetto"), and attempted to argue facts not testified to at trial. Furthermore, he repeatedly tried to explain the law to the jury, despite several warnings from the trial judge.

Despite this troublesome (and in some respects unprofessional) conduct, I cannot say that trial counsel was ineffective. First, he did elicit inconsistencies in the officers' testimony as to where the drug-filled bag was recovered. He also tried to undermine the officers' testimony by suggesting it was improbable. (See Tr. at 510-11 (arguing that officer's story that he went to walk alone in dark area where shots had been heard was not believable); Tr. at 513-14 (arguing that officers' testimony—that there was no one around except for Scott and no debris in the area except the bag of drugs—was not believable since it was a crowded city location and it was just after midnight on New Year's Eve).) Second, defense counsel pointed out that one of the officers at the scene never saw Scott throw anything to the ground, let alone a bag a drugs (Tr. at 516), while the other officer only saw him throw an object, not necessarily a paper bag, and lost sight of the bag at some point (Tr. at 520). In any event, due to the overwhelming evidence against Scott, which included eye-witness testimony from two witnesses, I cannot say that the result of the trial would have been different if trial counsel's inappropriate statements had not been made. More importantly, I cannot characterize as unreasonable the state court decision rejecting the claim. (See infra Part B. 1.e.) [FN 10]

✳ ✳ ✳

e. *Prejudice*

Even if trial counsel was constitutionally deficient in any of the above areas, Scott could not have suffered any prejudice. Thus, Scott cannot make out his ineffective assistance of trial counsel claim.

The evidence against Scott was overwhelming. According to the People's evidence at trial, three plain-clothes police officers on patrol in an unmarked car in Jamaica, Queens heard guns shots at approximately 12:20 a.m. on January 1, 1998. (Tr. 205-08, 255.) Once they began to canvas the area, they noticed Scott in the middle of a courtyard between the buildings of a housing project where the shots were heard. (Tr. at 209, 346, 351.) One of the officers exited the car to speak with Scott, who was about fifteen to twenty-five feet away from the police car. (Tr. at 209, 260-61, 336, 347.) At that point, he asked Scott, "Excuse me, sir, could I have a minute of your time? Police Officer." (Tr. at 211.) Scott immediately fled towards the street. (Tr. 211, 337.) The officer ran after him. (Tr. at 348, 352, 359-60.) Approximately fifteen seconds later, Scott threw a brown bag to the ground. (Tr. at 212-13, 338.) No one else was on the street at that time. (Tr. at 339-40.) About two minutes later, the officer caught Scott (Tr. at 213-14), while in the meantime, the other two officers who had been waiting in the police car drove around to meet them (Tr. at 214, 338, 363). The first officer told the other two that Scott had thrown a bag, and where it was, so that they could retrieve it, which they did. (Tr. at 214-16, 340.) Inside the bag they found 333 vials of crack cocaine. (Id.)

*9 In those circumstances, Scott cannot persuasively argue that, but for the challenged conduct of his trial counsel, the result of his trial would have been different. Therefore, I agree with the state court that counsel was not ineffective under Strickland.

2. Ineffective Assistance of Appellate Counsel

Scott contends that appellate counsel erred in not presenting an ineffective assistance of trial counsel claim based on trial counsel's failure to request a Dunaway hearing to challenge the allegedly unlawful seizure of Scott, and to seek suppression of the evidence discovered as a result of the seizure. (Pet. at 5(B).)

Although the Supreme Court formulated the *Strickland* test in the context of examining a claim of ineffective assistance of trial counsel, the same test applies to claims regarding the performance of appellate counsel. *See* Mayo v. Henderson, 13 F.3d 528, 533 (2d Cir.1994); Claudio v. Scully, 982 F.2d 798, 803 (2d Cir.1992). The second prong is different, however; the petitioner must establish that "there was a reasonable probability that [his] claim would have been successful before the [state's highest court]." Mayo, 13 F.3d at 534 (brackets in original, quotations and citations omitted).

It is well-established that, on appeal, counsel need not present every nonfrivolous argument that could be made. *See id.* at 533; *see also* Evitts v. Lucey, 469 U.S. 387, 394, 105 S.Ct. 830, 83 L.Ed.2d 821 (1985) (emphasizing that appellate counsel "need not advance *every* argument, regardless of merit, urged by the appellant.") (emphasis in original, citation omitted). Rather, counsel is expected to winnow out the weaker arguments and focus on the stronger ones. Jones v. Barnes, 463 U.S. 745, 751-52, 103 S.Ct. 3308, 77 L.Ed.2d 987 (1983). Reviewing courts should not employ hindsight to second- guess an appellate attorney's strategy choices. *See* Mayo, 13 F.3d at 533. A petitioner, however, may establish constitutionally inadequate performance if he shows that his appellate counsel omitted material and obvious issues while pursuing matters that were patently and significantly weaker. *Cf.* Jackson v. Leonardo, 162 F.3d 81, 85 (2d Cir.1998) ("[R]elief may be warranted when a decision by counsel cannot be justified as a result of some kind of plausible trial strategy.").

Under these standards, I find Scott's claim to be meritless. Appellate counsel filed a substantial brief in which she raised a claim of ineffective assistance of counsel based on four different grounds, as discussed in detail above. Tellingly, Scott now relies on these claims and his appellate counsel's brief to make out his ineffective assistance of trial counsel argument.

✵ ✵ ✵

3. *Ineffective Assistance of Pre-Trial Counsel*

Scott also challenges his conviction based on the failure of his pre-trial counsel to obtain a <u>Dunaway</u> hearing to suppress the physical evidence against him. Specifically, he claims that his pre-trial counsel was ineffective because he filed an omnibus motion that contained incorrect information—that when he was apprehended the police found drugs and drug paraphernalia on his person, when that was not true. Scott asserts that due to this misinformation, coupled with the motion's deficient factual statement, the state court denied a hearing. (Pet. At 6(D).) Respondent maintains that I cannot examine this claim because review is barred by an independent and adequate state procedural rule. (Resp't Aff. & Mem. Law Opp. Writ at 7.)

✵ ✵ ✵

CONCLUSION

For the foregoing reasons, the petition is denied. Because Scott has failed to make a substantial showing of a denial of a constitutional right, no certificate of appealability shall issue.
So Ordered.

✵ ✵ ✵

The Sixth Amendment also guarantees the accused the <u>right to a speedy trial</u>. This right is directed towards two goals. The first is to minimize the emotional distress and fear caused to the accused. The second is to help prevent the destruction or loss of evidence that may occur as time passes.

✵ ✵ ✵

CASE #9-5 Speedy Trial

UNITED STATES v. BENITEZ
2003 WL 23024543 (N.M.Ct.Crim.App.)

DORMAN, Chief Judge:

*1 A military judge, sitting as a general court-martial, convicted the appellant, contrary to his pleas, of the divers use and distribution of methamphetamine. The appellant's offenses violated Article 112a, Uniform Code of Military Justice, 10 U.S.C. § 912a. The adjudged and approved sentence includes confinement for 5 years, forfeiture of all pay and allowances, reduction to pay grade E-1, and a dishonorable discharge.

After carefully considering the record of trial, the appellant's assignments of error, and the Government's response, we conclude that corrective action is required. Following our corrective action, we conclude that the findings and sentence are correct in law and fact, and that no error remains that materially prejudiced the substantial rights of the appellant. Arts. 59(a) and 66(c), UCMJ.

Motion to Suppress

In his first assignment of error, the appellant asserts that the military judge erred when he denied a defense motion to suppress portions of the appellant's confession.

The specific concern on appeal is that the Government failed to provide evidence to corroborate the appellant's statements that he had used methamphetamine on two occasions in February 1999. In addition to challenging the confession by a motion to suppress, the appellant also made a motion for a finding of not guilty.

In its effort to corroborate the appellant's confession concerning his use of methamphetamine, during the motion phase the Government presented the statements of two individuals who had purchased methamphetamine from the appellant. In Appellate Exhibit XI, Lance Corporal Lanier stated that he went to the appellant's apartment in February 1999, along with Lance Corporal Arnold, and purchased $20.00 worth of methamphetamine from the appellant. He also stated that he purchased methamphetamine from the appellant in late April 1999. In Appellate Exhibit XII, Lance Corporal Arnold stated that in the first week of June 1999, he went to the appellant's apartment with Lance Corporal Lanier. Once there he gave Lanier $20.00 to purchase some methamphetamine from the appellant. Arnold did not see the transaction, nor did he see any drugs while in the appellant's apartment. After they left the house, Arnold asked Lanier if he had bought the methamphetamine. Arnold said that he had, and just before dropping Lanier off, he gave Lanier some crystal methamphetamine contained in a small clear zip lock bag. About a week later, Arnold made another purchase of methamphetamine from the accused, but this transaction was completed at a gas station off Interstate 805. No other evidence was presented on the motion.

During the Government's case-in-chief, Lanier and Arnold were called as witnesses. They testified consistent with their statements. Additionally, one of them testified that some individuals who use methamphetamine develop nosebleeds and some get nauseous from its use. Both witness testified as to the quantity of methamphetamine they had purchased as being a $20.00 amount. In his confession, the appellant stated that he had used methamphetamine twice in February 1999, and that he had used a "twenty" amount. Additionally, contemporaneously with his written confession, the appellant told the investigator that he only used it twice, because he had gotten a bloody nose and it had made him sick. This evidence was presented through the testimony of the Naval Criminal Investigative Service Special Agent who interrogated the appellant on 11 June 99.

☆ ☆ ☆

*4 The appellant also moved to dismiss, alleging a violation of his right to a **speedy trial** under Article 10, UCMJ. The Government and the appellant stipulated to a chronology concerning the appellant's pretrial confinement and pretrial processing of his case. Appellate Exhibit IX. Key dates—all in 1999—include the following: The appellant was placed in pretrial confinement on 11 June, and 4 days later he was advised that he was being held in pretrial confinement for a violation of Article 112a, UCMJ. On 7 July the charges were preferred. The appellant's **trial** defense counsel was detailed to the case and the appellant was informed of the charges on 9 July 99. The Article 32, UCMJ, investigation was held on 27 July and on the following day the appellant submitted his first request for a **speedy trial.** The appellant submitted a second demand for **speedy trial** on 8 August. The next day the charges were referred to **trial by** general court-martial. Then, on 19 August, the appellant was arraigned and the **speedy trial** motion was litigated.

During the litigation of the **speedy trial** motion, the Government presented the testimony of Major Miller, the Military Justice Office at Marine Corps Air Station Miramar. He detailed the steps he had taken working with the Senior Defense Counsel at Miramar to get counsel assigned to the appellant. At the time there were only two defense counsel assigned to Miramar, and since there were multiple cases that were potentially related, defense counsel from other commands were needed. Additionally, counsel was not normally assigned to a case until there were preferred charges. To facilitate appointment of counsel, Major Miller talked to the Regional Defense Counsel—the supervisor of the Senior Defense Counsel. Following presentation of the evidence and arguments of counsel, the military judge announced his findings of fact and denied the motion. (Record at 59-63.). Finding no clear error in these findings of fact we accord them substantial deference and adopt them as our own. Cooper, 58 M.J. at 58.

In applying a de novo standard of review, we do so conscious of the requirements of Article 10, UCMJ, that the Government is required to exercise reasonable diligence in bringing an accused to trial, but that constant motion is not required. United States v. Kossman, 38 M.J. 258, 262 (C.M.A.1993). We are also conscious of the four factors contained in United States v. Birge, 52 M.J. 209, 212 (C.A.A.F.1999); specifically: the length of the delay; the reasons for the delay; the assertion of the right to a speedy trial; and the existence of prejudice. See Cooper, 58 M.J. at 61. Applying those standards and factors to the case before us, we conclude that the appellant was not denied his right to a speedy trial under Article 10, UCMJ.

Post-Trial Delay

*5 In his fourth assignment of error the appellant seeks relief, citing United States v. Tardif, 57 M.J. 219 (C.A.A.F.2002), for the delay in the **post-trial** processing of his case. Specifically, he claims that the 13 months it took between the dates he was sentenced until the date of the convening authority's action was an excessive delay. As relief, he requests that we disapprove the adjudged and approved dishonorable discharge. He alleges no specific prejudice based upon this 13-month delay.

We are cognizant of this court's power under Article 66(c), UCMJ, to grant sentencing relief for **post-trial** delay even in the absence of actual prejudice. See id. at 224. However, having carefully reviewed the record in light of our authority and responsibility under both Articles 59(a) and 66(c), UCMJ, we find no prejudice or harm to the appellant, nor do we see any other basis to afford him relief for any post-trial processing delays that occurred in his case. We, therefore, decline to grant relief on this ground.

The Fifth Amendment provides that no person in a criminal case shall be required to be a witness against himself. This right has become known as the right against self-incrimination. It provides that no defendant must take the witness stand and that the state must prove its case beyond a reasonable doubt without the testimony and help of the accused. This right does not extend, however, to fingerprinting or photographing by the police or participation by the accused in a line-up, or to the giving of handwriting samples.

✳ ✳ ✳

CASE #9-6 Self Incrimination

UNITED STATES OF AMERICA v. BAILEY
No. 02-50571. D.C. No. CR-98-00043-AHS-2

✳ ✳ ✳

MEMORANDUM [FN*]

FN* This disposition is not appropriate for publication and may not be cited to or by the courts of this circuit except as provided by Ninth Circuit Rule 36-3.

[1] Mark Bailey appeals his jury conviction and sentence for willfully subscribing false tax returns in violation of 26

U.S.C. § 7206(1). Bailey argues that (1) the district court violated his Sixth Amendment right to compulsory process by allowing his co-defendant to assert her Fifth Amendment privilege against testifying, and that he was entitled to a continuance until his co-defendant was sentenced; and (2) the district court erred in applying a two-level upward adjustment under U.S.S.G. § 3B1.1(c) to Bailey's offense level for supervision of another's criminal activity. We have jurisdiction under 28 U.S.C. § 1291 and 18 U.S.C. § 3742(a), and we affirm both the conviction and the sentence imposed.

Because the parties are familiar with the facts, we include here only those facts necessary to explain our decision. During Bailey's trial, the district court conducted a hearing outside the presence of the jury, at which co-defendant Morgan asserted her privilege against compulsory **self-incrimination**. The court found her claim to be valid, and denied both Bailey's request for a continuance and his alternative request to compel a grant of use immunity for Morgan's testimony.

I. Sixth Amendment right to compulsory process

A criminal defendant has a Sixth Amendment right to compulsory process for obtaining witnesses in his favor, but "[a]n accused's right to compulsory process to secure the attendance of a witness does not include the right to compel the witness to waive his Fifth Amendment privilege." United States v. Moore, 682 F.2d 853, 856 (9th Cir.1982) (citing United States v. Trejo- Zambrano, 582 F.2d 460, 464 (9th Cir.1978).

We apply de novo review to Morgan's assertion of the Fifth Amendment privilege against compelled **self-incrimination**. United States v. Rubio-Topete, 999 F.2d 1334, 1338 (9th Cir.1993). For her assertion to be valid, she must be "confronted by substantial and real, and not merely trifling or imaginary, hazards of **incrimination**." United States

v. Apfelbaum, 445 U.S. 115, 128, 100 S.Ct. 948, 63 L.Ed.2d 250 (1980) (internal citation and quotation marks omitted).

We conclude that Morgan faced a genuine possibility of **self-incrimination** if she testified at Bailey's trial. As a convicted but unsentenced defendant, Morgan retained her Fifth Amendment rights. United States v. Paris, 827 F.2d 395, 399 (9th Cir.1987). See also Mitchell v. United States, 526 U.S. 314, 119 S.Ct. 1307, 143 L.Ed.2d 424 (1999). Morgan had pled guilty to only one count of a two-count indictment. See Moore, 682 F.2d at 856; United States v. Valencia, 656 F.2d 412, 416-17 (9th Cir.1981). Additionally, the plea agreement was binding only on the U.S. Attorney for the Central District of California, and did not protect Morgan from prosecution by a state authority, or by the Department of Justice outside of that district. Finally, the statute of limitations on the crimes charged is irrelevant to Morgan's Fifth Amendment privilege, because the district court "may consider as relevant conduct for sentencing purposes actions which may be barred from prosecution by the applicable statute of limitations." United States v. Williams, 217 F.3d 751, 754 (9th Cir.2000).

[2] We review for plain error Bailey's claim, made for the first time on appeal, that Morgan waived her Fifth Amendment privilege in her plea agreement. See Paris, 827 F.2d at 398. We are unpersuaded by Bailey's argument. It is well-settled that a voluntary plea pursuant to a plea agreement "is a waiver of the fifth amendment privilege only in regard to the crime that is admitted; the defendant retains the right against **self- incrimination** as to any crimes for which [she] may still be prosecuted." Moore, 682 F.2d at 856.

The district court's decision to exclude testimony based on an anticipated invocation of the Fifth Amendment privilege is reviewed for abuse of discretion. See United States v. Klinger, 128 F.3d 705, 709 (9th Cir.1997). Since Morgan's claim of privilege was valid, the district court did not abuse its discretion, nor did it commit plain error, in finding that Morgan should not be called as a defense witness nor required to answer Bailey's questions.

[3] The district court's denial of the motion for a continuance was not an abuse of discretion. *See, e.g., United States v. Rude,* 88 F.3d 1538, 1550 (9th Cir.1996). Bailey has not established that Morgan would have testified, or that any testimony would have been favorable. *See United States v. Sukumolachan,* 610 F.2d 685, 687 (9th Cir.1980) (per curiam).

[4] Similarly, the refusal to compel a grant of immunity to Morgan was not error. It is well-settled in this Circuit that an accused's Sixth Amendment right to compulsory process does not entitle him "to compel a prosecutor to grant immunity to a potential defense witness to get [her] to testify." *Trejo-Zambrano,* 582 F.2d at 464. The district court, on the other hand, can compel a grant of immunity only in limited circumstances, where such a measure is required by due process. *See United States v. Lord,* 711 F.2d 887, 890 (9th Cir.1983); *United States v. Westerdahl,* 945 F.2d 1083, 1086 (9th Cir.1991). Even if Morgan's testimony would have been relevant and noncumulative, Bailey has failed to establish that the government violated due process by intentionally distorting the fact-finding process. No prosecutorial misconduct is present in this case: the government asserted correctly in the district court that Morgan's plea agreement was not binding on any authority other than the U.S. Attorney for the Central District of California, and Morgan decided to invoke her Fifth Amendment privilege on the advice of counsel. *See United States v. Duran,* 189 F.3d 1071, 1087 (9th Cir.1999). The district court did not err in refusing to compel a grant of use immunity.

II. Two-level upward sentencing adjustment for supervision

[5] The district court's factual determination that a defendant qualifies for a role adjustment is reviewed for clear error. *United States v. Maldonado,* 215 F.3d 1046, 1050 (9th Cir.2000). Although it is a close question, we conclude that the district court did not err in enhancing Morgan's sentencing under U.S.S.G. § 3B1.1(c), which provides for

a two-level increase "[i]f the defendant was an organizer, leader, manager, or supervisor in any criminal activity" not involving five or more participants, and that is not otherwise extensive.

In this case, Bailey directed Curtis to accept $310,000 in cash to purchase property, told him to place the money in escrow, and to spend it as instructed. On these facts, it was not clear error for the district court to find that Bailey supervised Curtis, and to impose the two-level enhancement.

AFFIRMED.

☆ ☆ ☆

The Eighth Amendment prohibits the infliction of cruel and unusual punishment on convicted defendants. This prohibition includes those types of punishments that society finds unacceptable, that are disproportionately large compared to the offense, that are inherently cruel, or that are imposed arbitrarily. Opponents of the death penalty argue that it falls within the constitutional prohibition on cruel and unusual punishment and should therefore not be permissible. The U.S. Supreme Court has not found this to be the case, but has been sufficiently sympathetic to this argument to place a variety of requirements and restrictions on its use.

Article Three, Section Two of the Constitution provides that all criminals shall have a trial by jury. This right, which may be waived by the defendant, has been interpreted to include any serious offense where the penalty may be more than six months imprisonment.

Many of these rights have been memorialized in the Miranda warnings required to be given to persons under suspicion of having committed a crime. These warnings are not really constitutional guarantees but are considered a necessary step in safeguarding that the constitutional guarantees are provided. The Supreme Court requires that the accused be told that he has the right to remain silent, that anything that he says can and will be used against him in a court of law, that he is entitled to a lawyer, and that if he cannot afford a lawyer, one will be provided to him free of charge. The Supreme Court feels that these rights have no meaning if one does not know of them. Therefore, the accused must be informed of these rights to insure that they have meaning and substance. If these warning are not given to the accused, then the courts are precluded from using any incriminating statements given by the defendant or any evidence gathered as a result of these statements. Miranda warnings are relevant to all offenses except for violations, where arrest is not a possible consequence.

The next two cases are concerned with the constitutional limits on police powers and the rights of the accused.

✲ ✲ ✲

CRIMINAL LAW CASE #9-7

Rochin v. California
342 U.S. 165, 72 S.Ct. 205, 96 L.Ed. 183 (1952)

FRANKFURTER, J. Upon some information that the defendant was selling narcotics, three deputy sheriffs went to the house in which Rochin lived. Finding the outside door open, they entered and then forced open the door to Rochin's room on the second floor. Inside they found the defendant sitting partly dressed on the side of the bed, upon which his wife was lying. On a night stand beside the bed, the deputies spied two capsules. When asked, "Whose stuff is this?", Rochin seized the capsules and put them in his mouth. A struggle ensued, during which the three officers "jumped upon him" and attempted to extract the three capsules. Rochin was handcuffed and taken to the hospital. At the direction of one of the deputies, a doctor forced an emetic solution through a tube into Rochin's stomach against his will. This produced vomiting. In the vomited matter were found two capsules which proved to contain morphine. Rochin was convicted of possession of morphine and sentenced to sixty days imprisonment. The chief evidence against him was the two capsules.

The proceedings by which this conviction was obtained do more than offend some fastidious squeamishness or private sentimentalism about combating crime too energetically. This is conduct that shocks the conscience. Illegally breaking into the privacy of the petitioner, the struggle to open his mouth and remove what was there, the forcible extraction of his stomach's contents—this course of proceeding by agents of government is bound to offend even hardened sensibilities. They are methods too close to the rack and the screw to permit of constitutional(ality).

...Use of involuntary verbal confessions in State criminal trials is constitutionally obnoxious not only because of their unreliability. They are inadmissible under the Due Process Clause even though statements contained in them may be independently established as true. Coerced confessions offend the community's sense of fair play and decency. So here, to sanction the brutal conduct which naturally enough was condemned by the trial court whose judgment is before us, would be to afford brutality the cloak of law. Nothing would be more calculated to discredit law and, thereby, to brutalize the temper of society.

☆ ☆ ☆

CRIMINAL LAW CASE #9-8

Miranda v. Arizona
384 U.S. 436, 86 S.Ct. 1602 (1966)

WARREN, C.J. The cases before us raise questions which go to the roots of our concepts of American criminal jurisprudence: the restraints society must observe consistent with the Federal Constitution in prosecuting individuals for crime. More specifically, we deal with the admissibility of statements obtained from an individual who is subjected to custodial police interrogation and the necessity for procedures which assure that the individual is accorded his privilege under the Fifth Amendment to the Constitution not to be compelled to incriminate himself.

...[W]e concern ourselves with the interrogation atmosphere and the evils it can bring. In No. 759, Miranda v. Arizona, the police arrested the defendant and took him to a special interrogation room where they secured a confession....In (this) case, the defendant was thrust into an unfamiliar atmosphere and run through menacing police interrogation procedures. The potentiality for compulsion is forcefully apparent...To be sure, the records do not evince overt physical coercion or patented psychological ploys. The fact remains that...the officers did not undertake to afford appropriate safeguards at the outset of the interrogation to insure that the statements were truly a product of free choice....The current practice of incommunicado interrogation is at odds with one of our nation's most cherished principles—that the individual may not be compelled to incriminate himself. Unless adequate protective devises are employed to dispel the compulsion inherent in custodial surroundings, no statement obtained from the defendant can truly be the product of his free choice....

To summarize, we hold that when an individual is taken into custody or otherwise deprived of his freedom by the authorities and is subjected to questioning, the privilege against self-incrimination is jeopardized. Procedural safeguards must be employed to protect the privilege, and unless other fully effective means are adopted to notify the person of his right of silence and to assure that the exercise of the right will be scrupulously honored, the following measures are required. He must be warned prior to any questioning that he has the right to remain silent, that anything he says can be used against him in a court of law, that he has the right to the presence of an attorney, and that if he cannot afford an attorney one will be appointed for him prior to any questioning if he so desires. Opportunity to exercise these rights must be afforded to him throughout the interrogation. After such warnings have been given, and such opportunity afforded him, the individual may knowingly and intelligently waive these rights and agree to answer questions or make a statement. But unless and until such warnings and waiver are demonstrated by the prosecution at trial, no evidence obtained as a result of interrogation can be used against him.

✵ ✵ ✵

LEGAL LIGHT

During the year 2008, the Federal Bureau of Prisons housed 201,498 inmates. Off this number, 165,693 were housed by the Bureau of Prisons, 22, 890 were housed in privately managed institutions under the auspices of the BOP, and 12,915 were in home confinement arrangements.

✵ ✵ ✵

E. CRIMINAL PROCESS

The criminal process formally begins with the issuance of a complaint by an authorized public official, such as, in the federal system, a U.S. marshal or a U.S. attorney. The submission of the complaint is then made to a U.S.

magistrate, who, if he or she believes that the complaint satisfies the need for probable cause, would issue a warrant for the arrest of the suspect. An arrest is the taking into custody of a suspect in order to bring him before an appropriate court of law. Arrests may also be made without a warrant if a crime has been committed in the presence of a police officer. After the arrest, the suspect is booked at the police station. Booking entails the photographing, fingerprinting, searching, testing for the use of drugs or alcohol, and any other reasonably related activity.

Our system, based as it is on the presumption of innocence articulated in the Fifth Amendment, requires that the arrested individual be afforded the opportunity to leave jail until the trial takes place. To ensure that the person returns on the trial date, the court requires that the suspect post bail with the court. Bail is a security, usually money, which the court will keep if the suspect fails to show. On some occasions, the court may deny bail to a suspect if there is a great probability that the suspect will not appear at the trial.

The individual must then be arraigned. The arraignment is the process in which the accused is brought to court, informed of the charge or charges against him, and given the chance to respond to the charges or make a plea. After the plea is entered, the state's attorney may offer a plea bargain to the accused. Given the huge volume of cases with which the state contends, this opportunity to plead guilty to a lesser charge is an expedient way to dispose of a case, while it gives the accused an opportunity to get a lesser sentence than he might have received after a trial. If no plea bargain is arranged, then the accused will have his day in court.

✳ ✳ ✳

CHAPTER NINE
KEY TERMS

Actus Reus
Arraignment
Bail
Booking
Felonies
Infractions
Mens Rea
Miranda Warning
Misdemeanors
Prosecutor

✳ ✳ ✳

CHAPTER SUMMARY

Criminal law serves to punish those individuals who engage in activity we, as a society, deem illegal. All criminal law is statutory in nature; no statute, no crime. Each criminal statute is comprised of two parts. The first is the actus reus, or the act that is prohibited. The second part is the mens rea, or the requisite criminal intent attached to the prohibited act. Crimes fall into three categories. The most severe are felonies, which are those crimes that carry a prison penalty of a year or longer. The next group is misdemeanors, which are those crimes that carry a penalty of less than one year. The least severe are infractions, which usually carry no prison time but are punishable by a fine.

Given the inherent inequities between the parties in a criminal action and the potential loss of part of one's life to prison, the Constitution provides a variety of protections for criminal defendants that are not provided to parties in a civil action. The Constitution protects against double jeopardy so that the state can't keep retrying individuals. It also provides for assistance of counsel, protects against unreasonable searches and seizures, guarantees a speedy trial, ensures that one need not testify against oneself, and protects against cruel and unusual punishment. The actual limits of these protections are, of course, subject to judicial review and interpretation.

THINK AND WRITE

1. Why do all crimes have both an actus reus and a mens rea?
2. Why do we need the <u>Miranda</u> warnings?
3. What levels of crimes exist?
4. Why do we need to protect criminal defendants with extensive constitutional guarantees, but not afford these rights to civil defendants?
5. What rights are constitutionally guaranteed to criminal defendants?

PROJECTS

1. Please visit your local criminal court. Spend a couple of hours observing, and take notes of your observations.
2. Watch a case on Court TV. Summarize and critique the analysis done by the talking heads. Is their analysis helpful? Do you approve of televising cases?
3. How does your state deal with minors who commit criminal acts? In what court are they tried and what consequences are available if they are convicted?

4. Under what circumstances does your state allow for the use of force to protect personal property? When does your state allow for the use of force to protect oneself or others?
5. Cyber stalking, which is the harassment of an individual by the use of e-mail or other electronic communication, is a new and growing problem. Does your state have a specific criminal statute prohibiting cyber stalking or can cyber stalking be prosecuted under another criminal statute?

ETHICAL QUESTIONS

1. While interviewing a client at the local jail, you overhear the person in the next booth tell his visitor that he is guilty of the crime with which he is charged. What are the ethical and professional obligations of an attorney (or a paralegal) in this circumstance?
2. You are working as a paralegal for a local criminal defense firm that is representing an attorney charged with the theft of a client's funds from an estate. That night, your neighbor happens to mention that he is going to the charged attorney the next day to do a will and some estate planning. What should you do?

WEBSITES

1. Site that provides information about the death penalty: http://www.deathpenaltyinfo.org/
2. American Bar Association site about criminal law: http://www.abanet.org/crimjust/home.html

3. Links to sites concerning criminal law: http://www.hg.org/crime.html
4. Site about the federal criminal law: http://www.fedcrimlaw.com

GLOSSARY

ABA—The American Bar Association.

Abandoned property—Property that has been given up completely and finally with no intention of reclaiming it and belongs to no particular person.

Acceptance—In contracts, agreeing to an offer. One of the essential contract elements.

Accession—The right to own things that have become part of something already owned.

Accord and satisfaction—An agreement to pay and to accept late payment or less than all a debt or obligation is worth as full payment for an obligation, along with a payment.

Accretion—The gradual adding on of land by natural causes, such as any deposit of dirt by a river on its bank.

Actus reus—A wrongful deed or action. When combined with the mens rea, it produces a crime.

Adjudicative authority—The quasi-judicial power of administrative agencies.

Administrative law—1. Laws about the duties and proper running of administrative agencies that are imposed on agencies by legislatures and courts. 2. Rules and regulations written by administrative agencies.

Administrative law judge—An official who conducts hearings for an administrative agency. Also called a "hearing officer."

Administrative Procedures Act (5 U.S.C. 500)—A federal statute that proscribes how U.S. administrative agencies must do business and how disputes go from an agency to court.

Administrator—A person appointed by the court to supervise the estate of a dead person who died without a will. "Administratrix" is the feminine form of this term.

Appellate courts—A higher court that can hear appeals from a lower court.

Arraignment—To bring a criminal defendant in front of a judge to hear the charges and to enter a plea.

Articles of Confederation—The document that held together the thirteen original American colonies before the adoption of the Constitution.

Automatic stay—The statutory freezing of assets and debts in a bankruptcy proceeding.

Bail—Money or property put up to allow the release of a person from jail. It guarantees the person's return before the court.

Bailment—A temporary delivery of property by the owner into another person's custody.

Beneficiary—A person who receives property under a will.

Bequest—Giving personal property in a will.

Booking—The writing down by the police of facts about a person's arrest and charges, along with identification and background information. This is recorded on the police blotter in the police station.

Breach of contract—The failure, without legal excuse, to live up to a significant promise made in a contract. Breach also includes refusing to perform your part of the bargain or making it hard for the other person to perform his or her part of the bargain.

Causal link—That which reasonably connects an action with its effects.

Chapter 1—The first section of the Bankruptcy Code. It contains definitions and general procedural rules.

Chapter 3—The section of the Bankruptcy Code that deals with the administration of bankruptcy statutes including rules relating to professionals who work on the proceeding.

Chapter 5—The section of the Bankruptcy Code that contains rules governing creditors and claims, the debtor, and the estate.

Chapter 7—The section of the Bankruptcy Code that deals with liquidation bankruptcies.

Chapter 9—The section of the Bankruptcy Code that deals with municipal reorganizations.

Chapter 11—The section of the Bankruptcy Code that deals with reorganizations.

Chapter 12—The section of the Bankruptcy Code that deals with farm reorganizations.

Chapter 13—The section of the Bankruptcy Code that deals with individual reorganizations for people with regular income.

Compensatory damages—Damages awarded for the actual loss suffered by the plaintiff in a contract action.

Confusion—Mixing or blending together.

Consequential damages—Damages awarded for indirect losses suffered by the plaintiff in a contract action. Also sometimes called special damages.

Consideration—The reason or main cause for a person to make a contract; something of legal value received or promised to induce (convince) a person to make a deal.

Constitutional law—The study of the law that applies to the organization, structure, and functions of the government, the basic principles of government, and the validity (or constitutionality) of laws and actions when tested against the requirements of the Constitution.

Contract—An agreement that affects or creates legal relationships between two or more persons.

Copyright—The right to control the copying, distributing, performing, displaying, and adapting of words (including paintings, music, books, and movies). The right belongs to the creator, or to persons employing the creator, or to persons who buy the rights from the creator.

Criminal law—The study of the law that has to do with crimes and illegal conduct.

Dedication—The gift or other transfer of land or rights in land to the government for specific public use, such as a park, and its acceptance for that use by the government.

Devise—Giving real property in a will.

Disbarment—The revocation of the license to practice law.

Duty of care—A legal obligation to another person who has a corresponding right.

Easement—The right of a specific nonowner of a piece of land (such as a next-door neighbor, the government, or a public utility) to use part of the land in a particular way.

Election of remedies—The act of choosing between or among viable solutions for harm done.

Eminent domain—The government's right and power to take private land for public use by paying for it

Escheat—The state's getting property because no owner can be found.

Estates—1. The interest a person has in property; a person's right or title to property. 2. The property itself in which a person has an interest.

Executor—A person selected by a person making a will to be the individual responsible to hand out the property after the maker's death.

Exemptions—Items that may be excluded from bankruptcy proceedings.

Extradition—One country (or state) giving up a person to a second country (or state) when the second requests the person for a trial on a criminal charge or for punishment after a trial.

Family law—The study of the law that relates to the home and to the relationships between or among the people in the home.

Federal Records Act (44 U.S.C. 29-33)—The federal statute that defines the kind of records that administrative agencies must keep.

Federal Register—The first place that the rules and regulations of administrative agencies are published.

Freedom of Information Act (5 U.S.C. 552)—A 1966 federal statute that makes all records held by the federal government, with some exceptions (such as certain military secrets), available to the public.

Freedom of religion—The First Amendment right to hold any religious beliefs and to practice these beliefs in any way that does not infringe upon public safety or infringe upon important rights of others.

Freedom of speech—The First Amendment right to say what you want as long as you don't interfere with others' rights.

Felonies—A serious crime, carrying a potential jail sentence of more than one year.

Fixtures—Anything attached to land or a building.

Hearing officer—An official who conducts hearings for an administrative agency. Also called an "administrative law judge."

Heir—A relative who inherits property from someone who dies without a will.

Holographic will—A will entirely in the handwriting of the person making it.

Infractions—A minor law, usually carrying a penalty of a fine or very short jail term.

Intangible property—That property that cannot be touched.

Intentional tort—The area of torts that deals with those civil wrongs that are deliberately done.

International law—The study of the customary law that applies to the relationships and interactions between countries.

Involuntary petitions—The document filed by creditors to begin a bankruptcy proceeding.

Intestate—Having died without leaving a will.

Jurisdiction—1. The persons about whom and the subject matters about which a court has the right and power to make decisions that are legally binding. 2. The geographical area within which a court (or public official) has the right and power to operate.

Liens—A claim against specific property that can be enforced in court to secure payment of a judgment, duty, or debt.

Liquidated damages—A specific amount of money that is agreed to in a contract as compensation for a breach of that contract.

Lost property—Property that can no longer be found.

Mens rea—Wrongful mind or criminal intent. When combined with the actus reus, it produces a crime.

Miranda warning—The warning that must be given to a person arrested or taken into custody by a police officer or other official. The warning includes the fact that what you say can be used against you and that you have the right to remain silent, to contact a lawyer, and to have a free lawyer if you are poor. If this warning is not given properly, no statement given by the defendant during custody may be used by the police or by the prosecutor in court. The warning is required by the 1966 case <u>Miranda v. Arizona</u> (384 U.S. 436).

Misdemeanor—A criminal offense less than a felony that is punishable by less than a year in jail.

Mislaid property—Property put somewhere by someone who then forgets where.

Mitigation of damages—The principle that a person suing for damages must have takes reasonable steps to minimize the harm done, or the amount of money awarded will be lowered.

Mortgagee—One person putting up land or buildings as security for a loan. The real property is collateral for repayment of the loan.

NALA—The National Association of Legal Assistants.

NFPA—The National Federation of Paralegal Associations.

Negligence—The failure to exercise a reasonable amount of care in a situation that causes harm to someone or something. It can involve doing something carelessly or failing to do something that should have been done.

Nominal damages—Token or symbolic damages awarded because the actual damages have not been proved or are too small to measure.

Nuncupative will—An oral will.

Offer—A proposal to make a deal. One of the essential elements of a contract.

Patent—A grant of a right (given by the federal government to a person) to exclusively control, for a limited number of years (usually seventeen), the manufacture and sale of something that person has discovered or invented.

Primary sources of law—Binding legal authority.

Private law—The law of relationships among persons and groups.

Product liability—The area of torts that deals with the responsibility of manufacturers (and sometimes sellers) of goods to pay for harm to purchasers (and sometimes other users and even bystanders) caused by a defective product.

Property—Anything that is owned or can be owned.

Prosecutor—A public official who represents the government in a criminal action.

Public law—The study of law that has to do with either the operation of government or the relationships between the government and persons.

Punitive damages—Extra damages awarded to punish a defendant and to help keep a particular bad act from happening again.

Quitclaim deed—A deed that passes on to the buyer all those rights or as much of a title as a seller actually has.

Reasonable care—That degree of care that a reasonable person would exercise under the circumstances.

Reformation—A procedure in which a court will rewrite or correct ("reform") a written agreement to conform with the original intent of the persons making the deal. The court will usually do this only in there was fraud or mutual mistake in writing up the original document.

Release—A document by which a claim or right is relinquished.

Reprimand—A warning to an attorney to cease a particular practice.

Rescission—The annulment of a contract.

Restitution—Giving back something.

Riparian rights—A landowner's rights to use water and the land around and under it

Rule-making authority—The quasi-legislative power of an administrative agency.

Secondary sources of law—Nonbinding authority.

Specific performance—Being required to do to do exactly what was agreed to in a contract. A court may require specific performance of a contract if one party fails to perform and damages (money) will not properly compensate the other side for harm done.

Statute of frauds—Any of various state laws, modeled after an old English law, that require many types of contracts (such as contracts for the sale of real estate or of goods over a certain dollar amount, contracts to guarantee another's debt, and certain long-term contracts) to be signed and in writing to be enforceable in court.

Strict liability—That area of torts that deals persons held responsible for damages or injuries even if you are not at fault.

Subpoena—A court's order to a person that he or she appear in court to testify in a case. Some administrative agencies may also issue subpoenas.

Subpoena duces tecum—A subpoena by which a person is commanded to bring certain documents to court or to an administrative agency.

Sunshine Act (5 U.S.C. 552b)—The statute that requires certain business conducted by administrative agencies be done in public meetings.

Suspension—The temporary revocation of the license to practice law.

Tangible property—Property that can be touched, other than real property.

Torts—A civil wrong, other than a breach of contract.

Trademark—A distinctive mark, brand name, motto, or symbol used by a company to identify or advertise the products or sells.

Trial courts—Those courts in which legal disputes originate.

Trust—An arrangement by which one person holds legal title to money or other property for the benefit of another.

Trust beneficiary—The recipient of the proceeds or assets of a trust.

Trust deed—A document by which a person transfers the legal ownership of land to independent trustees to be held until a debt on the land is paid off.

Trustee—A person who holds legal title to money or other property for the benefit of another.

Unauthorized practice of law—The crime of practicing law without a license.

Voluntary petition—The document filed by the debtor to begin a bankruptcy proceeding.

Warrant or grant deed—A deed that guarantees that the title of the land being sold is good and is complete.

Wills—Legal statements as to how a person's property is to be handed out after their death.

Zoning—The division of a city or county into mapped areas, with restrictions on land use, architectural design, building use, etc.

7351627R0

Made in the USA
Charleston, SC
21 February 2011